P9-DEY-542

THE SPY IN THE CORPORATE STRUCTURE

AND THE RIGHT TO PRIVACY

EDWARD ENGBERG

THE WORLD  PUBLISHING COMPANY

CLEVELAND AND NEW YORK

Published by The World Publishing Company
2231 West 110th Street, Cleveland, Ohio 44102

Published simultaneously in Canada by Nelson,
Foster & Scott Ltd.

First printing 1967

Library of Congress Catalog Card Number: 67–15223

Printed in the United States of America

TO H. S.

ACKNOWLEDGMENTS

SUCH PRIVACY as I was able to claim during the composition of this essay I owe to the resolute protectiveness of my wife, Catherine, and the restraint of four spirited progeny. The essay owes much to the legwork, interviewing skills and talent for parsing financial statements of John W. Hunter, Jr. Eileen Caulfield made a strong and capable effort to reduce the number of misquotations, errors of fact and other booby traps strewn along the path. All the conclusions, as well as all the mistakes, are irremediably mine.

Acknowledgment is gratefully made to the following copyright holders for permission to reprint previously published material:

Dr. George W. and Muriel Beadle, for excerpts from *The Language of Life,* by Dr. George W. and Muriel Beadle, Copyright © 1966 by Dr. George W. and Muriel Beadle.

The Business Lawyer, for excerpts from "The Government is No Gentleman," by Ray M. Harris, Copyright © 1963 by *The Business Lawyer.*

The Educational Foundation for Nuclear Science, Inc., for excerpts from "Special Chain Reactions," by John R. Platt, from *The Bulletin of the Atomic Scientists,* Copyright © 1961 by the Educational Foundation for Nuclear Science, Inc.

Faber and Faber Ltd., for excerpts from *Collected Poems 1909–1962,* by T. S. Eliot, Copyright © 1962 by Faber and Faber Ltd. in areas outside the United States, its dependencies and the Philippine Islands.

Harcourt, Brace & World, Inc., for excerpts from *Collected Poems 1909–1962,* by T. S. Eliot, Copyright © 1962 by Harcourt, Brace & World, Inc. in the United States, its dependencies and the Philippine Islands.

The Harvard Business Review, for excerpts from "Industrial Espionage," Copyright © 1959 by the President and Fellows of Harvard College.

Harvard University Press, for excerpts from "'Operations Research' for Management," by Hermann and Magee, as published in *New Decision-Making Tools for Managers,* by Bursk and Chapman, Copyright © 1965 by Harvard University Press.

Industrial Research Inc., for excerpts from an article by Anthony Baker, Copyright © 1962 by Industrial Research Inc.

Thomas Nelson and Sons, for excerpts from *The First and the Fifth,* by O. John Rogge, Copyright © 1960 by Thomas Nelson and Sons.

The New York Times, for excerpts from a July 1966 article, Copyright © 1966 by The New York Times Company. Reprinted by permission.

Rutgers University Press, for excerpts from *The Eavesdroppers,* by Samuel Dash, Copyright © 1959 by the Rutgers University Press.

Scientific American, Inc., for excerpts from "Control Systems," by Gordon S. Brown and Donald P. Campbell, Copyright © 1952 by Scientific American, Inc. All rights reserved.

The Wall Street Journal, for excerpts from a May 1966 article, Copyright © 1966 by *The Wall Street Journal.*

Yale Law Journal, for excerpts from "The 'Conspiracy' Theory of the Fourteenth Amendment," by Howard J. Graham, Copyright © 1938 by the *Yale Law Journal.*

CONTENTS

Straighten up their hair is all they ever do,
Why don't they straighten up the mess that's inside.

PROFESSOR HENRY HIGGINS

In a democracy, you have to put up with a lot of things.

REPRESENTATIVE JOE RICHARD POOL,
presiding over a subcommittee of
the House Committee on Un-American
Activities

Chapter One

A QUESTION OF PRIVACY

He sees, as have few of his generation, the social and economic perils of the industrial revolution; he understands the development of the machine and of the business corporation, are threats to liberty and to the general welfare.

—ALPHEUS THOMAS MASON,
of Justice Louis D. Brandeis

1.

WE HAVE "PASSED TO A SUBTLER CIVILIZATION," Mr. Justice Brandeis once told an interviewer, yet "the law must still protect a man from things that rob him of his freedom, whether the oppressing force be physical or of a subtler kind." The subtler means of oppression occupied Brandeis' thoughts during most of his public life. In 1890, at the age of thirty-four, he, together with his law partner, Samuel D. Warren, wrote for publication in the *Harvard Law Review* a pioneering essay toward defining, as they conceived it, "The Right to Privacy." "Recent inventions and business methods," they remarked, "call attention to the next step which must be taken for the protection of the person, and securing to the individual what Judge Cooley calls the right 'to be let alone.' "

In the late summer of 1960, nearly seventy years to the issue after publication of the Brandeis-Warren essay, Al Worthington, a relief specialist for the Chicago White Sox, abruptly asked to be traded to another team. He was troubled, he explained, by the practice the White Sox made before each game of posting a spy behind the façade of the center field scoreboard at Comiskey Park. The scoreboard agent's job was to peer through a spyglass, and thereby to pick up the signs by which the catcher made his opinions known to the pitcher as to the kind of pitch the pitcher should attempt to throw next—a slider, changeup, fastball, or whatever else the pitcher might have in inventory.

The agent relayed this information over an open telephone line to the White Sox bench. There it was converted back into sign language to be read by the White Sox's third base coach and thence relayed to the batter. The batter, knowing what to expect, would presumably be put at an advantage. The value of information thus obtained is of course limited, as is all intelligence, by the capacity of the recipient for making use of it. There are some batters to whom it would make little difference, one way or the other, were the pitcher to clearly enunciate his intentions before every pitch.

Even so, it is a sneaky business and over an extended period of games and at bats might make a considerable difference, particularly in a close pennant race. In all events, Worthington wanted none of it. He wound up with the Minnesota Twins. There can be no question that he did the right thing. In 1965, he was able to help the Twins win the pennant, and to collect a full player's share of the team's cut from a World Series with the Los Angeles Dodgers. The White Sox had to be content meanwhile with the scraps from the World Series table that go to teams who end the season farther down in the first division.

At the time of Worthington's departure, however, there was no reason to suppose that virtue would be so amply rewarded. It is therefore worth noting that the pressbox issued no protest to shame the White Sox into firing the perpetrator of the sign-stealing scheme, and to make the team promise by all that was holy to Judge Kenesaw Mountain Landis, which was quite a lot, never to do it again. No writer of any consequence felt called upon to dredge up Shoeless Joe Jackson from the nearly repressed memory of the Black Sox scandal of 1919. There was no one to recall the little boy, eyes stained with tears, pleading, "Say it isn't so, Joe."

On the contrary, one stylist for a New York newspaper explained Worthington's action to friends as having resulted from "some sort of religious hang-up." He would have been embarrassed had a fabricator of editorial opinion summoned up the lines memorialized these days principally by stand-up comedians in search of an easy laugh:

When the One Great Scorer comes to
write against your name—
He marks—not that you won or lost
—but how you played the game.

2.

That the world out of which Grantland Rice composed those lines existed almost exclusively in the literary imagination of his time makes it none the less real. A person possessed by a psychosomatic cold uses as many Kleenex as one ensniveled by any other kind. For pertinent illustration, I turn to Colonel Allison Ind, a retired U.S. Army intelligence officer and the author of *A Short History of Espionage:*

> The Hawaii disaster came about because in 1941 we had no intelligence apparatus worthy of the name. We still operated in an atmosphere of adolescent chivalry. . . . One of the principal reasons why we had no hint of Japan's naval capability for simultaneously exploding war over a fifth of the earth's surface was because one of our Secretaries of State had, in a burst of quixotic zeal, blinded us a dozen years before. In 1929, it was explained to the late Henry Stimson why we were so well prepared for the forthcoming Naval Limitations Conference. Our experts had succeeded in breaking the Japanese diplomatic cipher system and we thus knew Tokyo's instructions to its delegates. "Code breaking" had been practiced by all nations clever enough to do it for hundreds of years before we were ever a colony. But when Secretary Stimson was informed of the United States' activities in the field, he was so outraged at our "reading the other gentleman's mail" that overnight he acted to destroy invaluable machinery and scatter the experts.
>
> Since Stimson's day we have gone far and fast—maybe too fast. . . .

In the 89th session of Congress, which convened in January, 1965, no fewer than one half dozen separate committees addressed themselves to questions involving whether we had gone too far or too fast in reading one another's mail, let alone that of alien gentlemen. To their concern we owe confirmation of much that we had merely suspected, and much else that we did not. We know, for example, that the Post Office Department, upon request from other Federal agencies, regularly intercepts the mail of specified "other gentlemen" in order to study the envelopes for clues to their origin, or whatever else one can discover from an envelope.

We know also that the Department has stationed agents at peepholes in locker rooms and lavatories in connection with mail theft investigations, and that like the State Department it employs polygraph, or lie detector tests, to narrow its lists of suspects, and also the list of candidates for employment. We know also that the Internal Revenue Service does not rely solely on records and adding machines for its audits.

We have long known that the Collector of Internal Revenue pays informers a stipulated percentage of taxes recovered as a result of information received. We might not have known, though, that he uses lockpicking gadgets to gain entry into private offices, "snooperscopes" to find his way around in them after dark, and "bugs" by which to eavesdrop on conversations which show promise of being instructive, including, perhaps especially, those between a taxpayer and his accountant or lawyer.

The IRS upon sufficient provocation evidently uses bugs and see-through mirrors the way they are used in market surveys or by automobile dealers. In private practice a car salesman, say, after giving his pitch to a man and wife shopping for a car, will excuse himself to take a phone call. Actually, he repairs to an office where he is able to overhear the prospects voice their misgivings, as if privately, through a concealed microphone. He then returns to deal with these objections as best he can.

In similar fashion, a Federal tax agent who excuses himself from an auditing session with a client and his financial or legal advisor goes to where he may hear and also, with the aid of a one-way mirror or glass partition, observe the taxpayer for incriminating utterances or doings, such as hasty notewriting, or amendments to records. What he learns may not be evidence, but it sometimes helps point to evidence.

We know, moreover, that the Food and Drug Administration uses bugs and recorders to memorialize the spiels of anyone who sells food or drugs by word of mouth, including blackstrap-molasses-and-wheat-germ barkers who appeal to food faddists. The FDA also uses electronic recording and transmitting equipment "to make a record," in the words of a former FDA Commissioner, "of the things leading to and surrounding illegal sales without prescription of dangerous drugs. . . ."

We know of these practices in consequence principally of work done by Senator Edward Long, a Democrat of Missouri, and the staff of the Senate Judiciary Committee's subcommittee on Administrative

Practice and Procedure. In the House, meanwhile, Representative Cornelius Gallagher, Democrat of New Jersey and a member of the House Government Operations Committee's subcommittee on Invasion of Privacy, was inquiring into practices perhaps subtler even than Brandeis had envisioned.

From testimony before the Gallagher Committee we learned that subbranches of the executive branch, including the Peace Corps, were requiring of applicants that they submit, as part of their application, to tests aimed at obtaining an "inventory" of their psyche. We learned also, incidentally to the purpose of the hearings, that one test, the Minnesota Multiphasic Personality Inventory, was used also in the selection of candidates to the Episcopalian clergy, and by many private concerns.

The Gallagher Committee touched on use of lie detector tests, as well as upon the fact that in 1964

> For the first time . . . farmers were asked to detail their outside income, including the amounts they received from social security, the Veterans Administration, dividends and interest and other sources. They also were required to submit this information for everyone living in the farmhouse, including their own families and hired hands.

The Committee also brought out that the Bureau of the Census planned to include in the 1970 decennial census questions concerning religion and personal income, and revealed an idea entertained by the Bureau of the Budget to install a national data bank, or center. As conceived by its architect, a consultant to the Bureau, the center would consist of a large information retrieval system containing in one place a substantial part of the information about private citizens scattered here and there among the files kept by other agencies, such as the Census Bureau, the Internal Revenue Service, the Agriculture Department and the Food and Drug Administration.

Whether we have gone too fast or too far since the days of Secretary Stimson and Grantland Rice is, by the terms of the expression, a matter of taste and of judgment. There is little question that some members of Congress believe we have gone too far. Senator Long, during one session, accused the Food and Drug Administration of "police state tactics" and "bizarre and juvenile games of cops and robbers." Congressman Gallagher averred that "We have become a nation of snoopers," and that "All of us may some day stand psychologically naked." It is an alarming prospect, perhaps as alarming as testimony by Henry B. Montague, chief postal inspector, that lie detector tests had been helpful in enabling the Post Office Department to recover millions of dollars worth of valuables from mail thieves. Or the State Department's claim of having, with the help of various sorts of surveillance, culled out or prevented employment of scores of security risks, principally homosexuals.

Charles F. Luce, Administrator of the Bonneville Power Administration, testified to the purpose of the Minnesota Multiphasic Personality Inventory. If a man is applying for a job, he said,

> . . . in which his emotional constitution is an important part of his qualification for the job—a job in which if he goes to pieces, he may endanger the lives of others, or the property of the Government, then I would say, yes, he consents to relevant inquiry.

The Director of the Peace Corps has his hands full without the opportunity, even if he thought of it that way, to greet every applicant. Thus, Dr. Abraham Carp, director of selection for the Peace Corps, also defended the use of the MMPI. Through the use of these tests, he contended,

> . . . we can help to identify people . . . whom everybody would agree it is wrong to send overseas. And there is some likelihood that if we did not use the test, we might have in fact sent them overseas, both to their own harm as well as that of the Peace Corps and the country overseas.

The FDA, through its commissioner, pointed out that:

> . . . several different investigations by several different responsible groups over a number of years have shown illegal traffic in such dangerous drugs [as amphetamines and barbiturates] to be a serious problem. It has been described by some law enforcement officers as being a greater hazard to society than traffic in hard narcotics. Our investigations have shown the illicit distribution of barbiturates and amphetamines to be closely linked not only to destruction of the user's ability to contribute to society but also to destructive effects upon society as a whole—to broken homes, prostitution, thefts, kidnapping, and other serious crimes.

There is no point urging the view that the tax system does, or can, insure that everyone pay a "fair share." But everyone who pays his legally obligated share might be inclined to feel cheated if the Government did not exact as much from all citizens. Suppose also that mail "covers," as envelope interception and inspection is called, were used only upon known members of the American Nazi Party, the Communist Party, tax fraud suspects, suspected gamblers and narcotics peddlers. Would that be going too far?

Or suppose they were used as a routine security check on CIA and FBI agents, members of the Ku Klux Klan or signatories to a "Black Power" petition. Would their use in none, one, some, or all of these applications be going too far? Polygraph tests are used by police agencies to insure against hiring men with violent feelings toward racial minorities. Too far, or not? When does "surveillance" become "snooping" and a census unlawful search and seizure?

3.

"The Congress," as Robert Kasanof has observed, "is like the human digestive system, unappetizing to the sight, but efficient." As a source of information, and frequently of instruction, it is unparalleled. In keeping with the custom of nearly two centuries, we look to it also as the last protector of our innocence and of our possessiveness, and hence, at least in comparison with the executive branch, of our desire to be let alone. Yet, starting in 1929, and in numerous subsequent sessions, the Congress has tried and failed to work out so much as a legislatable wiretap policy.

It would be unfair on that acccount to say of the Congress, as Charles Joseph, Prince de Ligne, said of the Congress of Vienna, "The Congress doesn't run—it waltzes." The Brandeis-Warren essay was written in a different world. It appeared, to be sure, nineteen years after California adopted the first wiretap law, a prohibition against the interception of telegraphed messages, and fourteen years after Alexander Graham Bell took out a patent on the telephone; still, its appearance preceded by five years the Illinois State legislature's action enjoining the newspapers of that state from tapping one another's telephones.

It was a world in which the two essayists could still assert with confidence: "The common law secures to each individual the right of determining, ordinarily, to what extent his thoughts, sentiments, and emotions shall be communicated to others." Much has happened since then to "inventions and business methods" that confound deliberation upon the subject of privacy. Among other effects, they have given substance to another spectre which Brandeis thought bore watching, and which, indeed, has made the concept of privacy more urgent to consideration than ever.

"Through size," Brandeis wrote in 1932,

> corporations, once merely an efficient tool employed by individuals in the conduct of private business, have become an institution—an institution which has brought such concentration of economic power that so-called private corporations are sometimes able to dominate the State. . . . The changes thereby wrought in the lives of the workers, of the owners and of the general public, are so fundamental and far reaching as to lead [able, discerning] scholars to compare the evolving "corporate system" with the feudal system; and to lead other men of insight and experience to assert that this "master institution of civilized life" is committing it to a rule of a plutocracy.

"Opposition to size as such," Adolph Berle wrote in 1959, "became a form of liberal stereotype." There arose, he says, "what is sometimes called the 'Brandeis school,' the men who carry on Brandeis' famous battle against the curse of bigness. I knew Brandeis from my childhood. My first job was in his law office in Boston. I loved him to the day of his death. But I think were Brandeis in action today, he would be the first to deal with the facts and the last to fetter his view with fiction." For some recent facts on this matter, we may turn again to the Congress.

Chapter Two

NADER

When, therefore, you increase your business to a very great extent, and the multitude of problems increases with its growth, you will find in the first place, that the man at the head has a diminishing knowledge of the facts, and, in the second place, a diminishing opportunity of exercising careful judgment upon them.

—Louis D. Brandeis

1.

We are aware, most of us, in a literary, *Girl from Uncle*ish way, that more goes on beneath the waters of commerce we tread from nine to five daily than appearances would urge us to believe. A large American business corporation resembles a nation-state constantly at war. Several are even larger in point of resources and international political power than a few actual nation-states. General Motors Corporation is an example.

GM in 1965 received at retail for its goods and services an amount greater than the dollar value placed on the goods and services produced in all of Sweden, the nation which in the indexes commonly used to measure a "standard of living" ranks second only to the United States. GM's "population," employees plus stockholders, amounts to 2,945,000, which would rank about 98th among nations, between Laos and Sierra Leone. Like any sovereign nation, it spends large sums of money to protect against theft of its property and of information that if lost to an enemy might cause it, and perhaps the rest of us, hardship.

That GM should also make an effort to find out what its competitors are up to would seem no more than prudent. Moreover, its methods, along with any anguish of conscience these may cause, are generally considered to be of interest chiefly to the business community. Every so often, though, the Congress whistles up for inspection a witness to spout first-hand evidence of what life is like below water. One such instance occurred in 1937 when the La Follette Committee paraded out spies hired by GM, among others, to infiltrate and to betray labor unions in violation of the then two-year-old Wagner Labor Act.

Committees of Congress are somewhat limited in the scope of their investigations by their authorizing appropriations. Committees like the Long and Gallagher committees are restricted by their charters to studies of Government operations and practices. However, Senator Long and Congressman Gallagher found sufficient excuse in their mandate to examine some examples of espionage as practiced privately, as did the Senate subcommittee whose chairman in the 89th session was Senator Abraham Ribicoff of Connecticut. It is to the Ribicoff Committee that we owe such knowledge as we possess about Vincent Gillen's investigation of Ralph Nader.

2.

Ralph Nader, we may recall, was in early 1966 a lawyer of thirty-two who spent most of his time in Washington, D.C. Before November, 1965, he had neither in the practice of his profession nor in his avocation—represented by contributions to newspapers, magazines and *The Insider's Newsletter*—boasted any achievement likely to earn him a place on the eleven o'clock news. He was a graduate of Harvard Law School, and a man of seemingly ascetic tastes and habits. He commuted frequently between his mother's home in Winsted, Connecticut, and a room he leased in which to live and work near the business center of Washington. He was also as reticent about his private life as he could be animated in discussion of public issues. The event that brought watchers of television news to learn this much about his personal life was the publication of a book he had written, *Unsafe at Any Speed.* In it he contended that the design and construction of automobiles sold to the public exhibited a greater concern for the sales curves than, and in some instances at the expense of, the safety of those who bought them.

In the hiring halls where proprietors of book review columns decide an author's fate, Nader's book was at first murmured about, taken note of here and there, but not much reviewed. This annoyed and troubled

Nader. He had learned from experience that editors were not eager to retail his story about auto safety. After several attempts at trying to persuade them, his manner grew to be self-defeating. "I know you can't print the story straight out," he told one editor, "but I've angled it so that you can slip it in." He brooded over the seeming indifference of reviewers to his book. For as all enterprising journalists must, Nader subscribed to the "rise-up" theory of social reform. This theory holds, with Lord Acton, that the power possessed by a business corporation will eventually corrupt it into serious abuse of power. When the facts become known, the public—or the proletariat, the middle class, the Government, student, housewife, or whatever—will rise up and smite it a paralyzing blow.

In point of fact, as Nader was to learn, the impetus toward corporate defeat has to come from within. It is as the homely philosopher Charles Wendte said of success in life "a matter not so much of talent or opportunity as of concentration and perseverance." This is in part because there are some things men value more than life itself. Economists dispute whether the sales declines that followed Nader's disclosures were due anyway, or were caused by his revelations. In either event, it seemed likely by the fall of the year that some eight million automobiles would be made and sold, no matter how safe they were by design.

Moreover, labor leaders and politicians always avoid precipitous actions against great corporations. Perhaps they are fearful of being bored or angsted to death by having themselves to become automobile company executives. This is the only reason I can think of to account for the fact that on the occasions when a corporation has summoned itself to do something genuinely suicidal, it has customarily been rescued by the solicitude of those who are supposed to rise up. Some weeks after Nader's book was published, a Senate subcommittee was making a case in point.

Nader's study was one of several that had been made over a period of years, questioning the structural and operating safety of automobiles. One of these studies was written by the Federal agency concerned with the specifications of the $132 million worth of automobiles purchased annually by the Federal Government. This made the subject appropriate matter for investigation by the Senate's subcommittee on Government operations.

The committee began hearings on February 19, 1965. They were resumed in early 1966, and on February 10th Senator Ribicoff of

Connecticut invited Nader, on the strength of *Unsafe at Any Speed,* to appear as a witness. Senator Ribicoff knew enough of Nader's background to relieve himself of any concern that something would turn up to distract from the merits of Nader's testimony, or cause the committee any embarrassment. Otherwise, some staff work might have been required, particularly in light of the evident hostility shown to the investigation by Senator Charles Curtis of Indiana. Senator Curtis' interruptions at one point caused his colleague, Senator Robert Kennedy of New York, to snap out: "Is there any crime in writing a book?" Despite Senator Curtis, Nader was able to say what he had to say, which was largely an elaboration of the material in his book. The book included a strong case against the design of pre-1964 Corvairs, a matter about which GM had already spent several troubled months in court.

Like any sovereign power, GM resents intrusions on its prerogatives. The Ribicoff committee's resumption of hearings posed the threat that the Federal Government would interest itself in establishing safety standards limiting GM's elbowroom in the design and engineering of its cars. Since Nader was beginning to assume a prominent part in that threat, it would have been remarkable had executives of the company not expressed some curiosity about who he was and why he was so interested in a subject about which GM assumes it knows more than anyone. Precisely how GM came to take the steps it did to satisfy this curiosity remains a matter for conjecture.

In keeping with its many security requirements, GM retains its own policing force. If for no other reason than the millions of dollars' worth of contracts it receives from the Government ($459 million in 1965), it must keep tabs on employees. Moreover, in order to maintain proprietary rights to its designs, GM has to exercise "due diligence," and maintains for that purpose a large security force to shield them from outsiders. Yet any of the Big Three would be astonished to learn that its competitors did not know nearly as much about its designs as it did itself—long before the official unveilings.

The automotive industry is also no stranger to the use of outside agents. One of the uses GM has found for private detectives was revealed a short while after its encounter with Nader in an opinion by Mr. Justice Fortas. The opinion concerned GM's efforts to stop dealers in Los Angeles from selling cars to discount stores. GM jointly with associations of car dealers who had been offended by this practice agreed to

> . . . finance the "shopping" of the discounters to assure that no Chevrolet dealer continued to supply them with cars. Each of the associations contributed $5,000 and a professional investigator was hired. He was instructed to try to purchase new Chevrolets from the proscribed outlets, to put on tape records of the transactions, if any, and to gather all the necessary documentary evidence.

Moreover, Fortas remarks, "There is evidence that unanimity was not obtained without reference to the ultimate power of General Motors." A dealer had testified that the regional manager had "related a story, the relevance of which was not lost upon him, that in handling children, 'I tell them to stop something. If they don't do it . . . I can knock their teeth down their throats!' "

It should not be surprising, therefore, that, as GM's president, James Roche, was to testify, an executive of the company acted without his knowledge, or the knowledge of any member of the company's executive committee. Whoever it was, he or she telephoned Richard Danner, an attorney in Washington who represents GM on routine matters involving its relations with Washington. Danner, we may assume, did not have to consult the yellow pages in order to find the man for the job. He telephoned Vincent Gillen, president of Vincent Gillen Associates, Inc., of 370 Lexington Avenue, New York City, and a graduate of the Federal Bureau of Investigation, the *Cordon Bleu* of the private security business.

3.

An onlooker at GM *vs.* Nader would have learned that Gillen was paid $6,700, the fee plus $700 in expense money. He would not have learned from the news accounts, however, why $6,700 and not some other figure. The question is interesting to speculate on because the same figure has been mentioned in connection with other investigations often enough to suggest that it is standard. Gillen might in fact have been considered a member of a calling that is taking on some of the traits of a profession, including standard fees for a certain class of clients, with its own trade association and its own publications.

Investigators are said by those in the security trade to represent the most profitable end of the business. This is because customarily no self-respecting private agency would charge less than $6,000 to a great corporation. Yet agencies are frequently able to subcontract work at a cost that is, in sum, far less. A security agent who is sent to obtain regular work in the "mark's" factory or office, for example, might receive from the contracting agent only $25 per week spending money above what he receives in salary from the mark. From the amount of subcontracting Gillen had to do for the GM investigation, however, it would appear that his margin of profit could not have been far out of line with GM's own ($4 billion pre-tax or 19.3 per cent on 1965 sales of $20.7 billion). Between mid-January and the end of February he and his agents talked, in all, to "50 or 60" persons who had been associated with Nader in any way. Their reports were made in response to a memorandum from Gillen in which he warmed gradually to his subject:

> The above mentioned is a freelance writer and attorney. He recently published a book, *Unsafe at Any Speed,* highly critical of the automotive industry's interest in safety. Since then our client's client has made some cursory inquiries into Nader to ascertain his expertise, his interests, his background, etc. They have found out relatively little about him. . . . Our job is to check his life and current activities, to determine "what makes him tick," such as his real interest in safety, his supporters, if any, his politics, his marital status, his friends, his women, boys, etc., drinking, dope, jobs—in fact all facets of his life.

Among the first definite intimations Nader received of Gillen's interest was when a friend and former associate in a law office telephoned to congratulate Nader on his new position. Since Nader hadn't applied for a position, except in the book review pages, he asked for details about the visitor. It turned out that the investigator had proved particularly interested in Nader's sex life and, in addition to the specifications laid out in Gillen's memorandum, whether he had exhibited any anti-Semitic tendencies. Why this should have interested the investigators was left unexplained.

4.

A reporter who comes for the first time to suspect that he is under investigation makes a quick inventory of his past deeds and then makes a naive calculation. He believes either that he is protected by the potential embarrassment that may be caused the investigator at having to own up to having gathered the information, or he sets about whistling hymns of courage to himself. This is altogether commendable, but it overlooks the purpose of such investigations. While the subject may not care who knows that he once belonged to the Communist Party, or has used up three wives, or that he is a member of the Mattachine society, not to mention many lesser offenses to public sensibilities, any committee of Congress that has entertained the thought of using him as a favorable witness certainly will care.

Nader remarked after his ordeal that the "price paid for an environment that requires an act of courage for a statement of truth has been needless death, needless injury and inestimable sorrow." The purpose of such investigations, however, is not to induce cowardice in the witness but to prevent his ever being called to testify. That is, investigations of the type made of Nader are not made for the purpose of blackmail, which is hazardous no matter how much in the way of goods the investigator has. They are made as a public service to prevent a public forum from calling as witness someone who might turn out to be an embarrassment to it. Whoever asked that investigators discover if Nader had shown any signs of anti-Semitism was doubtless thinking of the possibility as a reflection on Nader's Lebanese background. It would be too much to believe, however—trying to follow the lines of thinking in these circles—that it hadn't occurred to the investigators that Senator Ribicoff, being of Jewish lineage, might find a witness who was vulnerable on no other score, offensive for that reason. One could easily, with a few moments' thought, practically reconstruct the conversation that led to this emphasis in the investigation.

Another thing that happens to a man who feels he's being investigated is that he tends to regard odd and suspicious occurrences as part of the pattern of the investigation. Gillen denied under oath that his investigators had followed Nader to a speaking engagement in Pittsburgh, as Nader thought they had, or that he had hired girls to learn whatever he had in mind in his memo when he asked for information about "his women, boys, etc." Nader was on two occasions approached by girls sufficiently attractive to have made an impression on him under circumstances he regarded as unusual: Once while making a purchase at a drug counter and another time while in a supermarket. In one case the girl wanted him to come to her apartment and discuss foreign affairs; the other wanted him to help her move some furniture. It has to be noted that soliciting by women is illegal in Washington, D.C., as in most places.

Nader may never know if he passed up opportunities to add to his knowledge of life's fortunes, nor will the public know, evidently, whether these encounters were in fact part of the investigation. What's more, a friend of Nader's said he had been interviewed by an agent who held an attaché case in his lap. This led the friend to conceive of the possibility that there might have been a tape recorder in it. Gillen said the case contained nothing but paperwork.

Nader brought his evidence and his suspicions to the attention of the Committee and also that of several journalists. They in turn, chiefly James Ridgeway of *The New Republic,* saw that it was put at the disposal of the public and of other reporters. Two auto-makers promptly denied having anything to do with the matter. Then, on March 9, GM conceded that

> . . . the office of its general counsel initiated a routine investigation through a reputable law firm to determine whether Ralph Nader was acting on behalf of litigants or their attorneys in Corvair design cases pending against General Motors. . . . The investigation was limited only to Mr. Nader's qualifications, background, expertise, and association with such attorneys. It did not include any of the alleged harassment or intimidation recently reported in the press.

The announcement was issued so late at night as to have drawn from Senator Robert Kennedy the recollection of a remark President Kennedy had made just before the Senator had been appointed Attorney General: "I'll open the door at 2 A.M. and say 'it's my brother.'" However, not even the collective bargaining breakthrough of Sandy Koufax and Don Drysdale, which was then in process, was enough to dampen open speculation as to who might have made the investigation Nader described. A *New York Times* reporter wrote that he had been assured by sources of his own in such matters that the investigation as reported by Nader was too crude to be the work of anyone likely to be employed by any company in the automobile industry. Verification of the works of living artists is, alas, chancy at best.

5.

On March 22, no less than James Roche himself, President of General Motors, went from the automobile capital to the nation's capital to confess and apologize. It appeared at first in the Senate hearing room as if the surrender might be conditional. Gillen and GM's lawyers sparred vigorously with the committee staff and with its members, particularly Senator Kennedy. One exchange began when Kennedy asked Danner, "Who raised the question of looking into [Nader's] sex life?"

MR. DANNER That came about during the discussion. As I recall in determination of his associations, if he was married, if he was not married, what sort of girl friend did he have.

SEN. KENNEDY How would that be helpful in finding out about the Corvair?

MR. DANNER Well, I think probably none really on the Corvair, but I think it might reflect in some manner on his background.

Senator Ribicoff later pressed the point.

SEN. RIBICOFF But there isn't anything in this entire report of this investigation that has any bearing on that fact [Corvair]. Your entire investigation, Mr. Gillen, had to do with trying to smear a man, the question of his sex life, whether he belonged to leftwing organizations, whether he was anti-Semitic, whether he was an odd ball, whether he liked boys instead of girls. The whole investigation was to smear an individual, and I can't find anything of any substance in your entire investigation over these weeks that had anything to do basically with whether or not he was tied up with plaintiff's attorneys that had to do with Corvair cars.

MR. GILLEN Senator, you have just said, and have said as though it had happened, that I had used the term "odd ball." I have heard no sworn testimony to this fact, and I don't think it is appropriate for me to come here as a witness and be smeared myself. I made no attempt to smear Ralph Nader. I attempted to do a job for my client, and I think we did a darn good one.

Senator Harris asked, "Does the question or the answer as to whether or not he had girl friends have any bearing on the purpose for which you were hired?"

MR. GILLEN I would say so, yes.

SEN. HARRIS Legally could that have been used in evidence?

MR. GILLEN I do not practice law actively, sir. I am concerned with doing a job.

SEN. HARRIS How would you have used it?

MR. GILLEN Pardon?

SEN. HARRIS How would you have used it except for blackmail or pressure?

MR. GILLEN What do you mean by "blackmail"?

SEN. HARRIS How could it have been used legally in case you had found out the opposite of what you did not find out, or you did find out? How could you have used it?

MR. GILLEN That would be up to my client. I do not make judgments.

When pressed further, Gillen volunteered that his curiosity about Nader's sex life had been prompted by the desire to do Nader justice. His assignment, he said, "was to get the complete life and background of Ralph Nader, and in order to get it, I thought that these things would in the normal course of investigation be covered. And if they were not covered, they would be suspect." Gillen explained that therefore he had to pursue the investigations into Nader's sex life out of "fairness to Ralph."

SEN. KENNEDY What is "fairness to Ralph"? You kept proving he is not anti-Semitic and he is not queer. In fairness to Ralph? Ralph is doing all right. You were just a public-spirited citizen rushing around the country in fairness to Ralph?

MR. GILLEN Well, I did not hear—all right. I was doing a job, and I still think it was a good one.

Later, however, as GM's lawyers sought to make a point, Roche cut them short. Done, he said in effect, is done. At this nearly everyone but

GM and Gillen were fairly pleased with themselves. Nader, magnanimous even in victory, took the trouble to seek Gillen out to give him evidence concerning the one question Gillen said he hadn't been able to answer; that is, whether Nader had a driver's license. Gillen had been snapping pictures in the hearing room throughout the afternoon with a miniature camera. He took the license from Nader, rubbed it between his fingers, held it up to the light, then handed it back without comment.

A spectator had to wonder if Gillen had merely been off his form on this job, or if he had been so consistently successful at getting incriminating evidence in previous investigations as never to have been called to account. A fraternity brother of Gillen's, an executive of a large security services concern, pondered the same question, then pointed out: "Still, he'll get some business out of this one." Roche, too, was to salvage some satisfaction. The next day's editions of the late *New York World-Telegram and Sun,* for one, carried a wire service story which extolled Roche for displaying once again his unfailing sense of public relations. Senator Ribicoff, for his part, earned the place reserved for the Quotation of the Day in the next morning's *New York Times.* He said: "There's too much snooping going on in this country." The statement was unexceptionable even by a Senator's standards. Who would deny that any amount of snooping is too much? The point at which differences arise is where to draw the line between "snooping" and, say, "necessary security precautions." Or to put it another way, what did Roche mean in his March 9 statement by a "routine" investigation?

Chapter Three

NOBODY HERE BUT US SECURITY AGENTS

"Executives of sound judgment are those who are best informed."

—The John T. Lynch Company
"Former FBI Agents"

1.

Routine may describe unvarying procedure, or the regular occurrence of some one activity in it. Like the conventional round of human sex life, investigations made by corporations may be said to be routine in the latter sense rather than the former. For they, too, comprise practices that have been going on a long time, that everyone knows are going on now, but about which no one can be sure as to who but himself is doing them, how frequently, to whom, or how. In the spring of 1966, there was only one study of corporate investigative methods worth troubling with, and that was seven years old. The study, entitled *Competitive Intelligence,* was made with the help of nine students by a professor of Industrial Management at the Harvard School of Business Administration. That work, including some 100 interviews with company managements, was then absorbed into a more ambitious survey made by *Harvard Business Review* for publication in the November-December, 1959, issue.

We ought, perhaps, to hesitate before making light of three dozen or so solemn columns of type (including charts) in a journal as sturdy as *HBR.* Having hesitated, we are left still to ponder the study's first two conclusions, set off in italics. The writer chosen to present these findings begins with the customary assurance that he is not trying to foist anything off on his readers. "Our quantitative findings are based upon 1,558 completed questionnaires—1,250 machine tabulated, the balance inspected and found to have no significant differences—which represents a 21 per cent return from our mailing to a cross section of *HBR* readers." Then, without a stammer, he goes to his first finding:

> *The vast majority of business executives who read* HBR *say that, although they would like to know many things about their competitors, they would gather this information only through methods that they considered open and aboveboard—no matter how tough the situation!* [Exclamation point his.]

Whatever the truth in this conclusion, doubt has been cast on the method of attainment. Witness the findings of an independent survey that was made of a stoop-full of virile adolescent males living in Brooklyn. All belonged to the same Boy Scout Troop. All said that they read *Boy's Life* regularly and learned much that was useful from it. They were asked a long list of questions designed to elicit information on how they gathered competitive intelligence on the subject uppermost in their minds. Their responses may be summarized as follows:

(1) "None of your damned business." (2) Muteness caused by severe anxiety paralysis at the mention of the subject. (3) "Wouldn't you like to know?" accompanied usually by a broad wink. (4) "First let me tell you about the last one." (5) "Gee, I wish I had what (4)'s got." (6) "Who knows?"

Researchers said they felt able to assign statistical significance appropriate to a serious study only to responses (1) and (6), but expressed the wish to know more about (2). They agreed, furthermore, that verifiable instances of (4) could not be usefully extrapolated to describe the incidence among the 79 per cent of teenagers in the block who did not respond. No doubts at all, however, have been raised concerning the Harvard study's second conclusion, that "*most business firms gather information about the immediate activities of competitors in order to meet competition more effectively at the consumer or customer level.*"

The study devotes considerable attention to how corporation executives normally obtain competitive intelligence. Survey techniques are not much help here, either; least of all without careful attention to definitions. Information of a kind that literally changes the life of a corporation may come to it in a variety of ways. The Haloid Company of Rochester, New York, learned about the process that turned it into Xerox Corporation from an item in a technical magazine. Whether information about a competitor's moves comes to an *HBR* reader in a way that would make its editors proud of him is frequently as much of a mystery to him as it is to them. This would be true if for no other reason than that subordinates have "ways" of obtaining information which in reporting they may tend to glorify or play down depending upon how they actually got it.

Three years before the appearance of *HBR*'s study a *Fortune* writer observed that, clear-cut cases of espionage aside,

> Industrial intelligence itself encompasses activities that extend from innocuous practices, like pumping a competitor, to reprehensible ones employing fake polls and phony letterheads. . . . But the line between business intelligence and business espionage is sometimes vague, and depends on what has come to be accepted practice.

Hovering close to the line, we might suppose, is a practice implied in the remark of an investigator quoted by *Fortune:* "Give me a company's waste paper for a couple of weeks and I'll tell you all about its operations." Moreover, while executives near the top can describe the formal arrangements they have instituted to "insure a constant flow of information," they may be in the dark, as any management consultant can testify, as to the channels along which the information actually travels and what happens to it during its journey.

In these connections, the Harvard study emphasizes that younger executives were much less troubled in their minds about some of the practices at the nether end of competitive intelligence than were their elders. As the study points out, this tendency may be traceable to any number of causes, one of which could have been that being closer to the source, the younger executives knew better from where, and how, to get the information as well as how to package it so as to spare their employers troubled consciences when they came to use the information in making decisions. By 1966, some of these men were presumably closer to the top themselves. Do executives as they become older also become more "ethical" or simply more judicious in their responses to survey questions?

2.

Methods apart, the *HBR* study's usefulness to an exploration of what Roche might have meant by "routine" is further hampered by its definition of subject. The General Motors investigations of Nader and of its dealers in Los Angeles do not fall under the heading of competitive intelligence as conceived in the Harvard study; the study is concerned only with betrayal as between corporations. Thus it has to do with practices such as planting a spy in a competitor's plant, use of wiretaps, comparison shopping, and, at some length, hiring away a competitor's key employees to obtain the information they possess concerning a process or formula of commercial value. This restrictiveness was particularly disabling in the account the study gave of interviews with investigators. For example: The article carries across the title page a photograph of John O. Camden, Vice President and General Manager of, as it was called then, Pinkerton's National Detective Agency. The caption is a reassuring quotation from Mr. Camden: "We are called in less frequently than in the past. . . . Spying is . . . unnecessary." The whole of Mr. Camden's remarks, though, are more provocative.

As an illustration of how ethical competitors have become, he relates an incident in which a businessman had told a competitor that someone had offered for "$50,000 or $100,000" information about a formula and process in which the competitor had invested millions of dollars. The competitor went to Pinkerton's. Pinkerton's men discovered that the seller of this information was only a broker acting for an employee of their client. "We, through investigation and certain other phases of our work, were able to determine the identity of the employee who was going to provide the information, and he was apprehended." Some elaboration on "investigation and certain other phases of our work" might have shed more light on what makes for "routine."

In the same backhanded manner, the study hints at other types of investigation that might be part of the routine. A caveat should be noted, though: "When asked about cases of outright spying to gain advantageous information for its own sake, most of the investigators were reluctant to answer, and could cite fewer cases than one would expect from earlier published statements. Only after lengthy inquiry would they indicate the frequency with which such cases are offered to them." Deception is, of course, an investigator's bread and butter. Without it, there is neither need for his services nor many ways he could supply them.

Let us, however, also assume that in this case there was significant correlation between length of interview and truth of response. We may then learn that in 1959 many investigators felt "that the number of cases involving personal perpetration or investigation of industrial espionage is increasing." Upon further questioning, the investigators reveal that

> . . . the majority of these cases consist of situations in which management *feels* [italics mine] that an employee is stealing material or embezzling funds. Many of the remaining cases are requests for "management audits" which consist of supplying the client with undercover operatives to be employed for the purpose of reporting on employee activities. Again, most of these audit cases involve thefts; others are the investigation of foreman bias, slowdown on a production line, or simply a check on the general efficiency of company operations.
>
> Another major category of cases which are referred to by the investigators concerns investigations for lawsuits or patent infringements. In these cases, the company counsel or attorney usually hires the investigator. Typically, the investigator has to find out about the activities of a competitor in order to get evidence on a patent infringement.

These, we may assume, are part of the routine. Again, however, there is no explication of who, how, and how often. I say this not as criticism of the study; it did not purport to look into these areas. I mean only to indicate that perhaps the least part of the activity described as industrial espionage is devoted to spying as part of competitive battles.

3.

As the *HBR* study notes, it is almost beyond possibility to find investigative agents who will talk for attribution or for the record. We found a few who would, but while on the subject of the study, I might be permitted mention of two who would not. They will swear over a lunch table, although not in court, that a Florida real estate developer hires private investigators at a stipulated fee per head in order to get a glimpse of an applicant who sends a completed form from New York State. New York state law forbids the developer to ask applicants to identify themselves according to race or color. The developer wants this information, however, before he invests in a routine credit check.

Similar allegations were made about an insurance company that offers to sell term insurance by means of magazine advertisements. It appears that because of actuarial differences between whites and nonwhites, the company, in order to keep its rates competitively low, is in fact making the offer to some citizens, but not all. Again, it was reported to us as common practice for employers to hire investigators in order to make spot checks on employees who phone in sick. This employment, to be sure, like that of truant officers, might be directed only against the chronically ailing.

HBR aims at a different class of readers than those who might feel affected by these revelations. One might have supposed though, that even a junior executive might be at least as interested to learn that his own telephone conversations were being audited as he would be in the more widely celebrated revelations involving the theft of trade secrets from manufacturers of pharmaceuticals and chemicals; this if for no other reason than that he might make whatever adjustments in his conduct and manner of expression that he might consider necessary.

For more detailed knowledge of what has come to be "routine" in these matters we are again indebted to the Long Committee. The evidence is from a less well-publicized hearing held only two days after the hearing that brought James Roche to Washington to confront Ralph Nader.

That reports on the Long Committee hearing were not as detailed nor as widely circulated as those on the Nader hearing is not surprising. It isn't every day that a Senate committee can feature the president of General Motors Corporation eating crow, together with witty dialogue about sex with Senator Robert Kennedy in the role of the interrogator. Moreover, the protagonist before the Long Committee, Hyman L. Moore, president of the H. L. Moore Drug Exchange, New Britain, Connecticut, brought up a highly complicated complaint. The thrust of it was that Smith, Kline and French, a pharmaceutical company headquartered in Philadelphia, had planted a spy in Moore's wholesale drug warehouse as part of an attempt to police SKF's prices and distribution. The effect, though, said Moore, was to seriously jeopardize his business.

The threat that Moore posed to SKF's peace of mind was his practice of selling pharmaceuticals to retail druggists at a price below that posted by wholesalers who held SKF franchises. He was able to do this principally by conniving with the franchised wholesalers. The scheme took advantage of the fact that SKF offered a choice of two discounts. A wholesaler who sells in bulk to a nonretail account receives a 6 per cent discount. Wholesalers who sell to retailers receive an additional 9 per cent discount in recognition of the costs they incur to maintain inventories and salesmen, and for shipping, handling, and repackaging. Wholesalers who acted more or less as brokers and way stations, moving products in much the same form in which they were received, gained the lesser amount. Wholesalers who were willing to receive SKF's products in bulk for repackaging, and who could also provide receipts, vouchers and other evidence that they had spent time and money on sales and promotion, received an earned services discount of 15 per cent. (In either case, 2 per cent was added for cash payment by the wholesaler to SKF upon receipt of goods.)

Franchised wholesalers discovered in Moore the opportunity to increase their volume of sales while enjoying something more than the 6 per cent discount but at no more trouble or expense to themselves. Moore had, by use of direct mail solicitation, built up a customer list of retail druggists, many of whom also sold drugs at below retail list prices to the public. He was willing to take shipment in bulk of SKF products at a price representing less than the 15 per cent discount he would have received as an SKF franchised dealer. The franchised dealer thus had only to transship SKF products to Moore's warehouse in New Britain and represent to SKF, with the help of faked vouchers, that it was entitled to the full 15 per cent discount.

Moore indicated that other manufacturers left more room in their discount policies—some as high as 50 per cent—to work with. SKF products, however, accounted at the time for approximately one-fifth of all U.S. pharmaceutical sales, including many of the items most in demand. SKF manufactures, for example, dextroamphetamine sulphate under the trade name Dexedrine, advertised and prescribed, customarily, as an appetite suppressant, but widely known as a "pep-pill." The relatively narrow profit margins Moore would appear to have received on SKF products were worth all the trouble and conniving because in addition to some profit they gave him the competitive advantage of being able to offer his customers a full line of products. As he told the committee, "You can't do business out of an empty wagon." It was imperative, of course, that he take precautions to see that neither SKF, nor any other manufacturer, learn where, or how, he obtained his supplies.

Thus, each day there came into Moore's warehouse, often to the door of a neighboring company's warehouse entrance, boxes labeled Kool Ray sunglasses or Alka Seltzer which actually contained prescription drugs. In addition to the amounts he ordered Moore received the numerous samples franchised wholesalers would have handed out had they been making the calls to druggists that they represented to the manufacturers they had made. (The samples were particularly burdensome to Moore because each pill or capsule had to be wiped clean of the sample marking, usually with acetone.) This practice, it was alleged, cost SFK some $90,000 in additional profits on a volume of $1 million annually through Moore alone. The figure is arrived at by calculating the difference between the customary 6 per cent discount, and the earned services allowance of 15 per cent on sales of $1 million.

Moore also managed to have shipped into his warehouse drugs that had been sold to exporters for sale outside the U.S. Some bore labels indicating that they were destined for Vietnam, Korea, Indonesia and Hong Kong. They included a type of quinine which at the time was reported to be in short supply for treatment of soldiers in Vietnam. Senator Long explained that exporters were quoted lower prices on drugs than domestic wholesalers. This put Moore to the trouble at times of having to send a truck down to the New York piers late at night to pick up shipments for which he paid exporters, who would then represent to the manufacturer that they had shipped the drugs out of the country.

Into Moore's warehouse on August 3, 1965, came also David Terpstra, 30, a former Dutch seaman. Terpstra applied for a job, explaining that he had only three weeks before been forced to leave Brunswig Drug Company of Los Angeles, second in size among drug wholesalers and franchised by SKF, after six years of employment, in order to be near his parents, whom he said were about to emigrate to Connecticut. Moore, as it happened, needed another skilled hand, and so telephoned Brunswig to check Terpstra's references. He received a high recommendation. Brunswig, in fact, wished they had been able to induce Terpstra to stay. It wasn't made altogether clear how this endorsement was arranged; in point of fact, though, Terpstra had worked at Brunswig only three months, if that, and doing much the same kind of work he was about to do for, and on, Moore. In the trade, it is called security work.

Chapter Four

A QUESTION OF SECURITY

The danger in Hollywood is to think this is the world. To me there's safety in thinking that this is just one of many different places. I used to have a friend who edited The Dry Cleaner's Monthly, *and it's the same thing in the dry cleaner's world. In that world there are leaders, too—dry cleaners whose names are magic, up-and-coming young dry cleaners. There are many worlds.*

—Mike Nichols

1.

The March, 1966, issue of *Security World,* a trade magazine, carries a full-page advertisement which asks, in large print surrounded by two-thirds of a page of white space: "What is 'security'?" Without going further, we have to take the question as being no more than rhetorical. Security is, of course, the warrant under which the nation's, the community's, the corporation's and the decent American's interests are these days most often asserted. Its place in the economy is as secure as the defense budget. Moreover, its provision rewards handsomely a segment of American industry about which, appropriately, one hears very little.

Members of most professional societies know a remarkable lot about what their brothers are up to, but leave outsiders to their own devices. This is particularly true, for evident reasons, of members of the American Society for Industrial Security. By comparison with them, members of the American Medical Association appear garrulous. All the same, the rising popular esteem in which the word "security" is held has gradually encouraged the society and its members to talk somewhat more openly about their work. Moreover, of the Big Four in the business, Pinkerton's, Burns International Detective Agency, Inc., Globe Security Systems, Inc., and the Wackenhut Corp., three—Burns, Globe and Wackenhut—have raised capital in the open market. While the annual reports they are therefore required to issue will win no prizes from the New York Society of Security Analysts, they are enough, when examined together with responses at interviews and the fraternity's two leading trade publications, to give some idea of how much business firms spend to purchase security services from independent contractors—in addition, again, to the very considerable sums spent by business firms that maintain their own security systems.

There is no hope of calculating how much private industry alone spends in payroll costs on devices and measures to fulfill their obligations as Government contractors, to plug inventory leakages, certify the honesty of employees, and to seal trade secrets and machines from the eyes of competitors. However, for the purpose of giving substance to these speculations, John W. Hunter, Jr., a financial analyst, has calculated as nearly as they can be reckoned the amounts spent under contract to firms in the security business outside the walls of industrial corporations.

In 1965, revenues to the security industry from business firms very likely exceeded $500 million, which by itself would place the industry in the Commerce Department's ranking just above pipeline installation, but below the sales recorded by travel agencies and related services. Some 30 per cent of this total was spent with the Big Four, who in turn derived between 5 and 10 per cent of their income from investigative work. The bulk of their work is accounted for by the provision of uniformed guards, installation of electronic alarm and inventory systems, polygraph machines and other services lumped together by a financial securities analyst as "guards, gates and gadgets."

After the Big Four come several medium-sized companies with sales ranging up to $5.5 million and several thousand smaller agencies—industry executives generally agree that 5,000 is a sensible estimate—engaged almost exclusively in investigation. An accurate measure of their business volume is difficult to obtain, in part because a substantial portion of their business is conducted for cash, and in part because many private investigators have taken to calling themselves consultants. What's more, some states do not require the licensing of investigators, and many practitioners in the other states do business without a license. Hunter estimates that the average 1965 income for the smaller agencies probably falls between $80,000 and $100,000—with an outside range of $10,000 to $500,000. About 80 per cent of this is derived from business; the remainder represents private clients seeking to resolve marital problems, recover stolen property and the like. That would amount to at least $320 million spent by industry among the smaller agencies; another $15 million or so is spent for investigative services from the large and medium companies who also sold approximately $170 million in 1965 in "guards, gates and gadgets." Total: $505 million.

2.

David Terpstra, to relieve any lingering suspense, was of course a security agent *extraordinaire*. At seventeen he had shipped aboard as a radar operator with the Royal Dutch Navy. At the age of twenty-three, he left the sea behind him and took a series of odd jobs as a handyman and electrician for various employers, including a Long Island country club. How he came to find a career in the security business was not explained. The committee's counsel, Bernard Fensterwald, Jr., hinted that perhaps Terpstra's nautical work as a radar man and electrician may have commended him to the attention of his employer, but he and his employer agreed that they made no use of wiretaps and so did not need this particular skill in their endeavor.

In any event, Terpstra was employed then, as he had been during the previous four years, by Inter County Surveys, Inc., at 280 Madison Avenue, in New York City. The company was at the time of the hearing celebrating its twentieth anniversary of service, principally to the drug industry. It was then as always the length and shadow of its founder and president, John L. Saviano. He had reared it from a small one-man office to a business employing forty-three agents. Saviano assured the committee that the bulk of his work consisted of audits ordered by managements of conditions in their own plants and offices. He could not recall a previous time when he had accepted an assignment to penetrate, as they say in the trade, a business other than a client's.

This seems plausible enough, especially in light of the fact that 90 per cent of Saviano's work had been done for competitors in the same industry. Saviano was in fact an associate member of two organizations Moore had tried to join only to be turned away: the National Wholesale Drug Association and the Federal Wholesale Drug Association.

Considering the thoroughness of the reports turned in by Terpstra, 142 pages closely typed, including specifications as to the length and width of new shelving Terpstra had installed in Moore's warehouse, Saviano's files must have been a gold mine of information. Since, like most investigators, he must have had to rely heavily on word of mouth for advertising, it would appear either that competitors in the drug industry have no choice but to trust one another, or that Saviano enjoys enormous trust and esteem among his clients. Perhaps both; Fensterwald elicited from Saviano the admission that he had retailed the same information he received from Terpstra on assignment from SKF to other clients; but, he was quick to mention, with SKF's permission.

SKF paid Saviano the apparently customary $6,000 fee for the job. Saviano, in turn, paid Terpstra $25 per week, plus expenses, for twelve weeks. Even after allowing a *pro rata* share of overhead, plus a between-assignments salary to Terpstra, the profit margin from the SKF fee probably was proportionately higher than SKF's own in 1965. Although Terpstra thus received more in wages from Moore than he received from Saviano, the latter offered him stable employment together with the relief from the boredom of having to work too long in any one place. In the four years that he had worked for Saviano, Terpstra had been assigned at least seven jobs in as many different locations, including Los Angeles, Washington, D.C., and New York City.

Moore and Terpstra came to terms at $85 per week. On coming to his office the day following, however, Moore found Terpstra already energetically at work. Impressed, Moore gave his new employee a raise on the spot of $5 per week. By that time, Terpstra had already cased the warehouse. The information he obtained consisted mostly of reports on what the boxes that had come into the warehouse actually contained, and where they had, in fact, come from. He was able to get this latter information from packing slips and vouchers that were inside the cartons. At one point, Terpstra discovered that a stock boy Moore had employed some time before Terpstra came along was also recording data from packing slips and vouchers. As Terpstra testified, he wasn't sure whether he was competing with another agent, or could believe the boy's story that he was entertaining ideas of some day going into the business for himself. In either case, the stock boy stood to queer Terpstra's act.

Terpstra did, of course, what security agents do in the movies. He went to Moore one morning asking if he could spare a few moments for a private chat. Moore made time later in the day. Behind his closed office door, he learned from Terpstra, obviously pained at having to tattle on a fellow-worker, that the stock boy had been copying information from packing slips and vouchers. Terpstra told Moore that the stock boy had "asked me to steal invoices for him." Moore thanked Terpstra and fired the boy. As far as anyone knew, the boy did, in fact, want the information to nourish his dreams.

Moore's faith in his own judgment was shaken first by an incident he was unable to overlook. This was when Moore received a midnight phone call from Terpstra asking if Moore would please come down to the local police station and put up $50 bail. Terpstra had been booked for a violation known in Connecticut, in another example of indifference to precision of definition, as a "morals charge." It appears that he had been cohabiting with some poor wretch of a girl on parole from a state prison who was living with her relatives in the same rooming house as Terpstra. She was, as a result, recommitted. Terpstra paid a fine and took a suspended sentence.

Moore's suspicions were not further aroused until several months after Terpstra came on the job. They began when franchised wholesalers started to cut him off, some without a word, some with the information that SKF had evidently discovered whom they were selling to and had threatened to lift their franchises unless they stopped. At least one was disenfranchised. One at last suggested to Moore that "you have got to have a spy or a stooge in there, because everything is being pinpointed; there could be no other way." This was late in February. It didn't take Moore long to run through in his mind a list of half a dozen employees, most of whom had been with him for years and were well known around the town. Perhaps SKF had not given sufficient thought to the consequences of a total war strategy. For once treed, cut off from sources not only of SKF products, but other staples in his business as well, Moore had nothing to lose by telling his story to whatever public official would listen.

On March 9, the day Terpstra was served a subpoena to appear before the committee, he almost instinctively, it seemed, went to his employer. "Does it have anything to do with immigration?" he asked. (Terpstra was here on a permanent alien visa.) Moore said he didn't know. Maybe, he speculated, it was in connection with the morals charge. Terpstra doubted if that was of a magnitude sufficient to interest a committee of the Senate. He left the warehouse and went immediately to a pay telephone. Moore did not lay eyes on him again until the day of the hearing, even though Moore still, as he told the Committee, was holding a paycheck for the days Terpstra worked before he left.

Saviano refused to testify as to whom, in addition to SKF, he had sold the information. He first claimed a sort of privileged relationship between himself and his client. When it became evident that this wouldn't work, his lawyer pointed out that the subcommittee's authorization envisioned an investigation of surreptitious security work by Government agencies, but not the activities of private enterprisers. Long was aware of that, he said, but had put into the record an incident which he felt made the hearing a proper concern for the committee.

This had to do with the fact that Moore's company had only a few days before the hearing been fined $1,500 on two counts of a thirty-two-count indictment charging shipment of a misbranded drug in interstate commerce and refusing access to its records to Food and Drug Administration inspectors. The charge was that the company had shipped out as Dexedrine, an SKF product, dextroamphetamine sulphate that was, in fact, not of SKF's making. Seven counts relating to adulteration were dropped when it was shown that the drug was dextroamphetamine sulphate, even though not SKF's.

Moore said he had received the drug through his own private channels as an SKF product and had shipped it that way "in good faith." Senator Long thought the circumstances were sufficiently provoking to warrant the attention of a Senate Subcommittee on Government Administration Practices and Procedure. The question on the minds of most onlookers was, of course, whether the FDA had lent itself to SKF's enforcement efforts. This part of the hearing found no place in the prominent accounts of the day's hearings, although Senator Long's staff said that it planned to make further inquiry.

SKF in a formal statement from its offices in Philadelphia said that it "prefers not to engage in this type of surveillance" but that the "procedure was necessary because under the law we are obligated to see that our wholesale distribution agreements are uniformly enforced" and further that the company had a "public responsibility to know that its drugs, many of which fell under the new Drug Abuse Act, are confined to legal distribution channels." The company also said that it was "deeply troubled" by the testimony.

Neither Saviano nor Terpstra exhibited any sign of anguish, however. Saviano thought it was terrible the way that SKF was being bilked under its Earned Services Allowance Plan. Saviano also stressed that Moore had bought for resale drugs intended for fighting men overseas. Terpstra summed up his position when he was asked by Fensterwald, "You were an industrial spy, is that correct?" Terpstra answered: "Yes, to a degree. I was a security man, not a spy."

3.

The Long Committee hearings left even more troubling questions floating in the air than had the Ribicoff Committee. One that belongs perhaps to a study of political aesthetics was why a committee that had devoted as much attention as the Long Committee had to snoopery by Government agencies felt obligated to drag in testimony concerning Terpstra's brush with Connecticut's wilting prurience respecting cohabitation. More to the point is why an official from SKF had not been invited to make the corporation's case. And why the Food and Drug Administration was not offered an opportunity to explain its suit against Moore. Having speculated upon these questions, the spectator was left, to be sure, with one advantage.

While the workings of the democratic process in substance bear small relation to the descriptions retailed in high school civics classes, the outward consequences frequently come close enough to escape attention, except of older and more experienced men unwilling to taint the innocence of the young. Thus, with the help of the Senate, the spectator was able to form some notion of what the president of General Motors had in mind as a "routine" investigation, and of the meaning the trade assigned to the word "security."

Chapter Five

SECURITY IS A SCHLAGE

It is a silly game where nobody wins.

—THOMAS FULLER, *Gnomologia*

1.

ONLY RECENTLY, as the genealogy of words is reckoned, has "security" become a term of art. The Romans put together the prefix *se* and the word *cure* out of the need for an adjective to suggest of persons and things the capacity to exhibit or provide the literal equivalent of "freedom from," and "care" or anxiety. Users of Middle English turned the adjective to use in order to form a noun to denote objects which gave peace of mind to traders conducting transactions at a distance. It is perhaps only within the past quarter of a century that usage has issued a charter of intelligibility to apposition of the nouns "security" and "measure" as well as security officers, agents, manuals, councils, arrangements, precautions, risks, devices, programs, systems, safeguards, along, as we have noted, with security industry.

The author of the following definition in a standard dictionary has attempted manfully to take account of this development, but has failed:

> 1. The state of feeling of being free from fear, care, danger, etc.; safety or a sense of safety. 2. freedom from doubt; certainty. 3. overconfidence; carelessness. 4. something that gives or assures safety; protection; safeguard. 5. something given as a pledge of repayment, fulfillment of a promise, etc.; guarantee. . . .

In (5) he has disposed of those things which give peace of mind to pawnbrokers, bankers and traders on the floor of the New York Stock Exchange. We are therefore left to find examples of his meaning in (4). What distinguishes the "something" of the definition from the art of a physician, a warm blanket, a moat, a pistol, $1 million in a safe place and other items so numerous that they have long ago had to be assigned their own words? A lifeguard is not a security; neither is a policeman, or a warm saloon on a cold night. And so on.

We are forced back, therefore, to the question posed by the advertiser in *Security World.* His question turns out, however, not to be rhetorical. The copy below the question, "What is security?" offers only this answer: "Well, for one thing we believe security is something that isn't advertised. . . . We think security is something that is discussed between security officers and security specialists." The advertisement is signed with a trademark made up of the word "Schlage." True to its definition, the advertiser offers little evidence of who or what Schlage is, except to make mention of a cylindrical lock, about which the reader might learn more by writing to a post office box in San Francisco.

2.

In matters of language, usage does as usage is. Perhaps like social and political scientists, security agents find it hard to define their work in respect either of subject matter or method, and so rely upon reference to those who practice it and what they do. A good practitioner to look at for this purpose is Norman Jaspan. We know this because businessmen in 1965 paid Jaspan some $5 million for his services, and he sells security. Jaspan went into business in 1927. He has worked his way up from a one-man operation into an association employing 500 persons. When challenged by a problem in theft either of information or of goods, Jaspan Associates works according to much the same plan. Most of the firm's employees came to it as their first job out of college. Each new agent serves an apprenticeship of three years as a member of a "fact-finding team." This conforms to the practice of large management consultant firms which assign men to gather information for analyses of a client company's operations, except that Jaspan's men work, as a rule, under cover as employees or whatever other guise seems appropriately effective to the assignment. They seldom put in more than three months on any one job.

When they have completed their work, they present the data to junior consultants. These are men who have put in their apprenticeships, having done at least a dozen jobs in a variety of settings. The consultants then move in to ask questions, expose wrongdoers and reform procedures to minimize the risk of future losses. These security measures include as a rule "compartmentalizing" an inventory, whether of goods or information, and the institution of better records of who has had occasion to work with specific commodities or data. It may also include "de-bugging," the trade term for searching out miniature microphones and transmitters, checking telephone lines for wiretaps and the like.

Jaspan's recommendations may also include adoption of employment contracts to protect loss of trade secrets by way of departing executives, inventors or marketing men. A study by the National Industrial Conference Board estimates expenditures on research by private corporations in 1965 at $15.5 billion, and observes that "Companies have traditionally protected their investment in research by requiring employees engaged in such work to sign patent and secrecy agreements that give the companies the exclusive ownership of all inventions developed at their expense." The conventional forms of these agreements have in recent years been challenged in the courts and by Congress, however, and have in turn required expert attention for their revision.

Jaspan estimates that in 1965 his firm uncovered $60 million worth of "inventory leakage," as it is sometimes known in the trade, 62 per cent of which was traced to men at the plant supervisory level, or higher. Jaspan, speaking from the experience of thirty-nine years in the business, asserts that the theft of merchandise, materials and components for resale on a subterranean market has grown steadily to reach proportions that are "unbelievable." He attributes this to a general deterioration in morals and, by commonly cited implication, to competition: "Everyone is told they must get good marks in school even if they have to cheat; everyone changes jobs three times in five years nowadays to get ahead and takes the former boss' secrets with them as coin to trade up." This suggests another source of anxiety.

Jaspan attributes a good part of the business he receives to the fact that of all products on the market on any recent New Year's Eve, 60 per cent were not available the preceding New Year's Day. The information that these products embody, and that is invested in the strategy for marketing them, constitute the substance created by large investments. The principal measure of the value of most of them is the look of surprise on a competitor's face when he sees a product, or an advertising campaign unveiled.

We might imagine what the effect would have been on the life of the corporation in its early days had, for example, Thomas Edison been employed by General Electric, had there been a General Electric. A number of persons whom the president of GE had not met would be on to the fact that tungsten turned the trick in the light bulb. The fact would be recorded in notebooks, tungsten purchases would have been detailed in the shipping room, mention would have been made of the fact over telephones and jotted on note pads in conference rooms. The advertising and marketing people would have had to know all about the "Dynamic Solid-State Improvement" in GE's All-New Dura-Glo Bulb in order to make plans that would in themselves cost heavily and be as easily stolen. Each year during the fifties and sixties, thousands of new products were placed on the market, supported in most cases by heavy investments in research and advertising. Thus, as Jaspan remarks, "at the first click on the telephone" a businessman "realizes that Howard Hughes wasn't so dumb to conduct business in men's rooms and on beach fronts."

3.

From what we know of Jaspan's operation, we may take as an initial formulation that a security measure is an activity directed toward increasing the peace of mind of whoever pays for it, usually by reducing the peace of mind of another. Thus bank guards and Secret Service agents increase the peace of mind of depositors and bank managers by inculcating feelings of insecurity in those who might otherwise he tempted to steal the bank's money or to attack the President physically. This definition would work also to explicate the Secretary of State's meaning when he says that security forces have been dispatched to Santo Domingo in the interest of national security. A moment's reflection reveals, however, that the definition is still too expansive; left in that form it would make a security measure out of Hitler's invasion of Poland, not to mention the theft of a patented invention from a competitor by a company that needed it to forestall bankruptcy.

In order to get closer to the meaning implied by usage, we may take as our text a circular distributed by the John T. Lynch Company, Professional Investigators and Security Consultants, "America's Largest Professional Investigation Company" with "Representatives throughout the United States and 35 Foreign Countries." The circular, a reprint from *The Legal Chronicle*, notes:

> If he suspects a competitor is violating the patent rights of his client, Lynch will put an undercover agent in the competitor's

plant. In every case so far, the agent was in and out without being discovered. In fact, no undercover agent of Lynch's has ever yet been caught. Needless to say, Lynch will never put a man in a competitor's plant to steal any trade secrets owned by that competitor. Only where his clients' rights are being infringed on will such work be permitted.

Thus we may amend our definition to: "A security measure is an activity directed toward increasing the peace of mind of a good guy who pays for it, usually reducing the peace of mind of a bad guy." Or, to be more specific, if a dishonest employee doesn't get you, Ulmont Cumming will.

Chapter Six

THE NUMBER ONE SPY

Were the eye not attuned to the Sun,
The Sun could never be seen by it.

—GOETHE

1.

VINCENT GILLEN was not long done with doing as he might to save General Motors Corporation from Ralph Nader when Ulmont Cumming was thinking of ways to make more trouble for that beleaguered corporation. In thirty-nine years of practice, Cumming has won a billing in numerous newspapers and magazines as America's Number One Industrial Spy. He has also in that time worked sometimes for, sometimes against, GM. Even so, he told an interviewer he was surprised when General Motors Acceptance Corp. refused credit to his own corporate person toward purchase of a new car. He was astonished, he said, when the dealer through whom Cumming made the application indicated he would make a special effort to get approval from higher up rather than accept the cash Cumming had offered in lieu of credit. "That must be some blacklist," he said. The dealer eventually got approval for the credit, as it turned out, while acknowledging the cause of the inconvenience as an investigation at GM which Cumming had made a dozen years back. "I'm not through with it yet," Cumming said.

Cumming was then, at sixty-nine years of age, the only prominent, genuinely private investigator to have bridged the two most recent epochs in the annals of industrial security. The first began in the late twenties, when the industry branched out from a preoccupation with simple thievery and labor relations into, as Cumming once deposed, "investigations pertaining to patents, trademarks, surveys and various types of industrial investigations." The other epoch began after the war ended in 1945. The war wove security consciousness into the fabric of the American way of life.

Cumming was not sure if he liked his "Number One" billing. "For one thing, it makes me sound as if I'm some kind of dirty sonafabitch." He has disclaimed the quotation frequently attributed to him that "there isn't a factory or office building I can't get into." He said, "I would never make a statement like that. It would be just the time when you would fail. All I say is that I will try. I don't say I won't fail, but let me tell you I have never had a failure in my life."

The part of his life in which he had earned his reputation began in 1927, the same year in which Jaspan set up shop. Cumming had been working for an uncle who owned and operated a chain of business clubs, called the "Colony Clubs," with rooms for salesmen, conference rooms and a business information service, including a bulletin-board type of exchange for messages and advertising for services. Cumming took charge of the service, in the course of which he met a number of patent attorneys. When the Colony Clubs went bankrupt, he surmised that there might be enough work in trademark and patent investigations to support him, his wife and young child. He couldn't have picked a better time. His first two years in practice were banner years for the security industry, including, as they did, the stock market crash.

2.

Several years ago, while Cumming was testifying in a trademark protection case, he was asked how many investigations he had made. "Up to yesterday," he said, "27,853." At the time, that worked out to three investigations a day, leaving out Sundays and major holidays. Cumming's services are particularly valuable for the work he lists in his job description as "surveys." As a witness during a deposition or trial, his long experience with the issues and procedures involved in patent and trademark litigation more than compensates for his lack of the type of prestigious authority which attaches to the better-known polling and survey organizations. For example: Not many years ago publishers of a mass-circulation magazine (since ingested into a larger group of publications) were attempting to prevent a then recently formed and small chain of stores from continued use of a name the publisher thought was hazardously similar to the name of the magazine. Lawyers for the magazine believed that the similarity might cause confusion in the minds of shoppers, and mislead them into believing that the publisher operated the stores or endorsed their merchandise.

The owners of the stores retained Cumming to conduct a survey. He was unable, as it happened, to uncover a single shopper who was led to the store by the magazine's reputation, or who thought of the two as being in any way related. Lawyers for the publisher pressed him concerning his methods, but without much success; for the techniques devised to ascertain these matters remain, so far as courts are concerned, outside the authority claimed by exact science. The opposition lawyers questioned Cumming also as to his experience and his references. He cited the number of investigations he had made and listed as presumably satisfied users of his services a roster which included Firestone Tire & Rubber Co., Goodrich Tire, General Tire, U.S. Steel, Wheeling Steel, Stevens Stamping, General Foods, Pillsbury, General Mills, Upjohn, Parke Davis, Johnson & Johnson, American Home Products, Kellogg and International Harvester. As questioning by the publisher's lawyers continued, Cumming felt obligated to mention to one of the younger lawyers that some years previous he had executed an assignment for the lawyer's father.

The incident suggests one reason that published accounts of Cumming's adventures invoke a spirit something like that of a *Reader's Digest* "Most Unforgettable . . ." feature, right through to the snap ending. "There are also industrial mata haris," a news magazine account chirps. "Cumming once sent his wife on a plant tour to find out how a particular machine worked. The machine was broken when she reached it, so she played the bright do-it-yourself housewife with, 'Oh, I bet I can fix it with a hairpin.' A patronizing plant official (male, of course) let Mrs. Cumming go right ahead. She didn't fix the machine, but was able to study the works in minute detail."

Then there was the time Cumming was asked to find out what kind of device was being used to eliminate poisonous diesel truck fumes in an Oklahoma zinc mine.

> Cumming could find no plausible pretext for descending into that mine. So he instructed his wife in the intricacies of diesel engines, told her exactly what to look for, sent her down in the guise of a magazine writer doing a piece on mining from a woman's point of view. "She was so successful," Cumming recalls, "that the mine officials not only told her everything she wanted to know, they even tried to date her."

3.

A biographical account of Americana is no more complete without Cumming than it would be without touching on Allan Pinkerton.

Cumming was born on January 21, 1897, in Seaboard, North Carolina. He attended public schools until the age of seventeen, when he joined the army. His office contains photographs and trophies of his service with the 308th Field Artillery of the 78th Division. They include awards for his triumphs on the polo fields for the army before going overseas, the Croix de Guerre and Soldats de Verdun. Two stuffed swordfish and a few firsts, together with several seconds, thirds and fourths won at New York City horse shows also decorate the walls. He rose from private to first lieutenant, is a commander of the American Legion and one of fifteen survivors of his regiment who in 1966 were still meeting regularly. He won the Harvest Moon Ball at Madison Square Garden in 1935 and is presiding officer of the Sons of Confederate Veterans chapter in New York.

Cumming came to New York in order to earn enough money to get married. Before joining his uncle, he sold stocks and bonds, but, without training and friends, could not make a go of it. He seemed to have been intensely devoted to his wife, whom he regards as "the best agent I ever had." For a man who in 1966 was just shy of seventy, he seemed in splendid health, about five feet seven inches tall, slightly boned but stocky, under a faintly florid face. It was easy to imagine him brazening his way into a factory, but hard to picture him monitoring a "bug" or a wiretap. And like most industrial security agents, he kept a standard repertoire of stories on hand.

Little has been left on the public records of Cumming's activities or those of his fraternity during the fifteen years after the stock market crash, save, of course, for labor relations work. This stands in marked contrast to the period fifteen years after the war, when anyone with a *Reader's Guide and Index to Periodical Literature* coupled with access to a used-magazine outlet might buy all the stories he could stomach at literally a dime a dozen. Mostly, they were accounts of events which seem to have happened in limbo, as if to illustrate a point rather than to burden further one's knowledge of what was happening in the world.

There is the one about the West Coast (or Midwest) supermarket owner (or restaurant operator) who has been known to bribe a printer (or printer's messenger) for an advance look at a competitor's weekly advertising (or menu) specials. A St. Louis manufacturer asks himself sadly why a Boston competitor can sell the same item in St. Louis more cheaply than he can. A spy brings back information on the competitor's production methods, cost of raw material, internal sales organization and the like. The St. Louis man whittles down his costs and gets back into competition. Wholesale thefts by employees, intended sabotage of a chemical plant, theft of customer lists, the undermining of a TV rating, attempts to mess up company office procedures, all form part of the frequently repeated pattern.

For comic effect: "One company had as many as 35 undercover agents inside a plant, none of whom were known to each other. Unwittingly, they frequently wrote reports criticizing each other's conduct." Also, of course: "Counterspies have been known to trail spies who were trailing the counterspy's client. Once, during an IE job, private eyes had to sneak into a plant at night—and were promptly arrested by guards working for their own agency." These are the outward manifestations of the phenomenon that has made up a large and disturbing part of the large corporation's postwar environment. S. O. Astor, president of Management Safeguards, Inc., has estimated that "The consumer is paying as much as a penny on every dollar because of management's need to protect itself against espionage, internal theft and fraud."

4.

Cumming's reminiscences appear not to vary greatly from telling to telling. He has used all of the standard methods and guises: the stockholder who says he's been receiving dividends from the company for years and thinks it's about time he had a look around "his" plant; the tourist whose son is interested in auto racing, or boating, or chemistry, or whatever and who thought that as long as he was in town maybe somebody could give him some information the son would like to have; the delivery man come to pick up a shipment; the maintenance man come to fix the wiring; the salesman; and the like. The women he retains for special jobs customarily pose as writers working on magazine features.

Two adventures from his standard repertory serve to illustrate the characteristics that have brought Cumming such abundant success: a directness of method and a determination that gains force with each intermediate setback. In the first instance Cumming was retained in a patent dispute which centered on the early development of the GM system for automatic transmissions. His client wanted to know one fact: the date of the first prototype drawing of the design which eventually produced the Hydromatic and Dynaflow systems. Cumming went directly to the GM laboratory and asked to see the man in charge of transmission design. Told the man was absent he settled for number two, explaining to him that his son, a hot rod buff, had a passionate interest in the development of automatic transmissions. Did the designer possibly have any early drawings of the system that Cumming might study and report back to his son? Within five minutes Cumming had the original document in his hands and its data in his head.

In the second instance Cumming was asked to study some machinery in a plant in Cleveland. He made a deal with a fire inspector to take him along on a routine inspection of the plant, sealing the bargain with $50. But when the inspector learned which company Cumming had in mind he balked, claiming that its manager was a personal friend. Cumming agreed that this might be awkward and let the man off the hook but allowed him to keep the $50 in return for a promise of silence about the project. Later he attempted to enter the plant in the company of a building inspector only to be hustled off to the manager's office and grilled by a group (which included the $50 fire inspector) as to the identity of his client. "That got me mad," Cumming said. When it became clear that threatened legal action would not make him talk, the manager released him and an angry "Monty" Cumming went right to work. "I went downtown and rented a Hertz truck and hired a driver and bought myself some blue denim work clothes," he recalled in an interview. The next morning he and his driver arrived at the plant's loading platforms at 6:30 to await a fictional delivery. Half an hour later Cumming joined a line of early workers and entered the plant. He had cased the entire layout and was back in his truck driving away before the loading platforms opened at eight o'clock.

He sometimes has to get more persuasive help than that available from building and fire inspectors, as in Toledo at one time when he got the local police to get him into a plant on the pretext that there was a murderer inside that only Cumming, as an eyewitness, could identify. He has taught himself a good deal about machinery and production methods. Thus, when as the result of a feature in the *Wall Street Journal,* he received calls from businessmen who wanted to know why they were being undercut in competition, he was able to tell them. One, a cheesemaker in Ohio, learned that his competitor in Kansas ran a "filthy operation" spending no money on sanitation. The other, a Milwaukee bolt manufacturer, learned how his competitor had managed to eliminate two steps on the production line.

Like many another private investigator, he avails himself of a telephone company service one can't find listed along with Princess pastel-colored telephones. Evidently, if one knows how, one can get someone at the company to sell lists of the numbers called long distance by any given subscriber. This service can be useful in many ways, especially in tracking down a "plant" who has to report to someone out of town, or in harvesting a salesman's customer list. New York Bell Telephone, however, does not know that it offers this service. "Look here," Cumming has been quoted, "I'm employed by some of the most respected law firms and some of the biggest businesses in the country. If they're not worried about the ethics of the job, why should I be?"

Not until after the war of 1939–45, however, did Cumming gain the notoriety he now enjoys. Industrial espionage, he told an interviewer, represented a much smaller share of his business in the thirties than it does today. We estimate that in the decade of the fifties, purchases of security services by private industry, directly and by subcontract, rose 160 per cent to $285 million. In the three years corresponding to the nation's preoccupation with the late Senator Joseph McCarthy of Wisconsin, business broke into an even steeper climb.

Cumming, to be sure, does not lay claim to being a security agent. He takes that role, though, when he invades a corporation's premises to ascertain for a client whether the invadee is using a device upon which the client holds a patent. Thus, his attitude toward Al Worthington might be guessed as "live and let live." Jaspan, in common with Worthington, deplores eavesdropping among competitors. Jaspan, though, would allow as necessary and therefore justifiable eavesdropping on employees of a corporation by the corporation itself. This, I assume, is out of solicitude for the privacy of the corporation. Now, looking at the other side of the balance scale, is there some notion of privacy from which the employee may take security?

Chapter Seven

"RECENT INVENTIONS . . ."

Give me a fruitful error any time, full of seeds, bursting with its own corrections. You can keep your sterile truth for yourself.

—Vilfredo Pareto

1.

Supposing Patrick Henry had proclaimed to the Virginia convention: "Is life so dear, or peace so sweet, as to be purchased at the price of chains and slavery? Forbid it, Almighty God! I know not what course others may take, but as for me, give me privacy or give me death." We may safely assume that generations of schoolchildren would have been spared at least one exercise in rote memory.

Among active and sociable legatees of a revolution particularly, the ambition to draw a line around oneself and to withdraw seems at best, in our crowded circumstances, to be a daydream; at worst, cause for suspicion. In some circles it may be regarded as a neurotic constriction of personality, in others as snobbishness, or worse. In either event, who wants to stake his life on that privacy with which Andrew Marvell taunts the coy mistress?

The grave's a fine and private place,
But none I think do there embrace.

Revolutions are not fought, unless through successful deception, solely for that privacy cherished by private entrepreneurs, as entrepreneurs. Nor for private ends, either, although some, like Hilaire Belloc's Lady Poltagrue, "a Public Peril," might foment a skirmish here and there.

The Devil, having nothing else to do,
Went off to tempt my Lady Poltagrue.
My Lady, tempted by a private whim,
To his extreme annoyance, tempted him.

For this reason, every essayist whose safari of concerns leads him into exploration of privacy as a "right" feels obligated to point out that no such right is enumerated in the Constitution and to account for that deficiency. A standard conjecture maintains that it does not occur to the navigators of an undermanned ship of state afloat on an ocean of land that anyone might feel as Robert Browning did in *Paracelsus:*

> I give the fight up: let there be an end,
> A privacy, an obscure nook for me.
> I want to be forgotten even by God.

It might with equal force be argued, though, as some popular anthropologists have argued, that the reason why the British appear to be more civil toward one another and to exhibit a stronger respect for privacy than we do is that they have had to suffer one another at close quarters for a much longer period of time. We might, for all we know, be agreeably surprised were some young, enterprising sociologist to tap a bit of the money lying around for urban studies in order to learn if persons crushed in New York subways at rush hour today act any more or less civilly than they did ten or twenty years ago. Moreover, the city, because it is crowded, affords the greatest opportunity for anonymity, which is a form of privacy. It would appear to me, therefore, that the population explosion already bears more than its share of the burden for the explanation of things that go bump in the night without adding the load of blame for peephole inspectors in Government lavatories.

Another speculation places the blame on advances in the discoveries and inventions of which Justice Brandeis spoke. This argument is based on the coincidence in these advances and the rise nationally in security consciousness. The argument has some merit.

2.

Henry Mencken was much taken with the use of the word "bug" in its various meanings because of its usefulness to illustrate the differences that separate the "English" from the "American" language. Yet his monumental work of lexicography, *The American Language,* makes only one mention of the word "bug" in anything like its use in connection with eavesdropping. That was in reference to the underworld slang meaning, "an alarm device." For as recently as 1948, when the second and last supplement to Mencken's work was published, a rig for tapping into and recording a telephone conversation, or for eavesdropping on conversations in a room, was still a cumbersome business requiring wires, bulky hardware and the constant attention of the eavesdropper. They were scarcely small enough to be called bugs, and by the standards that obtained ten years later might even be considered unwieldy. During that decade "bug," as applied to eavesdropping, reverted to the meaning intended by its origin in the Celtic tongue, "a hobgoblin" or "spectre."

One of the reasons we know so little about this spectre is the lack of effective guidance by which civil servants may measure their words. Without a clearly formulated policy, they are forced to operate on their own, which tends to make liars, effectively, out of the most diligent and scrupulous of them. The Federal Bureau of Investigation, for example, is under injunction not to install wiretaps except under certain conditions. These conditions were once explained in testimony by Attorney General Katzenbach before a Senate committee. Since 1940, he said, wiretapping "has been done only with the personal authorization of the Attorney General and only in cases involving national security or human life." What's more, every year, when it comes time for the Bureau's director to come to Capitol Hill to support his request for appropriations, he gives some assurance similar to that he made in February, 1963:

> We have throughout the entire country at the present time less than 100 telephone taps. As a matter of fact the actual number today is 95. All are in security cases. In accordance with policy of many years' standing telephone taps are utilized only in cases where the internal security is involved, or where kidnapping and extortion may bring about the jeopardy of a human life. The F.B.I. does not have authority to authorize any wiretap. Each one must be authorized in advance and in writing by the Attorney General.

On May 24, 1966, though, a memorandum from Solicitor General Thurgood Marshall to the Supreme Court indicated otherwise. In the spring of 1964, Fred Black, Jr., a public relations advisor and business associate of Robert G., or "Bobby," Baker, was sentenced to fifteen months to four years in jail and fined $28,000 on tax fraud charges. The Supreme Court denied a petition for a hearing; the petition was based in part on the allegation that the Government's evidence had been gathered through eavesdropping by FBI agents. The memorandum from Solicitor General Marshall was to inform the court that contrary to his prior understanding, the FBI had, indeed, during its investigation, implanted a microphone in the wall of Black's suite at the Sheraton-Carlton hotel.

It came to light shortly afterwards that the FBI had also, in the course of an investigation into gambling activities, been eavesdropping on citizens of Las Vegas, Nevada; this time by means of bugs implanted inside telephones. On June 30, 1966, the District Attorney of Clark County said that he would prosecute the agents for violating a Nevada state law against the use of any form of electronic eavesdropping device. What's more, a "security supervisor" for Southwestern Bell Telephone Co. in Kansas City told a Senate subcommittee that the FBI leased lines running from office and residence phones there to the local FBI office.

In point of technical fact, neither of these cases made liars out of Katzenbach and Hoover, since the agents had not directly intruded on a telephone line. In the one case, they used a wireless device and in the other devices which required only that they lease telephone wires, an opportunity that is available to all good customers of A.T.&T. and its subsidiaries. However, in trying to determine whether private conversations, including those between a lawyer and his client, are to be treated as if they were private "mail," the distinction would appear to the layman's eye to be without a difference.

3.

A New York lawyer who because of the nature of his practice has some reason to believe that others may be interested in conversations he conducts with his clients writes to the New York Telephone Co. at irregular intervals to remind the company of its obligation to him as lessor of its services, and to request that his telephone lines be checked. With him, this is mere sport to while away the intervals between earnest engagements with established institutions. "I wouldn't say anything over a telephone I wouldn't be willing to shout through a megaphone in Grand Central Station," he says.

Many others have reason to regard the admonition as sound. In *The First and the Fifth,* O. John Rogge quotes a scary but anonymous description of wiretap practices by the Government. I pay it heed, though it is without attribution, because Rogge is a former assistant U.S. Attorney General, and he cites it as if to suggest that his own experience would make it creditable:

> For despite the statutes and judicial decisions which purport to regulate wiretapping, today this practice flourishes as a wide open operation at the Federal, state, municipal and private level.
>
> A wealth of collected information discloses that the conversations of public officials in every sort of government agency, bureau and political subdivision have been tapped. Reports are legion that private citizens have had their conversations recorded. All kinds of business organizations and social, professional and political groups have been listed as victims. There are charges that wire tapping may be an essential part of the Federal Bureau of Investigation's population-wide "loyalty" probe. And recently complaints have been made that telephones of United Nations delegates and employees are under surveillance, as well as telephones of foreign embassies, legations and missions in the United States. . . .
>
> In short, although wire tapping is a crime in almost every state, and although there is a Federal law prohibiting the interception and divulging of the contents of telephone communications, wire tapping is carried on virtually unimpeded in the United States today.

J. Edgar Hoover is not the first law enforcement officer to have been caught astride a credibility gap on this matter. Kenneth P. O'Donnell, appointments secretary to President John F. Kennedy, has said that the President "despised that kind of thing and never authorized it." Presumably someone did, though, because Bill D. Moyers, President Johnson's press secretary, said that "shortly after taking office" the President prohibited wiretapping by any Federal official or employee except in national security cases. That may be why James Riddle Hoffa, while attending the Teamsters Union convention in Miami in the summer of 1966, refused to enter a room until Bernard Spindel, his personal de-bugging specialist and himself a master snooper, had checked the woodwork. Those who hold with the security doctrine may invoke Proverbs 28: 1, "The wicked flee when no man pursueth: But the righteous are bold as a lion." To which we might add from that same text, verse 16: "Be not righteous over much."

For there are others besides those who contemplate trouble with the law who exhibit signs of nervous flight. *The New York Times* for July 24, 1966, recorded that in Washington, "The prevailing mood is that eavesdropping—by industry, political opponents, jealous spouses or perhaps the Government—is here to stay."

The account goes on to note that "This atmosphere has generated a number of do-it-yourself gimmicks for beating the bugs":

> One lawyer takes an inflatable plastic tent to hotel-room conferences. The conferees inflate the tent and sit inside, supposedly insulated from microphones hidden in the walls by the air between two layers of plastic.
>
> When another individual confers in a strange room, he always sits in the middle of the room, knee-to-knee with his conferees. His aides stand in pairs against the walls, talking constantly to muffle the discussion.
>
> Others bring old fluorescent tubes that blink and buzz, or ancient electric diathermy belts. When plugged into a socket, these set up radio static calculated to drown out the weak signals of any hidden transmitters.
>
> The situation has inspired more formal counter-eavesdropping devices. Ivan W. Conrad, an assistant director of the Federal Bureau of Investigation, was recently named "inventor of the month" by *Science Digest* for his patent on a bug-proof room. Several concerns market static-producing instruments.
>
> About half a dozen detective agencies here have experts who "sweep" or "sterilize" rooms to detect eavesdropping devices. This is done primarily by using instruments that detect metal inside the walls and radio emissions from hidden transmitters.

Another person who believes he has cause for concern is Joseph A. Beirne, president of Communications Workers of America. He testified before the Long Committee that local telephone companies used electronic monitoring equipment—such as a microphone installed in a desk calendar at company offices—to eavesdrop on conversations between their employees and customers. Beirne said he was concerned about such devices being "inflicted" on union members and about the "dangers posed by bribers and corrupters" who might try to use members to eavesdrop for them. Beirne said telephone companies were leaders in developing secret listening and transmitting devices, and he recommended strict Federal limitations on the manufacture, sale and use of all eavesdropping equipment.

Meanwhile, three telephone company subsidiaries in three different parts of the country have had to make it known that they spot-tap subscribers' telephones, although for reasons that remain obscure. An official of the Chesapeake and Potomac Telephone Co. acknowledged that electronic devices were used and said they were "a service aid to make sure the customer's problems are being taken care of." Another, in Massachusetts, caught up by a state committee investigation, explained that the taps were made to check on the quality of the signal in the system.

4.

A good part of this nervousness has doubtless been inspired by the publicity attending the Long and Gallagher committee hearings. The Senate committee hearings particularly brought out evidence of the extent to which executive agencies had used electronic eavesdropping devices. They also brought to light the range of eavesdropping equipment available to anyone who wants to use it, including martini olives that were really pickup and transmitting units, tie clasp microphones, and a dart gun able to lodge a microphone in a target from a mile away.

This last could easily be made obsolete, however, by the device described by Paul W. Blye, a retired Bell Telephone Laboratories engineer. He said that a laser was being developed as an eavesdropping device which could be aimed at a room several blocks away to obtain a television picture of everything that happened in the room, with sound. Microcircuits then coming on the market as a result of Government expenditures in the space program promised to make cigaret-pack sized hardware seem as bulky as an old windup Victrola.

Sherman Delmage, a retired major of Army Intelligence, has written in *Security World* that "the electronics of producing an unsophisticated 'bug' from readily available, completely 'innocent' components is within the skill of many high school students." Major Delmage shows a commendable resistance to the common temptation to exaggerate the state of the art. All the same, anyone who has leafed through the catalog issued by Continental Telephone Company, New York City's leading supplier of "investigative accessories," would go beyond Delmage's modest observation. In point of fact, there is no longer any reason why anyone with skill and patience enough to work a jigsaw puzzle, some spare time for experimentation, and less money than would be required to become a versatile shutterbug could not install an effective, well-concealed eavesdropping system capable of recording every sound in a room on a tape, and one that the eavesdropper may stop by and recover whenever it seemed convenient.

Anyone of a mind to eavesdrop would have had his fancy caught by the pitchpipe bug loosed by Emanuel Mittleman, who does business in lower Manhattan as Wireless Guitar Company. Like all eavesdropping systems, the pitchpipe bug consists of a detector, a link and a responder. Most genuinely effective bugging systems also require for each of these components an outside power source, such as a small battery. Miniaturization of power sources hasn't advanced as far as that of components. As a result, a pinhead microphone coupled with a microcircuit transmitter, about the size and thickness of a postage stamp, may require a bulkier object to supply power. I say "may" for word is around that innovators have conceived a way to get power from the light in a room, or even more reliably, from a commercial radio station signal, at least one of which in most major cities broadcasts around the clock. These, however, are not readily available. In the meantime, the pitchpipe bug may serve.

The pitchpipe bug detector is attached to the telephone in the area to be bugged. The link, responder and power supply are all supplied by the telephone company. The person who carries the pitchpipe, usually in the form of a one-note harmonica, may hear all conversations in the bugged area from anywhere in the country while the telephone to which the detector is attached remains on its cradle. If the eavesdropper is in Phoenix, Arizona, for example, he merely dials the number of the bugged telephone—in Honolulu, say. When he hears the click indicating that the circuit has been completed and the phone is about to ring, he blows the pitchpipe into his receiver. This cuts out the bell signal at the other end and activates the detector, which uses the power supply in the phone to relay into the responder, i.e., the telephone he is using. If the bugged phone is taken off the cradle, the signal cuts out.

5.

All the same, to assign to instruments the force of cause results in hazardous confusion, as if a physician, having prescribed chocolate butter to ease the discomfort of chicken pox blisters, took it that there was nothing more he might do. The confusion leads to the inevitably demoralizing endeavor to legislate the unlegislatable, such as alcohol in the twenties, and more recently a narrow band in the spectrum of the mood-changing drugs arrayed in the pharmacopoeia. Like the income-tax laws and injunctions against gambling except at approved locations, such as Aqueduct Race Track and the floor of the New York Stock Exchange, narcotics laws are a greater drain on enforcement facilities and a greater threat to community morale than seems, on balance, desirable, or for that matter, necessary.

It might be none the less instructive to speculate on the extent and nature of the uses the founding fathers might have found for the pitchpipe bug had it been available. We might, that is, learn something about either their conception of the world and of human conduct, or our notions of their conception. To that end, I suspect it might be even more productive, though, to speculate on the uses they would have made of the instruments which today make possible scenes like those that occur daily at 10 A.M. in the briefing room at United Airlines headquarters in Chicago.

Chapter Eight

". . . AND BUSINESS METHODS"

A merchant's desire is not of glory, but of gain; not of public wealth, but of private emolument; he is therefore rarely to be consulted on questions of war or peace; or any designs of wide extent and distant consequence.

—Samuel Johnson

1.

A drone buzzing around Darryl Zanuck's desk in a suite at the Hotel Plaza in New York City was asked by a newspaper reporter why Mr. Zanuck needed six telephones. "It gives him a sense of controlling his environment," the drone explained. As it happens, Zanuck has more means by which to lift and move things in his surroundings than most of us do in ours. The drone did establish, though, that he is plugged into the new world of systems science. In this world, the word "environment" finds uses undreamt of in the world of old-fashioned biologists. It is now part of the nomenclature of the study which enables an airline to concern itself hour to hour with a network of operations in which a multitude of events, of flights and transactions involving allocation and reallocation of equipment, people, freight, baggage, food, parts, tools, cash and credit, occur simultaneously, some in and some around the weather.

So as to be able to envision these occurrences all at once, as it were, United Airline's executives meet every morning in a briefing room at the front of which are two maps, one depicting the line's routes, with clocks at the top to indicate the hour in each time zone, the other portraying the most recently available weather information. Along the sides of the room are illuminated panels containing whatever other data one needs to guide the fortunes of an up-and-doing airline, all of them computed into manageable terms not long after the events they represent occur. The machines and methods that make this possible have made business corporations a great deal more pleasant to live with than they were before the most recent of the Great Wars.

Like most Americans, private corporations have grown to adopt the habits and outlook of city dwellers. They have little experience, nor would it make much difference if they had more, with life in the rural boroughs in which most of them grew up. Citizens there formed and wore their reputations the way tropical fish do. A banker or merchant could learn as much as he needed to know for the prudent conduct of his business by taking some time to talk and chat while walking the street.

Roughly the same condition obtains among prominent citizens of the community served by *The Wall Street Journal.* Those in finance and industry who occupy the brain pans of large corporations make occasion to see one another face to face, know who matters and who doesn't, and therefore form fairly definite ideas about who can be trusted, and for what. Moreover, they are privy to at least as much gossip as circulates through the nation's capital.

The corporations whose fortunes they tend are required, though, to solicit paid help and buy-now-pay-later custom from among persons they have never seen, or of whom they have never heard. Inevitably, they have gotten burned once and again and for many years retired to that form of twice-shyness easily mistaken for sullen unresponsiveness. The bigger they grew, the sulkier they seemed to get, until they became barely sufferable. We can only guess how balky these behemoths might be today were it not for their employment of one or another or all of the ideas gathered together as part of systems science.

2.

The late Fred Schwed, Jr., told of the time that a New York retailing pioneer was being chided for the accounts he kept in his large and prosperous East Side Manhattan department store. As rejoinder, the retailer led his critic to the room containing the pushcart with which he began his life in the United States. "You see this?" he indicated. "Everything else you see is profit." It is not as easy, of course, for the president of a large, scattered and variously occupied corporation to keep an eye on things as it was for, say, Alfred Bloomingdale. A trait that was charming in him is something less than engaging when discovered in the Secretary of Defense, or the president of a department store syndicate in which one has invested money.

These men have to keep a watch on persons, places and activities they may see at first hand only rarely, and perhaps never. That they are able to do this with greater self-assurance than in the past is attributable in large part to improved methods for keeping an eye on things, and for visualizing where the corporation has been and where it is going. These include, in the terms of modern accounting, improved standards and controls for reporting, to keep track of cash flow, inventory leakage and of the other animal and mineral energies at the corporation's disposal.

Other improvements have added to the scope and variety of the information available to the corporation's accounting. Survey techniques and the science of statistics have made the corporation's environment more readily available to view than at any previous time in its history. By being able to apply roughly the same principles as are involved in construction of actuarial tables, a corporation can put together a serviceable guess of what the market for its products will be in future months and even years, and make reckonings of the audience for its advertising.

Systems analysts and researchers can obtain an inventory of the risks entailed in introducing a new product without the cost of actual introduction. (At least 75 per cent and perhaps as much as 95 per cent of new products fail for reasons other than lack of sufficient capital.) The record of employment of systemic methods in reducing this figure has been spottier than in application to internal controls, but has contributed all the same to the increased willingness of many corporations to make innovations.

Retail Credit Corporation receives more than $100 million annually in return for information from its memory bank. It contains data on 42 million Americans, which is supplied and kept up to date by some 7,000 investigators. The magnitude of this achievement can best be appreciated by noting that the Department of Defense central index comprises information on only about one-half this number of individuals, some 21.5 million. It may be, of course, that the Federal Bureau of Investigation keeps a bigger file, but I have no grounds for conjecture.

In 1964, the National Industrial Conference Board reported on personnel "audit" techniques of 132 companies, employing approximately 2,237,000 persons. The report said that 37 per cent of the respondents used attitude or opinion surveys, and that 18 additional companies made sociological or psychological studies:

> Employees who are chronically absent or involved in lost-time accidents can be studied in relation to social characteristics such as age, sex, marital status or residence [in a poor community?]. . . . All inquiries into the motivation of employees fall within the category of psychosociological studies.

The employment of psychology in assessing credit risks appears not to have advanced nearly as far. Some firms have dabbled in graphology and associative techniques for analyzing applications for credit, but the practice does not seem widespread. The motivation to continue research is not purely risk-reduction. It may be that patterns will show up indicating that some installment plan buyers are better risks for purchase of some goods than others. If an automobile, for example, is vital to a man's ego, he may be relied on to keep up payments on it while perhaps challenging the creditor to come and retrieve his wife's furs. Knowing this could make credit decisions more discreet and improve business.

3.

Improved methods of gathering and organizing information would, of course, be useless without a means of storing it and making it accessible when it is needed. Here technology has been of help, in the form of information retrieval systems. The first customer for a giant system of this type was the census bureau in 1951. Since then they have proliferated throughout industry. They have so reduced the number of clerks, the amount of office space and furniture and other impedimenta needed to keep files as to have made economical and manageable the keeping of many times the number of accounts and personnel records that were available to corporations in the time before World War II.

An information retrieval system is, in summary, a device able quickly to compute a question put to it into the terms of its own operations, to search out, again by a series of computations, information required by the question, and to display it in some form to the questioner. The information may be stored in the form of punched or magnetic tape, microfilm or old-fashioned punch cards, to mention only the most prominent forms. It may be made accessible to the questioner in the form of display on a small television screen, on typed sheets, or even by voice, as in some teaching machines and devices that respond to questions put to them about investment decisions and results asked by securities analysts.

Thus equipped, a few large creditors have come full cycle in their relations with persons who owe them money. There was a time when customers were dunned by a credit manager, backed up with drawers of files and squads of file clerks. With the introduction of the first of the modern machines, customers were dunned by machines and forbidding form letters, as indeed some are still. In recent years, however, many delinquents have again received the personal touch, from a man or woman seated at a desk equipped with what appears to be a small television set.

By means of such a system, RCA, for illustration, is able to keep on tap data on job applicants who were turned down for lack of an opening, as well as on its existing and former employees. What's more, by pressing the right buttons, an executive at RCA can learn quickly, from a TV screen image, where in or out of the company he might find someone able, say, to translate from Spanish a communication from a customer in Peru. If a customer gives his telephone number to the girl who answers at the business office of New York Bell Telephone, she can in a twinkling supply name, address and credit standing. Also computation machinery makes easier the cross-referencing and checking of information required on application forms.

Perhaps the most highly refined techniques of all have been developed by the College Entrance Examination Board at Princeton to detect falsehoods in applications submitted nationally by parents applying for financial aid for sons and daughters planning to attend college. Presumably as these techniques become more manageable to ordinary credit decisions, they will enable managements to concentrate full attention on other causes for the phenomenal growth of the second martini.

Chapter Nine

ANIMAL CRACKERS

Art goes yet further, imitating that Rational and most excellent work of Nature, Man. For by Art is created that great Leviathan called a Commonwealth or State (in Latin Civitas*) which is but an artificial Man; though of greater strength than the Natural, for whose protection and defense it was intended; and in which the Sovereignty is an Artificial Soul, as giving life and motion to the whole body.*

—THOMAS HOBBES

You're not a man, you're a machine.

—GEORGE BERNARD SHAW
Arms and the Man

1.

THE ANONYMOUS AUTHOR of the short essay in Diderot's Encyclopedia headed "Automaton" defines his subject as an "instrument which moves by itself, or machine which contains within itself the source of its motion." He traces the word from the Greek origins into French that looks to an English translator as if he thought "maton" means "I am excited, ready to move," which may come as a surprise to Horn and Hardart, operators of Automat cafeterias. The essayist means the word to apply to the:

> Flying Pigeon of Achitas, mentioned by Aulus Gellius in Book X, chapter 12 of *The Attic Nights,* if one is willing to admit, of course, that this "Flying Pigeon" was not just a fable.

> Some authors include among automata mechanical instruments that are put in motion by springs, internal weights, etc. like clocks, watches, etc.

Some today might also include the devices by which Westinghouse Electric Company seeks to make one sure if it is Westinghouse. At the Westinghouse Tele-Computer Center in Pittsburgh, a Univac 490 "real time" system, a part of a network populated by 71 other computers, keeps track of the vital happenings of a company that sprawls here and there on two continents. Among other services, it handles orders, tells the warehouse nearest the customer about it, makes sure there is enough, but not too much, of the things Westinghouse sells taking up space in warehouses, keeps track of all the company's cash in 230 banks, advises the controller of the company's financial health once a month and on the day following the day on which divisions report. And it pays workers and pensioners, keeps track of and pays dividends to a rapidly churning stockholder population. The scene gives the presence of urgent reality to a vision long cherished by numerous philosophers our educators regard as being worth imposing upon the attentions of the young.

2.

The French philosopher Bertrand de Jouvenal sets it out as "the truth" that "there has never been a time—the case of Menenius Agrippa shows it—when in discussions on Society analogies have not been drawn from man's physical body." Menenius Agrippa, a Roman patrician and statesman sent to reason with the first seceders to the Sacred Mount, recited to them the fable of the belly and its members. We may fetch even farther back, though, than the sixth century B.C.; as far, at least, as Isaiah.

"Why should ye be stricken any more?" he asks the people of Judah, "ye will revolt more and more: the whole head is sick, and the whole heart faint. From the sole of the foot even unto the head there is no soundness in it; but wounds and bruises and putrefying sores. . . . How is the faithful city become a harlot!" We may observe, further to M. de Jouvenal's observation, that transformations in the picture naturalists have entertained of the human anatomy have been attended by corresponding changes in the conception philosophers and rulers mounted in their heads of political constitutions.

Modern philosophers have only recently gotten over the fear of their debt to Aristotle, and now willingly point out that he was a great naturalist, while to be sure pointing out the respects in which he went wrong. With the scheme Aristotle formed two centuries after Menenius Agrippa, the State became

> . . . by nature clearly prior to the family and to the individual, since the whole is of necessity prior to the part; for example, if the whole body be destroyed, there will not be foot or hand, except in an equivocal sense . . . the proof that the state is a creation of nature and prior to the individual is that the individual, when isolated, is not self-sufficing; and therefore he is like a part in relation the whole.

Some early notions of the human circulatory system may have given rise to the network of roads which bound Rome into a civilization, although it is doubtful if after-orgy speakers were as given then to dwell much on the "free flow" of goods and ideas we hear extolled at banquets today. For this we ought perhaps be grateful to William Harvey's liberating work concerning the circulatory system. Conceivably his work in embryology is related also to the conception of the underdeveloped nation.

Descartes looked upon the human and the social constitution as being each a species of divinely manufactured machine. In this he was later joined by Thomas Hobbes, whose Leviathan, however, was a contrivance of human, and not divine, art. Jeremy Bentham thought of the community as "a fictitious *body*, composed of the individual persons who are considered as constituting as it were its *members*. The interest of the community then is, what?—the sum of the several members who compose it." His reference to "members" would appear to make Bentham a throwback to Greek biology, but it is obvious from the argument he draws from this concept that he was thinking of Robert Hooke's work.

Muriel and George Beadle point out that Lavoisier and Cavendish had

> . . . prepared men to accept the idea that seeming entities *may* be composed of smaller units. Then, to the English Hooke's seventeenth-century discovery that living matter is made up of "an infinite company of small boxes"—that is, cells—was added the eighteenth-century finding of the French scientist Bechat that all tissues of the body are basically

similar, and the French Lamarck's assertion that tissues are a mass of cells. By the middle of the nineteenth century, the fact that cells had individual walls and nuclei were the basic unit of all living things was known and accepted.

3.

The time may not be far off, though, when in discussions on society no analogies will be drawn from man's physical body. Biologists do not talk much any more of "creatures" but of "systems," as the human biological system. This system is spoken of commonly as an automatic control system, which may be in part a tribute to the obstinacy of the French. More than three centuries after Descartes we arrive at the pages of *Scientific American* to discover a *maître assistant* in biochemistry at the University of Paris, Jean Pierre Changeaux, asserting that:

> The analogy between a living organism and a machine holds true to a remarkable extent at all levels at which it is investigated . . . in all their functions [living things] seem to obey mechanistic laws. An organism can be compared to an automatic factory. Its various structures work in unison, not independently; they respond quantitatively to given commands or stimuli; the system regulates itself by means of automatic controls consisting of specific feedback circuits.

To convey the idea of a feedback circuit, men occupied with such matters employ the familiar example of the household thermostat. As described by Gerard Piel, the system works this way:

> A mechanical sense organ absorbs a little of the heat generated by the household heating plant and thereby makes a measurement of its output. This small fraction of the output is fed back to the form of a signal to correct the input of fuel to the heating unit. By this feeding back of output to input, the household heating plant is made to regulate itself.

An illustration somewhat more complicated than this, but less so than the biological system, is offered by Gordon S. Brown and Donald P. Campbell:

> A radar dish tirelessly sweeps a beam of tiny electromagnetic pulses across the sea and sky. A target is discovered. The

> reflected pulses close a feedback circuit and freeze the radar on the target. Now the tracking of the dish puts computers to work, integrating the target position with weather and ballistic data. The solutions to these equations, fed through feedback circuits, start guns tracking the point in the sky where the trajectory of the shells and the course of the target will intersect. The final link in the system is a proximity fuse, which explodes a shell as it nears the target. This is diverse control, cutting across a half-dozen fields of engineering. Signals are translated with limitless virtuosity from discrete digital to continuous analogue statements, from electric and electronic impulses to mechanical and hydraulic actions. But already these achievements in control technology are shaded by more recent developments in guided missiles.

However one may feel toward the issue of "discrete digital" versus "continuous analogue" statements, it is at least clear, as Gilbert King, a physical chemist, points out, that "the lifeblood of automatic control is information," and that "to receive and act on information is the essential function of every control system from the simplest to the most complex." Biologists correspondingly have found it convenient and productive to expose the systems which occupy their concerns in terms such as that implied in the title of the Beadles' exposition of genetics, *The Language of Life*, and in such questions as "What causes cells whose nuclei carry identical genetic information to use that information in so many diverse ways?" The Beadles tell a story as instructive on this point as it is charming:

> When it was announced in 1958 that G. W. Beadle had won a Nobel prize, he received the following telegram from the virologist Max Delbruck. After he had separated an unbroken line of 123 letters—A,B,C, and D only—into triplets, the message read:
>
> ADB ACB BDB ADA CDC BBA BCB CDA CDB BCA BBA ADC ACA BDA BDB BBA ACA ACB BBA BDC CDB CCB BDB BBA ADB ADA ADC CDC BBA DDC ACA ADB BDB DDA BBA CCA ACB CDB ADC BDB BBA
>
> Beadle was hopelessly stuck until a botanist friend, David Smith, noted that BBA was the only triplet with a B in the middle, which suggested that it had a special function. It did:

it marked the end of a word. This clue, by delineating word lengths, was the key to the solution. The message read: "BREAK THIS CODE OR GIVE BACK NOBEL PRIZE."

Beadle responded by sending an acknowledgment in a code of *his* devising, one which Delbruck also required help to break. The score thus seemed to be 1–1. But Delbruck's gamesmanship was superior. At a formal lecture Beadle gave in Stockholm following the Nobel ceremonies, he was presented with a 10-inch helic made of toothpicks, the tips of each "nucleotide" stained with one of four colors. Delbruck had airmailed it to the presiding officer. When decoded, this message read: "I AM THE RIDDLE OF LIFE. KNOW ME AND YOU WILL KNOW YOURSELF."

4.

If a corpus such as the State or the business corporation may profitably be looked upon as analogous to a biological system, and if a biological system is a feedback system, of which information is the lifeblood, then. . . . The next step is tempting, but there is a hitch; or, more appropriately, there is static to overcome. An instance of it brought a show of petulance from the director of the Bureau of the Census, A. Ross Eckler, in an appearance before the Gallagher Committee.

"For businessmen as well as local authorities," the *Wall Street Journal's* writer recorded, "the 1970 census will be able to serve up its immense array of statistics from any geographical area, even an area as small as one side of a city block. Telephone companies, for example, already buy census data to help determine where they might sell the extra-cost Princess phones." And all this at a "relatively modest cost to the user."

The *Journal* noted, though, a "certain hesitancy among census bureau workers to pursue questions about family planning, church-going habits and amount and source of income." It also pointed out that "if asked, a person must answer any census question despite his feelings. Federal Law calls for fines and imprisonment for refusing to answer a question or for answering falsely." On August 23, Eckler appeared before a Congressional subcommittee inquiring into invasions of privacy. *The New York Times* reported:

> Mr. Eckler said the bureau is considering seeking more information on commutation habits, the assimilation of persons of foreign birth into American society, physical or mental handicaps and quality of housing. He indicated the bureau would also sample the growth of color television and ultra high frequency television, and the increase in two-home families.
>
> Most citizens probably would not object to answering a question about religion if it were included in the 1970 census without prior publicity, Mr. Eckler said. But a number of groups are strongly opposed to it, he said, and it has become an "emotional issue."

The story also noted that the American Jewish Committee had issued a statement reaffirming its position that, in the *Times'* phrasing, "compelling a person to profess his religious belief or lack of affiliation would violate his freedom as guaranteed by the First Amendment to the Constitution." It may console Eckler to know that the AJC was not the first to become "emotional," as the Census Director sees it, on the subject of privacy.

Chapter Ten

A QUESTION OF BALANCE

The last temptation is the greatest treason;
To do the right deed for the wrong reason.

—T. S. Eliot
Murder in the Cathedral

1.

William Howard Taft, twenty-seventh President and tenth Chief Justice of the United States, and the only man ever to have occupied both seats, may have seemed to Oliver Wendell Holmes on that account to have been living proof of the wisdom of the founding fathers in separating the powers of Government. Shortly after having attended the funeral for Taft's predecessor, Edward D. White, Holmes wrote to Harold Laski, under date of May 27, 1921:

> Now people speculate as to who will take White's place—Taft is much mentioned. I would rather have Hughes but I think he doesn't want it. Hughes is very hard working. Taft is said to be indolent. He has been out of judicial place for 20 years or so—and though he did well as a Circuit Judge I never saw anything that struck me as more than first rate second rate. . . .

Holmes appears not to have seen any cause to have changed this initial impression, least of all in Taft's opinion for the majority in *U.S. vs. Olmstead,* which came up on appeal the year before Secretary Stimson tore up the Japanese code.

Olmstead's complaint was not addressed against either the business corporation or, except in a metaphorical sense, the machine. In his eyes, it was more a matter of unfair competition on the part of the Government. He had been doing business in contraband spirits at the rate of about $200,000 per month when Treasury agents caught up with him. The evidence used to convict him had been obtained by tapping his home and office telephones. His lawyers contended that their client had thereby been deprived of the Fourth Amendment's protection against unreasonable search and seizure, and the Fifth Amendment's against being forced to incriminate himself.

Taft seems to have regarded Olmstead's plea as one of those exhibitions of cleverness which men have been inclined to look upon with suspicion since long before Socrates was made to quaff hemlock. ". . . The Amendment does not forbid what was done here. There was no searching. There was no seizure. The evidence was secured by the use of the sense of hearing and that only. There was no entry of the houses or offices of the defendants." Moreover, Taft wrote for the majority, by using the telephone Olmstead indicated that he meant his words to go out into the world. Although the Court had agreed not to consider the admissibility of wiretap evidence—wiretapping was then a misdemeanor in the State of Washington—Taft felt obligated to mention that he could not "subscribe to the suggestion that the courts have a discretion to exclude evidence, the admission of which is not unconstitutional, because unethically secured."

It often happens in landmark cases that the majority is remembered for its decision, and the minority for its opinions. Three of the four dissenters wrote separate opinions. Mr. Justice Butler objected to the majority's literalness. The Fourth Amendment, he said, implied "safeguards against all evils that are like and equivalent to those embraced within the ordinary meaning of its words." He reminded Taft that it is "a *constitution* we are expounding." Holmes agreed that "It is desirable that criminals should be detected, and to that end that all available evidence should be used. It is also desirable that the Government should not itself foster and pay for other crimes, when they have the means by which the evidence is to be obtained."

Holmes, having weighed the issues in balance, asserted that

> We have to choose, and for my part I think it less evil that some criminals should escape than that the Government should play an ignoble part. . . . If the existing code does not permit district attorneys to have a hand in such dirty business it does not permit the judge to allow such iniquities to succeed.

Brandeis' dissent, while apparently no more persuasive than Holmes's, spoke more closely to what has come to be the human condition. The court had once said, he lectured Taft, that, "a principle to be vital must be capable of wider application than the mischief which gave it birth." He pointed out that "Subtler and more far-reaching means of invading privacy have become available to the Government. Discovery and invention have made it possible for the Government, by means far more effective than stretching upon the rack, to obtain disclosure in court of what is whispered in the closet."

Harlan Fiske Stone did not compose a dissent, but chose from among the three that were delivered. As Attorney General, he had in 1924 imposed an absolute prohibition against wiretapping by the Department of Justice. In that same year he appointed J. Edgar Hoover Director of, as it was known until 1935, the Department's "Bureau of Investigation." Indeed, in 1929, at the first of congressional hearings held to work out, in response to Taft's opinion, a Federal wiretap policy, Hoover expressed himself in favor of a general prohibition against the practice.

Interestingly, Stone attached himself to Brandeis' dissent. This may have been because he knew better than anyone on the bench of the means at the Government's disposal to "obtain disclosure in court of what is whispered in the closet." Or he may have been persuaded by Brandeis' belief as to what the framers of the Constitution had in mind:

> They conferred, as against the Government, the right to be let alone—the most comprehensive of rights and the right most valued by civilized men. To protect that right, every unjustifiable intrusion by the Government upon the privacy of the individual, whatever the means employed, must be deemed a violation of the Fourth Amendment. And the use, as evidence in a criminal proceeding, of facts ascertained by such intrusion must be deemed a violation of the Fifth. . . . And it is . . . immaterial that the intrusion . . . was in aid of law enforcement. Experience should teach us to be most on our guard to protect liberty when the Government's purposes are beneficent. Men born to freedom are naturally alert to repel invasion of their liberty by evil-minded rulers. The greatest dangers to liberty lurk in insidious encroachments by men of zeal, well-meaning but without understanding.

2.

Holmes's admonition and Brandeis' warning in the Olmstead case have so often been quoted that, like citations from de Tocqueville and

"The Grand Inquisitor" of *The Brothers Karamazov,* they have become a part of the surroundings. They are like the sounds of a carillon one hears from a distance, but never sees, ringing out "Home Sweet Home" punctually on the hour. And so of course they go unheeded. One of the reasons why they go unheeded is Holmes's weakness in his younger days for striking off lively figures of speech.

A mind as supple and imaginative as Holmes's may be as much of a bane as it is a source of pride to the law. For it is ever-mindful, as are good poets, of the incapacity of conventionally logical propositions to contain and assert all of the ambiguities and implications required of dicta having to do with the way men conduct themselves. Persons possessed of such a mind are therefore given to muster to their arguments metaphors and aphorisms.

Those who are held, though, to the standards of lawyers and politicians, and not of poets, frequently on that account let themselves off too easily. The rest of us are thus left to the mercy of the effects of the aphorisms as indulged in by successor, and frequently less fertile, intellects. This is particularly true of the metaphor taught in high school history and civics classes as underlying the fulcrum statement in judicial and legislative efforts to balance the rights of individuals against the interests of the community.

It is the figure Holmes chose in order to body forth what he intended by "near and present danger." The defendant in the case, Charles T. Schenck, had been convicted under the sedition laws of World War I for distributing socialist circulars contending that military conscription amounted to involuntary servitude. "The most stringent protection of free speech," Holmes asserted, "would not protect a man from falsely shouting fire in a theater and causing panic."

The deficiency of this analogy for employment as a legal principle has become apparent to all but high school debaters. How much time shall we allow for the smoke to rise in the crowded theater in which we live so as to ascertain whether a shout of fire is true or false? Is the time elapsed under the Sixth Amendment prescription of "the right to a speedy" trial time enough? Moreover, in what useful sense is the handing out of pamphlets setting out a judgment about the nature of military conscription like shouting fire anywhere?

Without benefit of the analogy itself, "near and present danger" in effect became, as the "clear and present danger" test, the tenth and one-half amendment contained in the Bill of Rights. In recent years, its principal application has been to contain the efforts of unfortunates seized by a theology so barbarous as to warrant clinical more than judicial martyrdom, and against pornographers. Dean Louis H. Pollak of the Yale Law School has remarked:

> Actually, most of the free speech cases which have come to the Court since Justice Brandeis' retirement in 1939 have not been couched in the classic pattern of prosecutions of those who allegedly threaten armed overthrow of the state. Free speech has turned up in a variety of contexts—e.g. picketing; the claimed right of a witness before a legislative investigation to refuse to discuss his political views and associations; the administration of governmental (and indeed of quasi-private) "loyalty" programs; the authority of the postal authorities, and of state and local regulatory agencies, to bar the distribution of "obscene" books and movies; the power of judges to punish vigorous criticism as contempt of court; the power of the United States to deport, and otherwise penalize, aliens for present and even long-past political activity; the law of libel, etc.

I am not sure if this is because speech is as free as we could reasonably hope, or if so many proprietors of the engines of communication have come to regard the First Amendment as a variety of special inducement legislation, like the oilman's depletion allowance, that there are none left with the heart and means to give it a test now and again.

Brandeis invoked the balance test eloquently, but perhaps not as skillfully, extensively or elaborately as Mr. Justice Frankfurter, who contrived a place for it alongside the great laws of physics. On his jeweler's scale of justice, there was no accommodation for "the most comprehensive of rights," as Brandeis termed the right "to be let alone." For the balance-scale metaphor, like the system of checks and balances and the theory of countervailing power, is borrowed not from biology, but from Newtonian mechanics.

Whose scales should we use? N. R. Hanson, the British philosopher, poses a conundrum as useful toward an understanding of the mechanics of the political as it is of the physical universe:

> Let us consider Johannes Kepler: imagine him on a hill watching the dawn. With him is Tycho Brahe. Kepler regarded the sun as fixed: it was the earth that moved. But

> Tycho followed Ptolemy and Aristotle in this much at least: the earth was fixed and all celestial bodies moved around it. *Do Kepler and Tycho see the same thing in the east at dawn?*

That two American voters chosen at random would assent to the proposition contained in Holmes's crowded theater analogy is, I believe, nearly as certain as that Kepler and Tycho would have assented to the proposition, "that is the sun in the east." Hanson's question, though, is what do they *see?* And it is as pertinent in the one case as in the other. Holmes in *Olmstead,* for example, seemed more concerned with the Government's decorum, Brandeis with the human condition. They appeared to be not only using different scales, but weighing different things in them.

In the hands of Brandeis, Holmes and Frankfurter, the limitations of the balance test tend to be obscured; it was used in a way to suggest that it was the best we could hope for. Thus we are forever, it seems, required to beg all of the assumptions, and to accept as being the only productive question involving "rights" and "responsibilities" some form or another of the question asked by Representative Benjamin S. Rosenthal of New York during the Gallagher Committee inquiry:

"I think most of the community and all of us concerned ourselves with the main thesis, the question of how do you strike a balance between individual rights and community interest, particularly in the field of law enforcement and national security?" How, indeed?

3.

Al Worthington, Secretary of State Stimson and the baseball writers of Stimson's time might by their deeds be said to exemplify the playing-the-game or share-the-risk doctrine of privacy. I shall refer to it hereon as the Yankee Doctrine. Like every doctrine that concerns the way men constitute themselves to a common purpose, it advances certain stipulations about man and his condition. Fundamentally, it construes us as having been entered at birth into competition for the goods of this world, and an independent shot at the Other. It recognizes also, though, that neither the proposition that virtue is its own reward, nor its obverse, that vice is its own punishment, has ever submitted to universally accepted forms of demonstration.

Thus, some rules have to be posted. Some are universal but unspoken. Some are reached by communal agreement, and hence made law. Some are endemic to the particular contests to which we choose to commit ourselves. The rule of thumb to obey in making the rules is that they should, as far as words and rules can, minimize obstructions to one's choice of grail, and the opportunity to make for it. One of the rules which holds across the board, generally and in all specific situations, is that no entrant should be compelled by circumstance, stealth or superior force, to give away more of his stratagems, strengths and weaknesses than he betrays by his own words and actions.

Moreover, he ought to be able to mete himself out to others according to his own calculation of the risks. "By privacy in this sense," Professor William Beaney of Princeton University told the Gallagher Committee, "I mean the freedom to determine to what extent you will share your life, your activities, your ideas, your thoughts and sensations with others." As a corollary, the Yankee Doctrine holds that confidences ought to be spared pressure from outside efforts to force betrayals. This may sound to A. Ross Eckler, the director of the Bureau of the Census, like Tom Sawyer down at the graveyard, but the doctrine is not so sodden with emotion as to be entirely without merit to a reasonable man like himself.

> . . . take this opportunity to declare that, whether under a fee or not (for in such cause as this I despise a fee), I will to my dying day oppose with all the powers and faculties God has given me all such instruments of slavery, on the one hand, and villainy on the other, as this writ of assistance is.
>
> It appears to me the worst instrument of arbitrary power, the most destructive of English liberty and the fundamental principles of law, that ever was found in an English law book. . . .

Among other things, Otis argued, the writ:

> . . . is perpetual; there is no return. A man is accountable to no person for his doings. Every man may reign secure in his petty tyranny, and spread terror and desolation around him, until the trump of the archangel shall excite different emotions in his soul . . . by this writ, not only deputies, etc., but even their menial servants, are allowed to lord it over us. What is this but to have the curse of Canaan with a witness on us; to be the servant of servants, the most despicable of God's creation?

Relieved of "emotionalism"—Otis' career, if not his life, was at stake—Otis' argument would seem to imply agreement on the basic tenet from which the security doctrine is obtained: that the comprehensive purpose of Government is to confer, by its presence, strength and courage upon the citizens who constitute it. Private knowledge and private property have value and are negotiable only as long as the constituency of the, let us say, system, agree in one way or another to make strenuous effort to see that it isn't taken from its possessor without his consent.

It would appear, therefore, no more than prudent that the propertied as well as the unpropertied view it as "the right of the people," in the words of the Fourth Amendment, "to be *secure in their persons* . . ." so as to make the compact worth everyone's while. For that reason, it becomes incumbent upon the Government to seek out and arraign the bad guys at a minimum of disturbance to the peace of mind of the nonbad.

In external affairs we must for evident reasons allow a large measure of discretion to elected officials in choosing the bad, and also limit our inquisitiveness to matters of policy, as distinct from strategy. In issues which arise among ourselves, however, the experience available to the founding fathers caused them to be acutely security conscious about permitting any single official, or autonomous body of officials, no matter how appointed, or under what charter of "right," up to and including Divine right, to act at one and the same time as judge, jury and enforcement officer.

James Otis had been dead four years, but was still much in mind, when twenty-six years after his ordeal, the separation of powers doctrine was incorporated as a Constitution. He was perhaps even more in mind during the drafting of the resolution by which the Congress on March 4, 1789, conveyed the proposed amendments containing the Bill of Rights to the several states. It begins:

> The conventions of a number of the States, having at the time of their adopting the Constitution, expressed a desire, in order to prevent misconstruction or abuse of its powers, that further declaratory and restrictive clauses should be added: And as extending *the ground of public confidence in the Government,* will best insure the beneficent ends of its institution: [italics mine].

These two passages exhaust all uses of the words "secure," "private" and "property" in the first ten amendments:

> The right of the people to be secure in their persons, houses, papers and effects, against unreasonable searches and seizures shall not be violated. . . .

and

> No person . . . shall be compelled in any criminal case to be a witness against himself, nor be deprived of life, liberty or property, without due process of law; nor shall private property be taken for public use, without just compensation.

2.

For lack of a better idea, in sum, we have resorted to a process which we covenant to be owed, or due, every citizen on account of his being a citizen. It may be irksome, but it ought not to be surprising, that the most frequent and exacting tests of the process occur as a result of its encounters with the disaffiliated, disadvantaged and dispossessed, and that these encounters should be our principal source of instruction upon the meaning of "privacy."

As an instance: New York City's police, in common with those in most major cities, periodically conduct a "roundup of suspects." It is part of the continuous performance rodeo chronicled by that part of the press Ambrose Bierce described as "journalistic masturbation"—that is, sensation without the benefit of reality. The police rely for these roundups on an injunction in the municipal code which prescribes that anyone found "loitering idly" in a place of public assembly, such as a restaurant, and "without visible means of support" may be picked up and taken in as a vagrant.

On occasion over the years, they have taken the trouble to bring in Frank Costello, whose means of support have been a subject of conjecture to numerous public prosecutors. Costello, though, is seldom long detained. Like the King's wardrobe, his means of support, even though not visible, may be reckoned by their effects, including the legal talent he is able to command. Not that much is required: All that liberation from such annoyances takes is a lawyer willing to come to court and to ask the arresting officer if he offered the defendant a job.

Costello's intermittent skirmishes help to give us some notion of what Justice Brandeis meant when he spoke of the right of privacy as "the right to be let alone" but not what he meant when he spoke of it as "the most comprehensive of rights." The Supreme Court in the summer of 1966 issued some further instruction on that matter when it ruled that *anyone* brought into a police station must be given protection of the right not to incriminate himself, as much as if he owned the biggest chunk of real estate in the neighborhood.

The lesson was made somewhat equivocal, however. In another ruling handed down the same day, the Court said that it would not look with disfavor upon the practice of extracting blood from an automobile driver against his will in order to ascertain if there is enough alcohol in it to warrant a charge of driving while drunk. Justice Black, a Yankee doctrinaire, had some difficulty distinguishing between involuntary self-incrimination by means of words, and that gotten by intruding a needle into a person's arm and extracting his blood.

3.

Given no more than this speculative outline of the meaning of "privacy," what might we suppose the balance test would show concerning the action taken by the Dean of Students at Wesleyan University in the spring of 1966? The occasion was a request made of him by an FBI agent for the names of students belonging to Students for a Democratic Society. He said, "We consider the student's activities his own affair." That carried no weight at all on the scales kept by J. Edgar Hoover.

"The Attorney General," Hoover noted in a letter to the student newspaper,

> . . . stated publicly in October, 1965, that he had instructed the FBI to determine the extent of Communist infiltration into the Students for a Democratic Society. . . . This was the purpose of our contact with an official at Wesleyan University, and at no time was any attempt made to intimidate any student or official of the university. . . . An FBI investigation of an organization is not a judgment but a gathering of facts, to be studied by duly constituted legal authorities.

Men and women of college age are just beginning to make a sizable investment in a thing of great value to them, their reputations. Not all of them would be likely to choose the files of the FBI as the strongbox in which to store them. Yet it is clear they have no choice in the matter, unless it is to negotiate: which is to say, to lay low. Professor Beaney, in testifying before the Gallagher Committee, hinted at the community's interest against encouraging citizens to lay low. He recounted that "one of my colleagues has raised a rather ironic thought, that the only people in the future who may really enjoy privacy are those who do absolutely nothing important."

Congressman Gallagher expressed difficulty at perceiving the pertinence of some of the questions asked in the Minnesota Multiphasic Personality Inventory and other tests used by executive agencies. The committee's staff, in order to solicit more instruction from the outside world than the committee had been able to elicit from witnesses, collected together a sampling to include in its report. The effect of some of the questions in the context they were used suggested to one member of the subcommittee that they were used to discriminate against Negroes. Other questions asked about family income and the respondent's religion. Others appeared to a lay observer to scatter shots willy-nilly. True or false? "I am ashamed sometimes of the way my parents behave." "Housekeeping in our house is very disorderly." "Once in a while I think of things too bad to talk about." "I pray several times a week." Students were asked if they were troubled by any one of these problems: "Having a troubled or guilty conscience." "Bothered by sexual thoughts or dreams." "Lacking in sex appeal." And so on.

Congressman Gallagher has fought a valiant battle against a syndrome I shall call Jennyanydotsism, in memory of one of Old Possum's Practical Cats:

> I have a Gumbie Cat in mind, her name is Jennyanydots;
> Her coat is of the tabby kind, with tiger stripes and leopard
> spots. . . .
>
> But when the day's hustle and bustle is done,
> Then the Gumbie Cat's work is but hardly begun.
> And when all the family's in bed and asleep,
> She tucks up her skirts to the basement to creep.
> She is deeply concerned with the ways of mice—
> Their behavior's not good and their manners not nice;
> So when she has got them lined up on the matting,
> She teaches them music, crocheting and tatting. . . .
>
> . . . .
>
> She thinks that the cockroaches just need employment
> To prevent them from idle and wanton destroyment.
> So she's formed, from that lot of disorderly louts,
> A troop of well-disciplined helpful boy-scouts,
> With a purpose in life and a good deed to do—
> And she's even created a Beetles' Tattoo.
>
> So for Old Gumbie Cats let us now give three cheers—
> On whom well-ordered households depend, it appears.

Jennyanydotsism on the scale of a $100 billion-per-year Government or a billion-dollar corporation is bound to convert a trait that may in Gumbie Cats seem amusing to one that is a source of monumental annoyance. All the same, on balance, the Dean of Students at Wesleyan and Congressman Gallagher are fighting a holding action in a losing battle.

Chapter Twelve

THE PRIVACY MONGERS

I could have wished that the reputations of many brave men were not to be imperiled in the mouth of a single individual, to stand or fall according as he spoke well or ill. . . . Man can endure to hear others praised so long as they can severally persuade themselves of their own ability to equal the actions recounted: when this point is passed, envy comes in and with it incredulity.

—PERICLES, Funeral Oration

1.

JUST ACROSS the East River south of Manhattan, and extending along the port side of a Staten-Island-bound ferry, is the section of New York City called Brooklyn Heights. It is referred to occasionally as being "fashionable" but in the sense that might bring a tinge of smugness to a regular reader of *The New Republic*. For it is thoroughly integrated, in race, color, creed, national origin, income, occupation, sex, drinking habits and styles of architecture. And those of its residents whom fortune has treated well are likely to treat with some deference those whom it has not. This is by way of explaining the response of a man who on drawing near to his brownstone apartment there late one afternoon saw outside his door, impatiently ringing the bell, a short, delicately built woman whom he took to be of Puerto Rican lineage. "She was plainly dressed," he related later, "and bore the proud expression of the dauntless put-upon. I quickly focussed my stereotype. The impression I was to receive, I decided, was that if she didn't bring home a weekly pay check, the six children of her deserter husband would go without. By the time I got to the top of the stoop, I had dismissed encyclopedias, Avon and magazines, so that my curiosity was aroused."

A witness to the encounter recorded it as follows:

"Can I help you, ma'am?"

"Yes, if you would, I'd like to ask you for a few minutes of your time."

"Certainly, ma'am, if it's for a worthwhile purpose."

"It's just to answer a few questions."

"I'm flattered. Are these *your* questions?"

"No, I work for the Harris organization. Perhaps you have heard of us."

"Yes, indeed. Perhaps you will answer a question for me?"

"If I can."

"It's rather personal."

"Oh? Well, I—"

"Do you know if Mr. Harris' name is really Lou? Or is it Louis? You see, it might give me some insight into his psychological process—"

Smiling: "I'm sure I don't know."

"That looks like pages of questions on your clipboard, perhaps—"

Now, mock-pleadingly: "They won't take long."

"I regret that I haven't the time right now. Here is my card. You may send it on to Mr. Harris. If he calls me at my office, perhaps we can work something out."

She refused the card.

"I don't understand."

"Well, as *I* understand it, Mr. Harris wishes me to spend, say, a half hour answering questions which he proposes to sell to someone for a profit. Now I have invested considerable time and money and sacrifice in creating that information. If I gave it away, and on uncompensated time at that, I would not find it easy to do my own business after I arrive at the office tomorrow."

"I see," she said, although she obviously didn't. "Would you at least give me your name and address so that they will know that I stopped here?"

"I take it Mr. Harris doesn't trust you. If he doesn't trust you any more than that, why should he trust you not to copy names and addresses out of telephone books?"

"Thank you *very* much, anyway."

"Not at all."

And so ended another skirmish in the information revolution.

A sampling of responses to this account, taken at random social occasions, would indicate that some persons will look upon the occurrence as relief-giving reinforcement to support their right to be irritated at pollsters. Others will express outrage, either at Harris' tactics or the protagonist's boorishness and, as was often said, "evident paranoia." Yet others will wonder why the teller of the yarn wants literally to make a Federal case out of what amounts, after all, to no more than a highly refined sales technique. Still others will wonder how the retailer of the incident came to forget the punch line.

2.

The incident illustrates simply that not everyone who values privacy of property readily perceives also its relation to private knowledge. This is why rich men who believe themselves to be conservatives ask that the Chief Justice of the United States be impeached for wanting to secure the Constitutional guarantee against self-incrimination are the first to defend wiretapping by the Government against some "them" and, of course, see nothing at all wrong in spying on workers on suspicion of an inventory leakage.

Apart from the fact that property is wholly a creation of the system, it stands in some relation to private knowledge like that of gold to currency. It is the physical embodiment, the pledge, of the guarantee of the right to be secure in our persons. It is possible to conceive of persons secure in a propertyless state, but not in the state of George Orwell's vision in *1984*. Faith that one's knowledge is private is a better test of one's own internal security than the satisfaction shown on any given day by the Senate subcommittee on Internal Security.

Currency, to be sure, stands also in a subservient relation to the right enumerated in the Fourth Amendment. In the eyes of a marketing systems analyst, it is a form of information, but it is first of all property. If it were infinitely multipliable, the way knowledge is, so that everyone could hoard the same currency, it would have no value as information or currency. Private knowledge is like currency only in that it is readily negotiable on account of a prior guarantee.

All governments, of course, require the power to tax property and knowledge, in order to guarantee security of persons, provide for the common defense, and to conduct whatever other business it is given to them to conduct. The word "statistics" was coined to denote that which "is" that the "stat," or state, needed to know about, including information not reducible to figures. A census was to the Romans a registering of the citizens before it became, in French antecedents, an opinion. Some statistics are, indeed, vital. We also take it as vital that a citizen accused of a crime ought not be made to incriminate himself.

That leaves a good deal of room for negotiation. The rise in demand by Government for information has at least kept pace with the rise in taxes upon property. Both increases have raised cries of extortion, as when Congressman Gallagher objected to the Farm Bureau census and the Census Bureau's plan for the 1970 census.

In the native organism's relations with private corporations, it is assumed that all the knowledge he possesses is negotiable. That is, if he wants a job or to receive credit, he has to give up some part of what he knows about himself, and agree to permit the prospective employer or creditor to verify for himself what the applicant avows to be true. Here, too, though, the highest of the higher primates is losing ground under his bargaining position.

This is attributable in part to private industry's now established and rapidly growing implication in the Government's national security mandate. Private contractors must be as certain as the Government itself that they hire trustworthy persons, and that they shield from view information of possible use to a common enemy. There appears to be a correspondingly greater tolerance toward the practices adopted by corporations under mandate of security to their own property. Thus have been created private as well as Civil Service friends of privacy of the kind that relieves it of the necessity for enemies.

Take, for example, Richard Lukens, who with his father does business as Inter-State Surveys, Inc. Mr. Lukens, upon request and prospect of payment, performs certain "fact finding functions," including administration of polygraph tests as part of the screening and auditing of personnel. Lukens believes that polygraphs have gotten a bad name because of their use by bunglers, and he has been instrumental in attempts to get New York State to license polygraph operators.

There is so little doubt in his mind that the employer is entitled to know everything he can find out about a job applicant or worker, that he considers discourse without that assumption wholly uninstructive. Once it is made, he wins. Polygraphs, he says, are better for all parties since they protect the privacy of the individual. He reaches this conclusion by pointing out that the only alternative the employer has is to hire at much greater expense a number of private investigators to do an investigation of the prospect "in depth." So he saves money. At the same time, the prospect does not have a number of investigators asking personal questions of his friends, neighbors, bank, former employers, credit agencies, bartenders, girl friends and so forth. So his privacy is protected.

Oscar M. Ruebhausen and Orville G. Brim, Jr., observe in the November, 1965, *Columbia Law Review:*

> . . . the One-Way mirror is a common fixture in facilities designed for bio-medical and behavioral research. Personality and ability tests are as familiar to researchers in these fields as a stethoscope is to the family doctor. The computer and electronic data storage and retrieval have become crucial to the intelligent and efficient use of research data. Socio-active and psycho-active drugs are ever more tempting research tools, as are the concealed camera and the hidden microphone. . . .
>
> When these and other scientific and technological advances are used by scientists, they are used by highly trained, well-motivated, professional people for a social purpose on which the community places a high value. But this fact by itself, obviously, does not warrant the invasion of private personality any more than it would warrant the taking of private property or the administration of live cancer cells to non-consenting patients.

Who is to prevent them? The law, Mr. Justice Brandeis said, "must still protect a man from things that rob him of his freedom, whether the oppressing force be physical or of a subtler kind." Brandeis' conception of "the most comprehensive of rights" has fared badly in the balance, though. The first of the few states to adopt legislation insuring a right to privacy was Georgia, and that was to prevent intrusion of Federal agents upon the manner in which Georgians chose to deal with Negroes. Such other guidance as exists is indicated in a brief filed in a Chicago Federal District Court on behalf of Jack Guzik, whose means of support are also a matter for speculation.

The brief was Guzik's reply to a plan mounted by American Broadcasting–Paramount Pictures, Inc., through its Chicago outlet, WBKB, to offer in collaboration with the Chicago Crime Commission a series of six televised biographies billed in a local newspaper as "the most notorious powerful underworld leaders operating out of Chicago." The brief holds that the Chicago Crime Commission had "formed a scheme" to violate Guzik's privacy for money. The Commission, it observes, "is a fund soliciting organization" which "professes to have enlisted in the war against crime." The Commission's "part in the campaign," the brief adds, "is to deplore vehemently the existence of sin and badness" and that "its success in raising money depends upon its skill in persuading right-thinking people that financial contributions to the 'Commission' will tend to wipe out sin and badness."

That the show was withdrawn by the station probably had less to do with what the brief said about the Commission, though, than with the uncontestability of the claims it made for Guzik. It asserted that "plaintiff is not charged with the commission of a crime; that he is not an athlete or actor; that he is not a candidate for public office . . . that he has never achieved fame in literature, the arts or sciences. . . ."

3.

The "if-you-don't-know-I-can't-explain-it-to-you" school of rhetoric may help to keep a congressional thumb in the dike; it will not avail in the end against authoritatively framed demands made in "the interests of the community" and national security. Consider the following exchange between Representative Benjamin Rosenthal of New York, Representative Henry Reuss of Wisconsin, and the Administrator of the Bonneville Power Administration:

Congressman Rosenthal asked Charles F. Luce in connection with the MMPI, "I don't know what the appropriate answer should be for a fellow who is looking for a promotion, when he is asked to make a choice between 'I like to read books and plays where sex plays a major part,' or 'I like to be the center of attention in a group.' Which do you think would be the most appropriate answer for promotion in your organization?"

Luce said, "I wouldn't know. I am not a psychologist."

A few moments later, Congressman Reuss inquired: "Didn't you ever have in your practice, as I surely did in mine, cases where as it turned out, a lot of learned doctors were wrong and hadn't sufficiently researched the matter, and where you, by perspicacity and dogged pursuit of the matter found out something about this occult medical matter that a lot of the medical men didn't know? Didn't you ever have that experience?"

Luce said that he thought he was dogged "and I hope I was perspicacious, but I don't recall any instance in which I uncovered a medical truth that I hadn't first learned from a doctor."

Mr. Reuss: "Well, you missed a very rewarding part of law practice."

All that Mr. Luce had to do, of course, was to concede that things were certainly a lot more interesting in the good old days, but now, ruefully, a man running a big operation like the Bonneville dam has to take whatever advice he can get from persons who seem to know what they are talking about. Like Edgar S. Dunn, Jr.

Chapter Thirteen

BUREAUCRATIC DUE PROCESS

There was reason to fear that the Revolution, like Saturn, might devour in turn each of her children.

—LAMARTINE, *Histoire des Girondins*

1.

WHEN EDGAR S. DUNN, JR., made a modest recommendation for which he had been paid as a consultant by the Federal Government's Bureau of the Budget, the copy desk and a reporter for *The Washington Post* could scarcely contain their irritation. "Center for Data on Everybody Recommended," the *Post's* headline read. The story, by George Lardner, Jr., began: "The Government needs a consolidated center where it can keep all of its information on people's lives, jobs and deaths, a Budget Bureau consultant says." Senator Long was quoted, "Somewhere along the line toward Government efficiency we must cease pushing our citizens into the computer."

I am sure that the Director of the Bureau of the Census and Mr. Luce would agree. So would Dunn. What, after all, was Dunn's purpose? He proposed, merely, that all of the bits and pieces of information about citizens contained in various files, and guarded with more or less diligence by each of various agencies, be consolidated into a single data center. Lardner wrote that Dunn believed "there is far too much duplication and waste in the Government's record gathering. Urban planners, education officials, highway planners, welfare administrators and a host of others, he says, ought to be able to compare notes." He was reported also to believe that "much valuable information is lost because confidences are kept and statistics made anonymous too early in the game."

The protest which silenced Dunn's plan for the time being was aimed not at the Government's mandate to collect the information it had requested, or its charter to reassemble the information for another purpose, but at the fact that it threatened the unwritten separation of bureaucratic powers and due process held out frequently to reassure civilians. Thus, when Dunn appeared before the Long Committee he bore the expression of a man who had been greatly misunderstood.

2.

The Bureau of the Budget has assumed a position in the scheme of checks and balances that the founding fathers had not envisioned. It is commonly thought that the executive branch proposes, and the Congress disposes. This is still true, with the important qualification that what the Congress disposes, the Budget Bureau has proposed, and also redisposes. It draws up for presentation to Congress a budget of $100 billion and up, the great bulk of which is spent by the executive branch. It enjoys somewhat the same affection among executive agencies as the expense account watchman in a newspaper office.

Then, too, there is nothing better calculated to summon long neglected thoughts about privacy in an executive agency than the threat of having its own storepile of information swept into someone else's bin. A memorandum quoted by Lardner said "Agency officials felt that letting anyone else peek at their files, much less have them would be a 'breach of contract' with citizens who have been assured over the years that 'none but the agency personnel would view their reports.' "

Dunn perhaps knew that this was nonsense, as did one of Lardner's co-workers, William Harwood, who reported several days earlier that "A 'confidential' report discrediting a Washington Post reporter—which later proved to be totally false—went all the way from the State Department to the White House, the CIA and the Defense Department and, ultimately, to the managers of the newspaper." Moreover, during the Gallagher Committee hearings, a Department of Defense witness testified that "investigative material collected under the industrial security program sometimes gets back to employers."

Reporters who labored on the Fund for the Republic's efforts to dissect the practice of blacklisting in the entertainment industry in the mid-1950's were told by agents retained or employed to police casting lists and author's credits that their connections with the FBI enabled them to obtain a "rundown" on specific persons, although not a look at the files. Congressman Gallagher said that he knew of a certainty that lie detector examinations were circulated freely among agency personnel. The Director of Internal Revenue has said that information in his files was available to other law enforcement agencies.

Harwood reported that "on an ordinary working day, the Federal Housing Administration tucks away in its files 'confidential' reports on the marital stability of approximately 4,000 prospective home buyers." Information for these estimates is collected, if possible, without disturbing the applicants with the awareness that their connubial fulfillment is being measured. The FHA explains, Harwood reported, that "The reputation and marital amicability of an applicant for a mortgage loan . . . are a vital part of our risk determination. One of the leading causes of foreclosure is divorce." The reason that Harwood placed the word "confidential" between quotation marks is that the reports are, or were in June, 1966, available to mortgage lenders at $1.50 apiece.

To Dunn, it seemed no more than logical that all this information ought to be stored in one place, where it might be available to form combinations useful to managing the affairs of Government. As Lardner described Dunn's position: "The Center, he said, could be set up so that more information would be available to Government agencies, business and research groups, and state and local officials, without any more danger to an individual's right to privacy than exists now." He should have quit while he was ahead, though, for he added: "If you have no confidence in the administrative and political process in this sphere, then I guess you don't do it."

It isn't faith that makes these files possible. If every man without faith in the administrative controls of the executive branch were permitted to retrieve his good—so far as he knows—name from them, the files would be made useless. This would be true not only because the files would be decimated, but also because the names remaining in them would belong almost entirely to minimum security risks, the aggressively right-thinking and the righteous. As it is, the rest of us have to take whatever sustenance we can find from hope and from charity.

3.

Apart from the mandate security gives to paternal meddling, it appears to be destined to make all that we see, hear, smell or conceive of into grist for the information machine. That process has proved until now to be merely unsettling. Now let us turn to the fact that there is in

New York City a detachment of the Central Intelligence Agency with the principal assignment of cultivating senior business executives, particularly those in companies whose international commitment require that they obtain intelligence that may also be of use to the CIA. An agent told an interviewer how he approaches his wards:

> I call the president of the company and, naturally, reach one of the secretaries. I tell her I want to speak to the president and that I am an employee of the U.S. Government. The reply I inevitably receive is that I must disclose something of the nature of my business before I can be put through. I then respond that it is a serious and confidential Government matter that I am not to discuss, that the purpose of the call is to arrange a private meeting with the president wherein I can discuss it, and that the secretary might want to mention that I am an employee of the Central Intelligence Agency. It works every time. Even if they don't cooperate with me to the degree that I require, the CIA thing makes them too curious to refuse. And once I have made the contact, at least they will come around to what I want—if not completely, at least in good part.

He cites examples of companies that *although*, as he sees it, in litigation at the hands of the Government still "trusted the CIA" enough to cooperate.

The approach is not much different from that used by others in and out of Government who would like to "get a line on" an existing or former corporation employee. He, of course, will not have much to say about what conclusions are formed about him. More than that: Yesterday's executive was likely to think that time is money. This isn't a highly popular slogan any more, especially after Chrysler some years ago fired a good part of its top echelon as a survival measure, and found that they weren't missed. Today's executive is inclined to think of information as money. If that doesn't occur to him in the course of his own business, as it surely will, the truth of it may be impressed upon him when he goes to approve a voucher to pay a college professor's consulting fee.

After a visit from the CIA man it might occur to him, too, that if not all information is intelligence, it is best to act as if it were. He will be helped along to this conclusion by an article J. Edgar Hoover wrote for the June, 1966, issue of *Nation's Business*. Hoover notes that Chinese

Communists have since 1949 "poured tens of thousands of dollars into the American economy through purchases of non-classified publications of myriad types and descriptions." By this means, he wrote, Communist nations have saved "incalculable time and resources in their race to overcome the camp of freedom."

Hoover tells how a Chinese Communist intelligence agency had over a period of time written letters under an assumed name from Berlin ("The writer vaguely implies that he resides in the free sector of that city") to business and industrial establishments, colleges and universities, publishing houses and technical societies in various parts of the United States, requesting maps, blueprints, scientific journals and other printed material of strategic interest and importance to the Red Chinese. Over a period of months, thousands of dollars worth of data vitally important to Red China was sent him—innocently and in good faith—by Americans in care of a post office box in the communist sector of Berlin.

Supposing that the President of the American Rocket Society (one of those approached by the Red Chinese in Hoover's account) stopped sending material to Berlin, or anywhere else for that matter. Presumably he has minimized the risk of getting material into the hands of the Red Chinese, but how can he be sure? Or consider the portent of a press release sent out some time before Hoover's article from The Advanced Systems Development Division, Data Processing Division, of IBM.

4.

The release was part of a kit, which itself is filled with information enough to establish the need for the new information retrieval system it touts. One of the releases notes that:

> Ralph O'Dette, of the National Science Foundation . . . cited the difficulty of keeping up with foreign literature as typified by a Russian paper entitled "The Application of Boolean Matrix Algebra to the Analysis and Synthesis of Relay Contact Networks." "Tardy discovery of this one important paper," O'Dette says, "caused $250,000 to be wasted in duplicating the work that it covered."

The implication of the example begins to creep up on us when in the next paragraph, there it is: "Russia is reportedly combating this problem with a huge task force of scientists assigned to an information retrieval center known as the All-Union Institute for Scientific and Technical Information of the U.S.S.R."

The principal function of this organization is to "burrow through" technical documents "from every part of the world, extracting and abstracting information requested by research and development laboratories throughout the Soviet Union."

The release goes on to hint darkly that the Russians are ahead of us at information retrieval. And then, of course: "Although qualified American observers are both impressed and alarmed at the magnitude of the Soviet effort, they do not believe in the creation of a single monolithic government agency to solve the problem here." The next question is "Why not?" If the protection of technical data is as vital to the national security as Hoover believes it to be, I should feel a lot safer were it kept in one place where it could be guarded effectively and at less cost than were it to be strewn about here and there.

The reason why not would be immediately evident, of course, were the Administration to propose with any weight and seriousness the construction of an All-American Institute for Scientific and Technical Information of the United States, to the exclusion of any such private facility beyond the size of those needed to keep tabs on credit risks and airline reservations. In the pages of *The National Review,* unless I overestimate its editors, the Fourth and the Fifth Amendments, somewhat tarnished from their frequent weighings on the late Senator Joseph McCarthy's balance scales, would acquire a luster to stir emotions likely to give even A. Ross Eckler, the director of the Census Bureau, pause.

It would seem, therefore, to be the better part of wisdom for corporations who wish to retain such privacy as they have remaining to them to limit their use of the security mandate—as have some universities in refusing, out of obligation to academic freedom, to take on Government contracts requiring security precautions to keep their researches secret. In the industrial corporation, though, we appear to be dealing with a creature that is becoming increasingly bored with itself.

Long before psychiatrists found clinical use for the name of the Austrian novelist Leopold von Sacher-Masoch, Samuel Johnson catalogued in his dictionary:

> seeksorrow. One who contrives to give himself vexation.

With the same disregard for the vital principle of one's own well-being which prompts a great corporation to send a private detective to dog the tracks of an author, manufacturers and purveyors of pharmaceutical potions are engaged in an effort to bring the security mandate to use so as to invest their own private knowledge with the attributes of private property, at considerable risk to the privacy of native organisms.

Chapter Fourteen

WHAT'S GOOD FOR MERCK . . .

The business of America is business.

—CALVIN COOLIDGE

1.

ON MARCH 1, 1966, Representative Harris B. McDowell, a Democrat whose constituency included E. I. du Pont de Nemours & Company of Wilmington, Delaware, introduced into the 89th session of Congress certain amendments to Title 18 of the United States Code, known, for ease of conversation, as the National Stolen Property Act. It will help toward understanding the purpose of Congressman McDowell's proposal if we make an effort to put an imaginative construction on events past. What would we suppose might have happened, all other circumstances holding equal, had Vincent Gillen, the FBI agent, not Gillen the private entrepreneur, made the investigation of Nader, and had Food and Drug Administration investigators rather than Saviano and Terpstra penetrated Hyman Moore's warehouse?

It would seem plausible to assume on the record of recent years, if not decades, that no matter what evidence Nader may have had that he was under surveillance, neither he nor the public would have been given confirmation of the fact by a committee of the Senate. In the highly unlikely event that the FBI would have owned up to such an investigation, it would also have given a reason to explain away its action. And the explanation would most likely have served to divide, if not subdue, editorial judgments about its propriety. This is, of course, because we assume that it is part of the democratic process that the FBI looks out for us, but GM makes do for itself.

Moore, having a greatly more complicated case to urge, was even more vulnerable. Had he charged that the Food and Drug Administration rather than a private investigator had planted a spy in his warehouse his chances for a hearing would have been considerably diminished. When a legislator looks into the activities of Government agencies, he customarily examines its practices over a period of time, the good along with the bad. It would be asking a good deal of a legislator to risk his political neck on a single case, and in opposition to an assertion from the FDA that it was only, for instance, trying to make sure the Drug Abuse Act of 1965 was being properly enforced through all channels of distribution. This would be particularly true in a case like Moore's; he had committed an indictable offense which did in fact confuse judgment about his case, whatever the merits of the law or of Moore's defense.

2.

These investigative forces were not, in the Spring of 1966, available to GM or SKF for their own special security problems, except for those involving theft of property or frauds in interstate commerce. Had the McDowell amendment been on the books, however, FBI and FDA investigators would have been available to the drug industry for a good many more security assignments than they had been before the amendment was passed. This helps to explain the industry's support of the measure, and also a passage in the Harvard study: An unspecified number of executives of "firms employed in industrial security," the report observed, "feel that many of the cases of wiretapping are internal company matters, and that the rare cases of outright spying activities have been blown up by the press, or used by industries as a vehicle for publicity."

The most casual reader of the general press, not to mention the trade magazines, felt the effect of these publicity efforts. It has been hard to escape the impression that, since the late fifties, drug and chemical companies have been raided mercilessly and systematically by spies who pirate commercially valuable secrets for their own use, or for sale to competitors in the United States and abroad. Sources that were rarely identified gave specific dimension to the problem. The most frequently cited estimate of the loss was set at $3 billion annually to all business, but mostly drug and chemical companies. Some accounts, as early as 1959, assigned estimates to the percentage increase in the incidence of industrial spying over a specified period.

A substantial part of this publicity implied quite clearly that the security of formulae and processes, many of them the products of large expenditures in money and talent, was bound up with the national security. The case was put this way by John Connor, then president of Merck & Co. and later U.S. Secretary of Commerce, in a quotation which appeared in *Reader's Digest:*

> Commercial espionage is a crime. It damages the stockholders of the company whose secrets have been stolen by depriving them of their property. It damages the employees by keeping the company from increasing employment and raising wages. And it damages the public: if the fruits of research cannot be protected, the incentive to develop new products and improve old ones is bound to suffer.

The case for more adequate protection against the damages wrought by industrial espionage is precisely what the McDowell proposal seeks to remedy. If the secrets of which Connor speaks were, in fact, property, all the publicity given to industrial spies would have been to little purpose. But there's the rub.

3.

Amendments to the National Stolen Property Act form a record of successful attempts to persuade the Congress that protection of some forms of possession exceeds the capacity of municipal and state enforcement—without, that is, involving such cost and inconvenience as to defeat justice. The act began by punishing interstate traffic in stolen cattle. Later it moved up to embrace interstate movement in stolen motor vehicles. This proved to be a boon in the capture of robbery suspects because they could be held on suspicion of having stolen a car even after crossing a state line. It has been amended also to mobilize Federal law enforcement facilities against traffic in stocks, bonds and other securities, as well as presses, dies, engraving tools and the like used to counterfeit securities and tax stamps. It was amended again to protect against fraudulently labeled phonograph records.

The first thing to be noted about this catalog of items is that it describes or has to do with objects that are recognized by law and in everyday use as being forms of property. Some are things; and as things, once they have been removed they leave the previous possessor without the object itself or the rights and benefits that come with it. Some are only titles to things, but having them or not having them makes a difference in the same way that ciphers in a bank account make a difference between $1 and $1,000,000. Among the several manifestations of the difference is that the man with the higher figure in his account will have considerably more time to contemplate the abstract forms of property. The other items in the stolen property catalog have to do with the fraudulent misrepresentation of property, the creation of false titles to property, or the misleading of buyers of property.

Information and ideas do not share in these attributes, and therefore neither do trade secrets or the information protected by copyrights and patents. Dozens of spies might break a drug company's security arrangements and each steal the same formula. The drug company still has the formula for its own use. The same spies might observe and take out with them the details of a process or of a piece of machinery. The company still has knowledge of the process, and the machine is still in as good working order as before the spies committed their thefts. What the company has lost, however, may be worth, in money, more than the cost of the machine, the building it is in and the land the building is on all put together: that is to say, the exclusive use and control of the information.

Recognizing as much, Federal law extends protection to the articulated forms of information and ideas: that is, to a particular arrangement of words and, if they are new and useful, to particular devices and processes (though not compounds). Whoever it was devised double-entry bookkeeping (an idea of enormous value and of great consequence to civilization) would have been able to obtain a U.S. copyright on any number of detailed forms for entering figures. This would have given him protection against someone producing precisely the same forms, but not from anyone using the method bodied forth in the forms, or from telling the world about it.

Similarly, the man to whose imagination it fell to devise the decimal system might have obtained a patent on a mechanism which, with the use of the system, comprised an adding machine. Again, in this case, and in this country, he could for seventeen years rely on duly constituted law to help him obtain damages from anyone who undertook to make and sell essentially the same mechanism, but not against use by a librarian who might want to adapt his system for arranging books, or for an inventor who used it in a genuinely new mechanism. These are but the essentials of the legal snarls which divide information from property. They stand in relation to the subject as a hive to a maze of hornets. However, with these, and one more observation, we may begin to understand the drug industry's problem.

4.

The additional observation is that the misappropriation of a copyright or patent is contemplated by law as being not *contra pacem* so much as to the scandal of the government. It is not usually a criminal, but a civil wrong. The courts will help the demonstrably wronged plaintiff recover what they think he has coming to him from an infringer. But they won't send the infringer to jail or fine him unless he refuses or is unable to pay the stipulated damages adjudged in a particular case. (Courts interpret such failings as contempt of their efforts to assist Justice to her feet.) This much is also true under certain conditions of trade secrets, although the conditions are so elusive of definition that no lawyer worth his fee would stake his reputation on any single statement of them.

Even so, one could probably obtain the services of a reputable lawyer in an effort to recover civil damages from the loss of exclusive title to such information, if he could show that he had taken strict precautions to protect it, as if it were a secret; that it represented an idea or series of facts which did not qualify for protection of copyright or patent (or the possessor did not want to solicit that protection), but was nonetheless valuable, that the value was demonstrated by someone's having obtained it, either by stealth or breach of confidence, and had used it to make money. This definition applies to things like jottings in a notebook that explain how to make, say, an oral contraceptive; charts of oil fields in which the charter has invested perhaps hundreds of thousands of dollars in test borings; the design of next year's automobiles, and so on.

The possessor of such things inclines naturally to think of them as if they were property. The state does not. Assuming, but only for the time being, that it ought to, the state is unable to afford them the protection that is due property. If the courts held out the promise to consider every application by persons who thought a new and useful idea had been stolen from them, they would have scant time left to read pornography, or advertisements for it, or to do much else that they judge most immediate to the responsibilities they have undertaken. Yet it becomes increasingly clear that in many instances, civil remedies are like a prescription offered as a palliative by a backsliding general practitioner who is without the means for accurate diagnosis.

A case in point dates back to July of 1964, when Eugene A. Mayfield, a graduate of a training program for junior executives at Procter and

Gamble Co., left the company at the age of twenty-six to return to his home in Evanston, Illinois. Four months later, Mayfield telephoned the Colgate-Palmolive Company in New York City from Chicago, where he had taken a job as a products manager for another concern. He offered to sell, for $20,000, a supplement of 188 pages to P & G's budget. The supplement outlined the company's marketing strategy for 1964–65 for Crest Toothpaste. Colgate's dilemma, as described by a reporter for *The New York Times,* "involved several factors. First, the offered budget could conceivably have been a fake intended to mislead. Then, it might have been stolen by a discontented employee of Procter and Gamble. In any case, the purchaser could clearly be put at the mercy of the seller. So Colgate decided to call in the FBI."

The FBI entered the case on the grounds that it was interested in a possible violation of interstate commerce regulations. This interest was enlivened by the possibility of a conviction under the National Stolen Property Act for use of a telephone to further a dishonest scheme. In any event, the FBI suggested that Colgate arrange a meeting with Mayfield. On November 14, a Colgate man met Mayfield, at Mayfield's urging, in a men's room in the Trans-World Airline terminal at Kennedy International Airport. The Colgate man carried $20,000 in marked bills; Mayfield carried an office-copier edition of the budget supplement.

The two men went into adjoining cubicles. Mayfield asked the Colgate man to remove his trousers and to pass them under the partition separating the two. Mayfield accepted the trousers, exchanged the budget for cash, and walked out into the custody of FBI agents. He was indicted, on April Fool's Day, 1965, not only on the telephone charge, but also for having come across state lines from Chicago with "goods knowing the same to have been stolen." In September, 1965, he pleaded guilty, but only to the charge of having used the telephone to further a fraudulent scheme. The more severe count had been dropped. He was put on two years' probation.

P & G estimated the value to Colgate of the budget supplement to be $1 million. This may have put too high a value on the use Colgate could have made of the information. In the working out of a strategy in a market, where the terrain is uncharted and unchartable, it would be impossible to know whether the advertising and promotion plans Colgate worked out on the basis of the information would have been much more successful, slightly more successful—or even whether Colgate might not have been better off without the information. Had Colgate accepted the deal and then been hauled into court, the courts would have been hard put to assign a value. This is no less true, as we shall see, of cases involving theft of trade secrets where the value of the stolen information appears to be more easily definable.

The purpose of Congressman McDowell's proposed amendments to the National Stolen Property Act was to enlist the help of Federal enforcement officers on a more regular basis by making theft of things like copies of secretly held budgets, and so on *ad infinitum*, punishable as if to be a crime. Specifically it would have made a felony out of taking, transporting or using for profit "any object, material, device or substance or copy thereof, including any writing, record, recording, drawing, sample, specimen, prototype, model, photograph, microorganism, blueprint, or map, which describes, depicts, contains, constitutes, reflects, or records a trade secret."

A draft of the bill dated February 4, 1965, together with the customary memorandum setting out arguments for the benefit of Congress, was circulated by the chief counsel of Merck & Co. at a seminar of the American Management Association. "The increasing thefts of scientific and technical information," it said,

> and the transmission of such information across State lines and abroad, constitutes a serious national problem threatening our economy and our security . . . the incentive and morale required to support the massive research effort of American industry are sapped if the rewards of discovery are reaped not by the innovator, but by the research thief and those to whom he delivers the stolen information. The national interest is further harmed when the stolen information is used by competitors abroad, and by our enemies as a cold war tool. The problem is national and international in scope, there are growing indications that organized crime is moving in, and only the Federal Government can deal effectively with it. But Federal authority has been hampered because existing law—the "National Stolen Property Act"—speaks more in terms of traditional forms of property than it does of property in the form of scientific and technical information, and because it imposes value requirements which may be difficult to satisfy when the value is not so much in the piece of information itself as in what can be produced with it.

One person the author of these lines very likely had on his mind while composing them is Robert Sancier Aries.

Chapter Fifteen

THE BOGY MAN

A phrase has spread from civilians to soldiers and back again: "This is a phony war."

—PERTINAX in *Grave Diggers of France*

1.

ON AN AUTUMN DAY in 1961, Robert Sancier Aries (born Sami Arie), at age forty-two the possessor of two advanced degrees in chemical engineering from Brooklyn Polytechnical Institute, a Master of Arts degree from the University of Minnesota and of science from Yale, forty U.S. patents, five inches in the parsimonious pages of *Who's Who*, considerable experience as a consultant to U.S. corporations, banks, brokerage firms and to the military, and, moreover, possessor of a U.S. passport stamped VALID FOR IMMEDIATE RETURN TO U.S. ONLY, somehow got hold of at least $46,000—"somehow" because Swiss courts had only a year before sequestered all of his visible assets; "at least" because that was all he had to post as bail to obtain his release from a Geneva magistrate in whose custody he had been languishing for nearly twenty-four hours.

It was also approximately the amount then being sought by Hoffman–La Roche, a manufacturer and distributor of pharmaceuticals, with offices in Basle. This amount represented the balance due from a successful claim the company had made that Aries had sold it rights he didn't own to a process for making a commercially valuable product. The amount due may have had something to do with the size of the bail demanded of Aries. Or it may have been that the magistrate, mindful that Aries was being sought also to answer criminal indictments held by an Essex County, New Jersey, court and a Connecticut Federal District Court, might have thought a bail of that size together with the passport restriction would deter the peripatetic Aries from further travels. Aries, however, had a good deal of unfinished business to see to.

Hoffman–La Roche was only one of four companies to whom Aries sold rights to the process. Since the time of the incident in Geneva, courts have held that Aries was liable for a total of $1.3 million to Sterling Drug Co., Hackensack, New Jersey, Burroughs-Wellcome, Ltd., London, and Synorga of Paris. Merck, rightful owner of the trade secret on which Aries based his patents, had already been told that the courts would stand ready to help it collect $6,637,499 from Aries. Since then Rohm and Haas and Sprague Electric Co. have also received permission to recover, if they can, respectively $2,288,600 and $3,600,000. These represent amounts a Federal district court thought Aries should have paid for having misappropriated and sold as his own the rights to trade secrets of their making. Total judgments: $14 million.

2.

Aries' birthplace has been fixed variously in Bulgaria, France and Hungary. He told a reporter in France in 1962 that at the age of eighteen he was graduated *cum laude* from the American University at Sofia. Some time after that he emigrated to the United States and by the time he was twenty-two had become a lecturer at Brooklyn Polytechnic. As a teacher, Aries had little patience for bookworms. He was a learn-by-doing advocate who urged his students constantly to get out and visit companies engaged in the frontier work in chemistry and to write detailed reports on "hot products, young products." As is the custom these days among enterprisers on college faculties, he also did a good deal of outside consulting. As the drug analyst for a brokerage firm that retained his services has remarked, "We used to marvel at how much he knew about what was going on in the industry."

To the casual inquirer there is no knowing why precisely, but in 1956 Aries and Brooklyn Polytechnic severed their connection. Popular accounts are full of suggestions that Aries was retailing to his consulting clients reports brought to him by his students. If that's true, Aries may have thought it no more than part of a teacher's covenant with his vocation to share what he knows with the community at large. No one has suggested publicly that any of his students suffered from the assignments they were asked to perform, nor from the penetrating questions one would suppose Aries asked while grading the reports turned in to him. In any event, after leaving the school Aries repaired to Stamford, Connecticut, and founded one of eventually six corporations formed by him, Aries Laboratories.

He began also to publish a newsletter, *Chemononics,* which helped him, in turn, to expand his consulting business. In keeping with another common practice, he enlisted correspondents, known in the periodical trade as "stringers," to supply him information. (Stringers are customarily reporters and writers not kept on a payroll but paid space rates or retainers for regular contributions.) Aries' stringers were drawn, though, not from the pool of moonlighting and unemployed journalists, but from chemists and technicians working in the laboratories of chemical and pharmaceutical companies. In his capacity as consultant and publisher he, in January of 1959, telephoned a former night-class student, employed as a chemical engineer by Merck, who had just returned from an assignment in Brazil. What, Aries asked, was new at his shop?

Merck at the time was well pleased with itself at having brought close to a point where the company might ask for a patent, a process for making a specific effective against a barnyard scourge called coccidiosis. The coccidia is a parasitic organism which kills the host, including poultry of every kind, by metabolizing its supply of a vitamin, niacin. Merck's coccidiostat, then known in its laboratories as MK-234, simulated the vitamin in a way that made it satisfying to the parasite, but did not provide its nutrition. The coccidia would starve to death, thus saving the host and its eggs for the food market.

Merck has said that it had invested on and off during several years some $1.5 million and the efforts of 200 persons in researching and developing the coccidiostat. It thought this to be more than justified by a market which it estimated to be worth $20 to $25 million annually in sales in the United States alone, not to mention extensive markets in Europe. Aries tried unsuccessfully at first, but more convincingly after several meetings, to obtain from his former student samples of MK-234, and details of the process used in making it. When they at last agreed, the young chemist was, he has testified, to receive 25 per cent of Aries' earnings from sale of the rights.

Merck has said that the first inkling it received that all was not well was in the form of an abstract published in a trade magazine of a lecture Aries was to give in Ottawa in September, 1960. The description Aries gave of his new coccidiostat, which he called Mepyrium, came painfully close to the product of the process Merck was about to patent and register as Amprolium. Worse, a Merck negotiating team, which had been in France closing a deal for acquisition of controlling interest in a French drug firm, Synorga, returned to report that among the new acquisition's assets was the right, for which it had paid Aries, to make and sell Mepyrium. Such coincidences are not unknown, but it would have been foolish of Aries to expect that Merck would shrug and write the matter off to experience. While Aries gave his lecture in Ottawa and went on to sell the Mepyrium rights to others, Merck took a calculated gamble.

3.

The gamble consisted in asking its new partially owned subsidiary, Synorga, for a closer look at what it had bought from Aries. It was a gamble because had Merck, upon examining the data, found nothing to suggest that it was stolen, Merck in marketing its own version of the product would have been vulnerable to lawsuits charging that it had violated a trade secret. (French law with regard to the theft of trade secrets includes provisions for criminal prosecution.) One account claims that Merck was emboldened to take the chance by something one of its engineers saw while visiting the Synorga plant. Two vats that had been installed for the Amprolium process in Merck's plant had proved useless but were left standing in the hope they might find uses elsewhere. Two vats much like them were lying idle, the account says, in the Synorga plant Mepyrium production area. In all events, Merck found that the details supplied to Synorga were, though crudely predated, sufficiently like Merck's drawings and sketches to cause it to begin a search for an employee who might have taken them out for Aries to copy.

Through examination of small clues, principally similarities in handwriting, the Merck legal staff narrowed its scrutiny down to a suspicion of Aries' former student, who was then on assignment in Asia. Summoned home and confronted with the evidence, he told all, including details of code names he and Aries had used, out-of-the-way rendezvous to transfer samples and copies of documents, and other paraphernalia familiar to watchers of the less stimulating television episodes of spy-thrillers. By the time officers of the court arrived at Aries' jerry-built laboratories in Stamford, however, he was on his way toward Europe.

Cases of violent assault on persons and property cascade over public prosecutors with such numbing regularity that they frequently haven't time or attention to spare on the nuances unfolding in other matters of law. This may help to explain a Merck official's irritation with the prosecutor in Merck's home county, Essex, New Jersey; the prosecutor was willing to try for a grand jury indictment against Aries, but only on the charge that he had received stolen property, the samples of MK-234, and not for having received the stolen documents containing process data. Similarly, the U.S. Attorney for Connecticut sought and obtained a Federal grand jury indictment against Aries for interstate transportation of the stolen product, but again not the documents. Their insistence on these distinctions, the Merck officials believed, helped to create the legal mare's nest which ensued.

Disentanglement of all these complications may some day prove to be instructive matter for a doctoral thesis by some student interested in the contrast between Roman, or "code," law and law cast in Anglo-Saxon tradition which Aries fled when he left the country. Suffice it to note here, though, that U.S. officials could not regain jurisdiction over Aries. The U.S. Attorney in Connecticut could not seek extradition because neither France nor Switzerland are constituted to reckon with crimes in interstate commerce; the theft of the trade secrets themselves would have been a crime in those countries. France was reluctant to grant the request, however, because while Aries had been a U.S. citizen since 1950, in France he could, and did, claim dual citizenship. This still left Merck an avenue, because French law also holds that if a French citizen commits a crime in another country which is also a crime in France, he may be tried in France.

4.

We ought to note in this connection another difference in the legal terrain Merck had to traverse. Speaking of another case, a Merck official noted:

> . . . there is very little on the continent in the way of satisfactory private investigation work. Most investigations are carried out by the police and their detective forces. Their search warrants are much easier to obtain and broader in scope than ours, although less protective of the individual. We found that these can be availed of if proper requests are made by United States police authorities.

Evidently, even the English are not unfailingly efficient in these matters. The official tells of a case for which Merck lawyers wanted a telescopic or long distance photograph of a former employee concerning whom they were gathering information. "Instead, the photographer appeared with one of those old style box cameras on a tripod with a hood and plunked it down right in front of" the suspect. Even so, Merck was able to obtain, through the efforts of the Essex County prosecutor, informal help from Interpol. The FBI, of course, had to withdraw after Aries fled the country. Interpol interested itself largely out of professional courtesy, since the international agreements under which it operates do not view trade secrets as property, either.

While Merck, the State Department, Interpol and the Essex County prosecutor searched out information and avenues of approach, they were joined by Rohm and Haas and Sprague Electric, who filed civil suits contending that Aries had made off with and sold in Europe the rights to two products which they held to be of some importance and value. They, too, got their evidence from employees who said they had peddled material to Aries. This brought to eight the number of criminal and civil actions pending against Aries, who by this time had himself or through agents filed patent applications for Mepyrium in some forty countries. Adjudication of ownership in most of these countries is based on date of filing rather than proof of invention, and many of these countries, in turn, make it a practice to issue patents to anyone who files. This confronted Merck with the prospect of a country-by-country legal battle to regain its rights to Amprolium.

The Hoffman–La Roche suit caught up with Aries late in 1960 when the authorities in Geneva sequestered $80,000 in visible assets and all the cash he had on his person. The Swiss, however, were still at that time making it a point not to track down assets in numbered bank accounts, a practice without which the Swiss might long ago have been gulped down by one of their larger neighbors. It would have seemed an easy thing to have found means to detain Aries when he showed up in Geneva a year later, but perhaps Swiss legal processes work at a more leisurely pace than in the United States. In any event, having bailed himself out with the $46,000 demanded by the magistrate, Aries slipped out of the country, probably over the border to France, where by this time he was also being sought.

5.

For after Merck sued him, Aries had sued Merck. He charged that the company had stolen his trade secret and bought controlling interest in Synorga in order to legalize the theft. He therefore also swore out a criminal complaint against the French company for having been a party to the theft. He asked for $36 million in damages. In court, he produced a University of Paris chemist who swore to having worked with Aries on the Mepyrium process in 1957, along with other corroborating witnesses. The ploy might have worked save for the fact that the chemist panicked and confessed that he had been bribed by Aries. Three other witnesses followed suit. As a result, Aries was wanted not only for having received stolen property, but also for having suborned witnesses.

At the time, in 1962, when a *Saturday Evening Post* reporter talked with Aries, he was about to be sent to jail on order of a French magistrate. A smattering of trade magazine reports after that said that he was, in fact, being held in a French jail. By January, 1966, when he again made the front page of *The New York Times,* however, he was living in an apartment in a fashionable section near the Bois de Boulogne. The *Times* reported that a higher court had ordered Aries released from jail while it took time to study his case. The occasion for his renewed notoriety came as a result of changes France and Monaco made in their trademark legislation. Like most Western European countries, Monaco and France have long permitted registration of trademarks within categories of the products they cover. Moreover, unlike the United States, they permit corporations to register trademarks without first having made some use of them. Both are also signatories to a West European convention which recognizes the earliest date that a trademark has been registered in one country as binding on the other countries in case of a dispute.

On August 1, 1965, France and Monaco, in recognition of the needs of the many corporations that had been formed to sell, not products, but services, created eight new classifications of trademarks in addition to the then existing thirty-four. The date went unnoticed by many corporations which had registered at one time or another under one or more of the old classifications. From August 2 to September 4, Dr. Aries and two companies, one called Prochina and the other (with which Aries said he had no connection) named Marques et Protection, filed separately for a total of 328 trademarks. Among them were: in banking, Chase, Morgan, Bankers Trust and Household Finance; in culture, N.B.C., C.B.S., B.B.C., *The New Yorker* and *Harper's.* They managed to find categories under which to register Sears, Sante Fe, Goodyear, Thyssen and Messerschmitt, not to mention "Never on Sunday," Harvard, Princeton, Jack Daniels, Wells Fargo, Texaco,

Sunkist, Formica, Schering (but not Merck) and others as numerous as they are familiar.

A lawyer in New York said that while his clients would rather fight than pay Aries to withdraw his registrations, he thought it possible that others might prefer a modest settlement to long, costly and involved litigation. Aries told a *Times* reporter that he and Prochina were acting as agents for third parties who had rights to the names. "He was asked who, for example, had rights to 'Sante Fe' and 'Erie.' 'Look around Lake Erie and you'll find somebody,' he replied."

Chapter Sixteen

FROM DU PONT WITH LOVE

And they asked me how I did it,
And I gave 'em the Scripture text,
"You keep your light so shining
A little in front o' the next!"
They copied all they could follow,
But they couldn't copy my mind,
And I left 'em sweating and stealing
A year and a half behind.

—RUDYARD KIPLING, *The Mary Gloster*

1.

WE ARE NOW almost ready to place ourselves in the position of a Congressman asked to consider the McDowell Amendment, or some variant upon it, to the National Stolen Property Act. We would know, that is, that its sponsor was a large and vital industry which considered "commercial espionage" to be a "crime" in some sense in which "audits of employees," "penetration" (all the quotation marks, I hope, may be excused by the technical nature of the subject) of a distributor's place of business, and a "routine" investigation of a pesky author are not crimes. In light of the Aries case, we may have concluded that civil actions are less than ideal for the purposes of deterring acts of espionage or remedying the losses that may result. Brief consideration of two more cases will put us on the doorstep of a question of public policy.

One was hailed by Robert Morgenthau, U.S. Attorney for the Southern District of New York, as the first successful prosecution of an industrial espionage case under the National Stolen Property Act. He had either forgotten about, or had thought to be less than wholly successful, the prosecution of Eugene A. Mayfield. In any event, this case concerns thefts from Lederle Laboratories, of Pearl River, New

York, a division of American Cyanamid. It begins in 1958, when a Lederle chemist, Dr. Sidney Fox, then thirty-seven, got to brooding about his station in life and his $10,000 annual salary. A cocktail party brought him into conversation with Nathan Sharff and Seymour Salb, owners of Biorganic Laboratories, a small drug firm located near Fox's home in exurban Spring Valley, N. Y. Fox and Salb had children attending the same school, and through frequent meetings their conversation progressed to the point where Salb—Fox says—proffered the idea that Biorganic Laboratories could market certain drug materials if Fox could supply them.

Fox, as it happened, was head of a research team working on antibiotics of the tetracycline family; tetracyclines account for perhaps more sales than any other drug in the world. Fox began to take home with him cultures of the drugs in various stages of fermentation together with documents containing parts of the recipe. Some of these he sold to Sharff and Salb. They, in turn, sold them to buyers in Italy, which does not think highly of patents as a means of encouraging research and invention, and so doesn't subscribe to international agreements. When it occurred to Fox that Sharff and Salb might be getting rich on his wile and risk, he decided to go into the marketing end of the business himself. He quit Lederle, made contacts of his own in Italy, and enlisted a former colleague, John Cancelarich, aged twenty-seven, to supply him with cultures and documents.

During five months starting in October, 1960, Fox and his assistant negotiated deals with five Italian companies. Since they agreed also to supply technical production advice, the pair flew often to Italy, under false names and on separate planes. They concealed the organisms in pocket cigar cases and the process data on microfilm. Once Fox's assistant got the hang of how to sell the material, he and another of Fox's partners—he owned a legitimate medical supply firm which gave Fox a cover for the operation—went into business for themselves, freezing Fox out. They suspected that Fox was retaining much of their share in the profits. Adding further to insult, they joined forces with Sharff and Salb, who by this time had bought a big shareholding in a small Italian drug firm to which they had already sold tetracycline cultures.

The process might have gone on like generations of leaves except that the successor to Fox's successor as the in-plant source of the secrets lost his nerve. Here we ought to pause just briefly to note a piece of business staged by Lederle's lawyer, Walter Mansfield, now a Federal judge, in the U.S. District Court for the Southern District of New York. Fox's successor in the plant, John Cancelarich, owned the house where his parents and sister lived. When *his* successor, Joseph Gerace, spilled the beans, Mansfield used Gerace's affidavit, which accused Cancelarich of having stolen organisms from Lederle, to obtain a civil judgment in the form of a lien on the house. Thus armed, he and Lederle's security chief, William Fulton, flew to Milan to explain the situation to Cancelarich.

2.

Roughly speaking, the message Cancelarich got was your confession or your house. After thinking it over, Cancelarich agreed to an affidavit and telephoned instructions to Leonard Fine—the former Fox partner with the medical supply firm—to put the stolen organisms into the hands of an independent accounting firm. That was in 1962. It took nearly two years more of legal maneuvering to bring Fox in. Mansfield put the squeeze on him by obtaining a civil decree ordering return of the organisms Fox had taken. Fox, of course, could not comply, and so was put in jail. Mansfield meanwhile had handed his evidence over to the Justice Department, asking for a criminal prosecution on the grounds of conspiracy provision contained in the National Stolen Property Act. With the by this time enthusiastic cooperation of the FBI Mansfield helped to secure an indictment by a New York Federal Grand Jury.

Mansfield pressed the civil action because it seemed to him that the Justice Department was slow in getting around to prosecuting the criminal charges. The Department was at that time constructing a case against Cyanamid, Lederle's parent, also alleging conspiracy, but in this case under the antitrust laws. It appeared to Mansfield on that account to be reacting sluggishly to his complaint.

After being put into jail on the civil complaint, and then placed under indictment on the criminal charge, Fox gave way. He told his story, confessed to perjury and pleaded guilty to an altered indictment. On January 20, 1966, nearly eight years after Fox had begun his rebellion, Judge Charles Metzner sentenced Sharff, Salb, and Dr. Caesar C. Bottone, a chemist who need not detain us here, to two years in prison.

Cancelarich, Fine and Fox received six-month sentences. Gerace was given a suspended sentence of six months as a token for his cooperation with the prosecution. Lyman Duncan, a vice president of Lederle, said the trial "is a firm step toward assuring the continued ability of industry to carry on the scientific work which has contributed so much to technological and social progress." Judge Metzner, in passing sentence, asked: "Don't you think . . . that there were hundreds of thousands of dollars expended by Cyanamid in this case, and wouldn't they have been a little better off if they paid their people with doctorate degrees higher salaries than students out of law school for two years are paid in law offices?"

Someone has suggested that in view of the fact that Italians seem to be the biggest spenders for drug secrets, Mansfield might have rationed his time more productively had he tried to convince the State Department to apply economic and political sanctions against Italy with the end in view of making Rome see the value of the patent system. Like all sensible proposals, however, that one, if adopted, would have been only partially effective. It would not have helped the courts determine what to do about Donald Earl Hirsch.

3.

Hirsch's case was outlined in a memorandum sent by the New York public relations firm of Hill and Knowlton to the editors of the *Saturday Evening Post* under date of November 11, 1964. Hill and Knowlton thought that it was a bad thing that Hirsch, then an employee of a client, American Potash and Chemical Corporation, was prevented from doing the work for which he was best equipped by inclination, training and experience. To the *Post,* devoted at the time to a policy of "sophisticated muckraking," the idea must have seemed fairly appetizing, particularly since the villain of the piece was the du Pont Co., a target favored after the turn of the century by the primitive muckrakers. However, for reasons of its own, the *Post* left the story for others to tell.

The story, as it unfolded in public testimony, began when Potash put in a request to du Pont for a license to use its exclusive process for the manufacture of titanium dioxide pigments by a chloride process. Du Pont said no. In September, 1962, Potash, whose headquarters are in Los Angeles, bought space in the newspaper serving du Pont's home town of Wilmington, Delaware, to advertise for a manager of plant technical services who "must have TiO_2 experience." (TiO_2 is the chemist's symbol for titanium dioxide.) It then contracted with a management consultant firm which advertised for the same position in a chemical trade journal. Hirsch was, in his mid-thirties, a senior chemical engineer with du Pont, knew about all there was to know about making titanium dioxide by du Pont's process, and earned, with bonuses, about $15,000 per year. He also looked upon management's coolness to his petitions for promotion as evidence that his work was not enough appreciated. So he replied to the Potash ad in the trade journal.

Potash spoke to Hirsch, satisfying itself as to his experience. It may also have learned that Hirsch had not contracted with du Pont to refrain from working in competition with the company after he left its employment. A short while later, Hirsch was notified that Potash would be happy to welcome him aboard. Hirsch gave his notice.

It is often charged against large corporations that they react to danger, as well as to opportunity, with the speed of a pinched hippopotamus. The charge is probably an unfair exaggeration. After trying to talk Hirsch out of leaving, du Pont put a motion for an injunction in the hands of Chancellor Collins Seitz, and shortly after that won a favorable judgment of the motion together with a temporary restraining order citing Potash as co-defendant with Hirsch to prevent Hirsch from going to work at Potash in any capacity having to do with development or use of processes for making titanium dioxide. Du Pont said it was willing to "challenge" Potash's motives, but, even apart from that, argued that it was "inevitable" that Hirsch would divulge du Pont's trade secrets.

Potash moved for a summary judgment to dismiss du Pont's petition and the order, arguing that du Pont's "inevitability" thesis was no more than "prophecy." Du Pont rejoined by introducing evidence as to the difficulty inherent in "scaling up" to a production of TiO_2 by a chloride process and contended that in view of the "frailties of mankind" situations would arise in which "disclosure will inevitably or probably follow from Hirsch's employment by Potash. . . ." Chancellor Seitz went along with du Pont's argument; he said he considered the inevitability argument relevant, and the facts appropriate matter for trial.

Hirsch went to work for Potash, but at a job having nothing to do with TiO_2. Du Pont seemed to be satisfied with the status quo. Hill and Knowlton's efforts to gain publicity for the case received only half-hearted support in the form of action from Potash lawyers. An illness of Chancellor Seitz postponed action on the injunction, and by the time he was able to hear arguments most of the witnesses were on the West Coast. Chancellor Seitz was quoted in a business magazine as saying that the case "has great social and industrial significance." That's the way matters stood when an author of a note in the *Virginia Law Review* commented: "It is not difficult for an observer to regard the entire situation with complacence, and to feel that without having had to face the most troublesome issues, and without noticeably clarifying the law, the [court has] left the parties just about where they ought to be."

To appreciate the author's complacence, we must refer to a statement of the "balance theory" (his phrase) to which he subscribes:

"Does the use of the knowledge by the employee involve a necessary and legitimate risk which the employer by reason of the nature of his business would stand, and will the employee be unduly handicapped in future efforts to obtain a livelihood if he is forced to forego the use of such knowledge?" In the balance theory there are no standard weights and measures, only comparisons—contingencies of the times and the moment. Since these have changed, so have the apparent merits of once highly regarded court decisions.

What do Holmes's, Brandeis' and Frankfurter's legatees say to Hirsch? "There, there, old man, everybody's got to suffer a little loss of freedom so the other fellow can have some." And to Hyman Moore? Perhaps: "On the facts as revealed by the Long Committee, we can only say, 'How else are we to know for sure that when we go into a drug store we get what we ask for?' " And to Ralph Nader? That seems clear on the record: "Stupid thing for GM to do, old man. Glad to see your book is selling so well."

Let us allow that the investigation of Nader was an aberration, an irresistible impulse indicating the "frailties" of human nature in the corporate structure. The "routine" that prompted it clearly was not. Moreover, not every worker "audited" by an undercover agent or citizen subjected to the routine has a book to sell, or owns a drug wholesale business. Nor have all scientists who may want to change their jobs been college teachers, as Hirsch was, a fact which added to the complacency of the *Virginia Law Review*'s author. He figured Hirsch could always go back to teaching.

We seem, in sum, to be drifting toward a circumstance in which the only activities that may be said to constitute an invasion of privacy are those that lack redeeming social value. How much weight ought we to give to the claims of the effort by private industry to enlist public security officers to the cause of protecting their trade secrets? We can't know in any reliable way unless we know what weight also to assign to the individual's own trade secrets, so to speak.

Taking a leaf from a strategic dictum concerning the best defense, we might first inquire into the reasons why the business of selling security has quintupled in the past decade, and why the industry confidently predicts a tenfold increase in the next ten. This exercise will require a speculative dash through some history, including a glance at the first and greatest of this nation's industrial spies.

Chapter Seventeen

THE SPIRIT OF INDENTURE

Where is the life we have lost in living?
Where is the wisdom we have lost in knowledge?
Where is the knowledge we have lost in information?
The cycles of Heaven in twenty centuries
Bring us farther from God and nearer to the Dust.

—T. S. Eliot

1.

Espionage is sometimes referred to as the second oldest profession. However, in order to assume that betrayal by spying came second, we should have to assume that the earliest practitioner of the oldest profession did not have to send someone regularly to see if the coast was clear. This hypothesis flies in the face of evidence gathered from observing apes. It suggests strongly that pre-Neanderthal males were as jealous and suspicious as any that came after. I am therefore inclined to look upon espionage as the older of the two, and an accompaniment of the human condition long before men kept records of anything, let alone of one another's credit standing.

Even so, while the realms, principalities and dioceses of William the Conqueror's time were no doubt busy snooping into one another's affairs, almost all of commercial value that was known was "imprinted," as a modern geneticist might say, on the mind and muscle of craftsmen. Spyglasses, tape recorders, parabolic microphones and postage stamp transmitters would not have availed to obtain, nor a Xerox machine to make transportable, either the brewer's art or the recipe in his head.

The most advanced of tools these craftsmen used would have been of not much more use to anyone outside the craft than Abercrombie and Fitch's best reel and fly rod would be in the hand of someone who has never set foot in a trout stream.

Exclusive possession of a range of skills made it possible for the forerunners of the modern business corporation, the enclaves of merchants and craftsmen situated along the European coastline, to exact from their Crowns recognition of their autonomy and freedom from feudal obligations. Late in the 1200's, perhaps a century before Parliament in 1383 paid official notice, the craft guilds in England began the practice of taking on apprentices. This practice might have posed security problems, save for the fact that by that time guilds throughout Europe were able to take some peace of mind from a magnificent conceit.

2.

Sir Ernest Barker elaborates on Aristotle's conception of the state's likeness to man's physical body:

> If the State is the end of its citizens' activities, as Aristotle everywhere assumes, it must be a system of which they are the organs or its instruments. Its function must be the function to which their separate functions are all so many contributions; its life must be the life in which they all partake, and by partaking in which they have any life of their own.

States, however, are differently constituted; no state, even among those generally classed as belonging to the "free world," resembles another in all of its specific organs or modes of operations. None has a constitution precisely like ours, some have bicameral legislatures and some don't, and so forth. What the *natural* state is meant to imply, I gather has to do with at least two other qualities.

One is that a living, breathing human organism is in some sense the same man at thirty-five that he was at twenty-five, although every cell in his body has been replaced at least once in the interim, with the trivial exception, I suppose, of foot callouses. Does the State, or Society or the Community, share in this attribute; is it, that is, a "living" being, irrespective of the persons who constitute it at any given time? Walter Lippmann, for one, supposes that it is, which is why "young men die in battle and old men plant trees they will never sit under." The royalty of the Middle Ages, moreover, with the help of schoolmen and philosophers who took their text from Aristotle, were in the habit of looking upon their subjects as incorporated not into an "as if" corporation, a creation of law, but an entity, a body politic as much a creature of God as living, breathing organisms, with a life independent of which particular subjects composed it at any given time.

Having won recognition as being in themselves organic corporations, operating under the divine charter of the king, the guilds would not have understood a single proposition of any argument devoted to the virtues of competition. It was probably worth an apprentice's neck to break his indenture agreement; but if he did, there were few if any places he could peddle his skills where he would be better off than he was in the guild. The chances are good that he was not so badly off at that. Out of respect, more or less, not only to the metaphysical and scriptural foundations of their prosperity, but also to the requirements of communities constantly under siege from a resentful countryside, the medieval craft guilds were great respecters of persons.

The guild rules for Southampton require that a guildsman be punished almost as severely for "speaking evil" of another guildsman as he would be for striking him. Moreover, "If any guildsman falls into poverty and has not the wherewithal to live, and is not able to work or to provide for himself, he shall have one mark from the Guild to relieve his condition. . . ." Guildsmen as a rule were required to be as attentive to their duties toward an apprentice as they were to the apprentice's obligations to them. If the rules promulgated in the City of Bruges were not exceptional, apprentices worked a 48-hour week, with Saturday afternoon off, and were assured other amenities requisite to human existence.

Work by the French historian, George Renard, indicates why the benefits of competition might not have occurred with force to anyone who bought from the guilds. He wrote that

> . . . the guild prided itself on letting nothing leave its shops but finished products, perfect of their kind; it examined and stamped every article, and further required that it should bear a special trade-mark stating where it was made and its just price. At Ypres, toward the end of the thirteenth century, the pieces of cloth thus officially accepted numbered 8,000 a year. Nor was this all; like Caesar's wife, the guild must be above suspicion; not only fraud, but the very appearance of fraud

> was rigorously excluded, all that might deceive the buyer was forbidden. In Florence jewelers might not use sham stones, even if they declared them to be such; in Paris it was forbidden to make glass jewels in imitation of real stones, or to put a leaf of metal under an emerald to give it artificial brilliance; plated and lined goods were not allowed, as they might be mistaken for solid gold or silver. . . . Sale was carefully watched over as production. Not only had the weights and measure to be verified and controlled in conformity with carefully preserved standards, but at Florence, for instance, the "iron ruler" of the Calimala was the standard for measuring woolen materials. . . .

As it happened, it was not the apprentices within the guild who made for the principal security problems, but the sons of freedmen without the walls who tried to gain, but were denied, the opportunity to serve as apprentices. For the guilds were becoming introvertly smug in their cozy monopolies. By the fourteenth century, manorial barons, too, were tiring of their dependence on the city and its imperious ways. They gave encouragement and protection to disappointed apprenticeship seekers as they went to the country and groped their way toward breaking the city's monopoly on commercial arts. And merchant trade, then expanding to new markets, was greatly aided by these new suppliers. The necessity to secure transactions at a distance, in time as well as geographically, created the need for negotiable titles to capital, which might be invested anywhere and in anyone able by his skill to turn it to profit. By the fifteenth century, the guilds were showing full-blown signs of security consciousness. Here we ought to return to Renard:

> A tragic example of what it might cost to be indiscreet may be found in a Venetian law of 1454: "If a workman carry into another country any art or craft *to the detriment of the Republic* [italics mine], he will be ordered to return; if he disobeys, his nearest relatives will be imprisoned, in order that the solidarity of the family may persuade him to return; if he persists in his disobedience, secret measures will be taken to have him killed wherever he may be."

Moreover, guild crafts were becoming more complicated. In Paris, Renard remarks, "the guild of the bird fanciers attempted, though unsuccessfully, to prevent citizens from setting on eggs canaries which they had caged, as it injured the trade of the guild."

Adding to the security consciousness of the Venetians was a phenomenon that might command sympathy from the group of young executives poignantly described in a newspaper feature concerning office copying machines. Each day these legatees and successors of Ford, Durant, Hill and Rockefeller were flooded with copies of letters and reports from the field, trade magazine items, pages from newsletters and the like with the result that it became too much for them. For much of the time they squirmed in their chairs as if paralyzed, their eyes glazed over, unable even to look at, much less to act upon, much of the information that was brought to them. These men, though confined to the arena of action within the arc inscribed by a swivel chair, are suffering the symptoms of dizzying pace.

3.

Eric Partridge says of the group of words which includes the word "information" that it "rests firmly upon L *forma,* s form-, shape, that which shapes, that which has been shaped, but esp the shape imparted to an object," which he takes to be "o.o.o.," or "of obscure origin." The Oxford "Concise" etymological dictionary suggests origins as far back as language as we know it can be traced, which is a remarkable achievement for a word in these days of "Winston Tastes Good Like a Cigarette Should" and "Superette," a word composed wholly of a prefix and a suffix headed in opposite directions.

Philosophers trouble themselves with the distinction, if only to reject it, between those objects given shape or informed by human intelligence and skill, or by other agents, such as wind, rain and dam-building beavers, and those which have, in Aristotle's statement, within themselves "a principle of motion and a stationariness (in respect of place, or of growth and decrease, or by way of alteration)." Such as men, trees and beavers. This principle he calls "nature" so that the distinction is between objects "constituted by nature" and those that are not.

Recent work in genetics promises that we ought before too long be able to order up children the way we do our needs out of the Sears, Roebuck catalog, and that this will coincidentally reduce the human method of procreation to a matter of preference. This advance will make it even more difficult, I fear, to reflect sympathetically upon a world in which great swatches of a person's environment, methods and routine as well as objects, were taken as having been informed, or constituted, by the principle Aristotle referred to as nature; and in which much of what was not of nature had been around so long that it might as well have been.

As far as I can learn from standard etymologies, it was not until the world of Middle English that the word "know" was put to use as a verb in the sense of "to be assured of." Philosophers then arrived at a distinction between "knowledge" and "contingent knowledge." Newton's laws and Euclid's geometry ranked as knowledge until Einstein's general theories described a universe, in only a subuniverse of which they could be said to hold true. Now it may be said to be true that to every action there is an opposite and equal reaction, provided. . . .

The most contingent knowledge of all, in a loose manner of speaking, is information. Its significance and its capacity to render assurance is contingent upon time, place and the requirements of the informing—again in the sense of conferring shape or structure—intelligence. Or, as we might say, upon the programmer. During the breakup and recomposition of the "pictures we carry in our heads," as Lippmann puts it, much that was knowledge turns to information.

If for no more than a period of three generations men reckon themselves and their circumstances as if through a kaleidoscope that sticks every time someone tries to turn it, they come to believe that they are looking instead through a powerful telescope. The first generation identifies and names the bits and pieces which form the pattern, the second constructs a curriculum around it, and the third celebrates it as part of the Divine plan. A sudden twist may so disconcert them as to cause dizzying pace and hence paralysis.

In those circumstances, it is best to stay loose. But how? It seems to me that the relation of accounting methods to a businessman's peace of mind is so taken for granted as not to have been sufficiently explored. Luca Pacioli, one of those irritatingly Renaissance mathematicians, educators, painters, geographers, men of business, poets, and so forth, knew the tranquilizing effects of knowing how "to arrange all the transactions in such a systematic way that one may understand each one of them at a glance."

The first recorded use of double-entry bookeeping occurred in the banking house of Francesco di Marco Datini in Tuscany, sometime during the fourteenth century. Before then, if a private investigator were to try to get an idea of a guildman's business, he would have gotten small help from a look at the books. They were kept in much the same way housewives today keep their budgets. In the front of his journal the guildsman listed money he received from whom and for what; in the back he cataloged his purchases.

The system was fairly well suited to a cash-and-carry, day-to-day world. The fourteenth-century merchant and banker, though, had to keep track of several different kinds of transactions begun one day and completed on another; of several different forms of assets; of receivables, balances with foreign correspondents, consignment sales and even a reserve for taxes, together with his own equity and miscellaneous matters.

The first systematic presentation of the method by which this became possible is contained in Part I in *Distinctio nona,* of Pacioli's *Summa de Arithmetica, Geometria, Proporcioni et Proporcionalità.* It is essentially the same as that used today by small business firms, by mayors and governors for the instruction of voters and journalists, and by the Congress to measure and apportion its own power, as well as to keep track of how the President uses his. As Pacioli observed, "without making their entries systematically it would be impossible for them to conduct their business, for they would have no rest and their minds would always be troubled."

4.

Among those who had become familiar with the uses and advantages of the accounting method Pacioli described was a contemporary of his, who is himself remembered more often for his understanding of the soothing qualities of information than for his other achievements. He was the Baron Jakob von Fugger (1459–1525). The Fugger family had built up very nearly a monopoly in the mining and trading of silver, copper and mercury. Jakob Fugger insured himself of control over his immediate environment. He lent immense sums to Emperor Maximilian I and financed the election of Charles V.

He also understood the value of that knowledge which may be termed contingent information: intelligence. A dated Navy manual provides a definition: "Intelligence is information upon which a course of action may safely be based." This definition might apply to all knowledge, including propositions that fall under metaphysics and theology, but we may assume that the action referred to is that required to best an opponent.

Competition among bankers, merchants and craftsmen for capital, raw materials and markets made valuable the sort of information classed today under the heading of strategy. Prices and terms of sales and purchase, location of buyers and of raw materials, negotiations for real estate and the political environment and court intrigues in foreign markets were matters about which a competitor's ignorance might make a sizable difference, though, even to a monopoly enterprise. Fugger and the other monopolists of his time seemed to understand what the craft guilds did not, that "nature" awards a better chance of survival to living corporeal things that make some disposal of the energies available to them than to those that don't; that growth, in short, is a condition of survival.

Out of this understanding grew the Fugger newsletters, the first systematic, global effort for gathering information of use to businessmen. It was, of course, circulated free of charge but to a highly controlled list of subscribers sworn, or assumed to be sworn, to secrecy. A recent account notes:

> Their international business connections assured the Fuggers inside information from politicians and clerics alike. News came through to them with amazing rapidity and was even smuggled through the lines of opposing armies. Amounting to sort of Kiplinger service, these newsletters either were based on direct eye witness accounts, or were rewrites of published reports collected by those diligent forerunners of Reuters . . . two alert Augsbergers named Jeremias Crasser and his successor, Jeremias Schiffle.

A casual reading of some of the Fugger letters would suggest that a part of the information contained in them was obtained by spying. It would suggest also that much of the information that in those days had to be obtained by spying would today be available from any equivalent of the Government Printing Office. Espionage, like voyeurism, is a contingent term. Just as one man's *voyeur* is another's crusader for sexual freedom, so one man's spy is another man's pioneering journalist. In any event, the foundation for industrial espionage as we have come to know it was laid not on the Continent proper, but among the Protestant-speaking nations, principally England, where businessmen had little ear for "clerics."

Chapter Eighteen

THE BREAKUP

Tennyson goes to the heart of the difficulty. It is the problem of mechanism which appalls him.

"The stars," she whispers, "blindly run"

. . . Each molecule blindly runs. The human body is a collection of molecules. Therefore, the human body blindly runs, and therefore there can be no individual responsibility for the actions of the body. . . .

—ALFRED NORTH WHITEHEAD

1.

THE INTELLECTUAL COMMUNITY has been riven in recent years by a disagreement over the scope and nature of the effects of automation, and all that it implies, on the human condition. There have been forebodings of men turned into robots, armies of unemployed, global destruct buttons pushed inadvertently, and a pace of decision and commitment made possible by machines that will defeat prudence, rob us of the cherished second guess in many vital matters, and catapult civilization into oblivion. Some of the participants in these conversations seem to be saying that we have done our damnedest to keep the House of Intellect in order. Yet we never know at what time of the day or night some monster sorcerer is going to come reeling home from his think tank with some notion or contraption that will cause heaven-knows-what damage.

It is as if their collective nerves had worn down trying to render the furies manageable, and they would happily settle for the role of the common scold. Some of the keening that has been heard in the more advanced forums puts me in mind of Molly Bloom as she might appear reading *The Feminine Mystique* to a group of Girl Scouts gathered around the last camp fire. There are many in the top ranks of management who would commiserate. But talent for exasperation or nostalgia does not command a high premium in today's executive job market.

Neither can erase a company president's night thoughts of awakening to find that Britain's Central Bank rate went in the wrong direction, or that the Venezuelan President in exile whom he had been too busy to take lunch with was President of Venezuela again, or that a Congressman had succeeded in an effort to tell him how to label his product.

Nor do they help matters when a competitor persuades the American Dental Association to love another toothpaste, or a company he thought was in the film coating business in upstate New York comes out with a dry-process office copier that makes his whole inventory of machines and copying paper, which he had hoped to sell the way Gillette sells razor cartridges, into nothing more than a tax writeoff; or a rival drug company takes the hottest thing to come out of his laboratories, adds a molecule, and walks away with a good part of the market.

But a man with concerns like these usually has gotten over the early stages of shrinking nerve. He realizes that forces working to shorten or snuff out the lives of his investments are the same socks, turned inside out, from which he made those investments and from which he will make more. He knows that inside of every Edsel is a Mustang struggling to get out. His anxieties, therefore, are closer to the top of his head.

Yet they run deep. Indeed, they run so deep that had the headstrong young Swedish Queen Christina not insisted upon getting a fifty-four-year-old Descartes out of bed every morning at five A.M. to teach her philosophy in the coldest of cold Stockholm winters, he might have lived long enough to have ironed out his differences with Sir Isaac Newton. As it happened, Newton was only eight when Descartes yielded. We might otherwise have been spared some of the acute schizophrenia which contributes greatly to our security consciousness.

2.

"God in the Beginning," Newton believed, "form'd matter in solid, massy, hard, impenetrable, moveable Particles, of such Sizes and

Figures, and with such other Properties, and in such proportion to Space, as most conduced to the End for which He form'd them." So it long appeared to the English entrepreneur and it was reflected in the way he chose, even before the Reformation, to regard the persons who labored for him. Henri Pirrene records, in *A History of Europe,* that by late in the fourteenth century

> . . . in conformity with the "common law," the employer and the employee entered into contracts directly, without the interposition of any authority or association. The one sold his labour, the other bought it, and the price depended only on their "free will." This meant that it was actually imposed upon the weaker by the stronger. Completely unorganized, whether in the city or the country, the workers of the new industries had to submit to the law of the capitalist. Since the workers elaborated the raw material supplied by the capitalists under their own roof, they were particularly liable to exploitation, thanks to the regulations of all kinds which the capitalist was able to impose on them. And in fact, from the beginning of the sixteenth century there is abundant evidence of the wretchedness of their conditions, and of their discontent.

Things were also bad for the workers on the continent, but for different reasons.

". . . treat of the network," the modern German philosopher Ludwig Wittgenstein admonished, "and not of what the network describes." To Descartes, the network was everything. "Give me space and motion," he said, "and I will give you a world." The network, moreover, was of a piece, a whole. To him, the human biological system was a machine, completely governed by the laws that governed phenomena outside it. The implication is clear in the *Analytical Geometry:* ". . . for, as I before remarked, although the things which I perceive or imagine are perhaps nothing at all apart from me, I I am nevertheless assured that the modes of consciousness which I call perceptions and imaginations, in as far only as they are modes of consciousness, exist in me."

While the continent went on in its own feudal way, it gave rise to the speculations of great mathematicians, Pacioli, Pascal, the philosophers of the Enlightenment and this entry on industriousness and invention by Jaucourt in Diderot's *Encyclopedia:*

> Inventions are the children of time, but, if I may say so, industriousness can speed the delivery. How many centuries did men walk on silk without knowing how to make use of it, how to adorn themselves with it. No doubt nature has in her storehouse treasures which are as precious and which she keeps for the moment when we least expect them; let us always be prepared to take advantage of them.

"Knowledge is power," Lord Bacon said. In contrast to the delight in invention evident in Leonardo's Notebooks, and in the easygoing Jaucourt, we have H. S. Harrison's no-nonsense, up-and-at-'em resolve in the Oxford *A History of Technology.* The heading is "Extreme Slowness of Progress":

> Man has progressed less by the pressure of his needs than by the insistence of his opportunities. Human progress has always depended largely upon opportunism—in the earliest times casual and obtuse, but later becoming intermittently persistent. . . . We have become far less dependent upon accident than were our distant forefathers.

An understanding of the Chinese puzzle box of cause and effect of which these differences are a part has been held to include whatever it is that makes England a monument to the Reformation and France sort of Roman Catholic; it might also yield clues as to why an Englishman discovered the cell as the "building block" in biology and a Frenchman tissue, why Merck & Co. had so much trouble getting salt on Robert Aries' tail, why in books intended to describe computer technology to laymen, one is more likely to find in the index Descartes and Cartesian than Newton or Newtonian, and perhaps even why James Watt didn't perceive his most significant contribution to the steam engine.

3.

While with one hand trying to stir up a counter-Reformation, James I with the other had to give away one by one the royal prerogatives attributable to his divinity, and to delegate the interpretation of God's law to others. One of the things he gave away was the Crown's right to charter monopolies. In 1624, not long after the Pilgrims landed, he agreed that the Crown would do no more than to issue letters patent giving inventors the right to the exclusive use and control of their inventions for a limited time. In exchange the inventor had to deposit with the Crown all the specifications someone competent would need to duplicate the device.

More than a century and a half later, James Watt made the contribution he supposed to have been the critical improvement to the Newcomen steam engine.

> I have gone to take a walk on a fine Sabbath afternoon, I had entered the Green and passed the old washing house. I was thinking of the engine at the time. I had gone as far as the Lord's house when the idea came into my mind that as steam was an elastic body it would rush into a vacuum, and if a connection were made between the cylinder and an exhausting vessel it would rush into it and might there be condensed without cooling the cylinder. I then saw that I must get rid of the condensed steam and injection water if I used a jet, as in Newcomen's engine. Two ways of doing this occurred to me: First, the water might be run off by a descending pipe, if an offlet could be got at a depth of 35 or 36 feet, and any air might be extracted by a small pump. The second was, to make the pump large enough to extract both water and air. . . . I had not walked farther than The Golf House, when the whole thing was arranged in my mind.

The passage is quoted in *A History of Mechanical Inventions,* by Abbot Payson Usher, first published in 1929. Professor Usher was concerned in part with the inadequacy of the *Eureka!* theory of great invention. This is the theory, greatly encouraged by comic-book plotting in the movies, which holds that the inventor, while looking into his girl's eyes, suddenly snaps erect, a light flashing over his head, and we have—the air conditioner!

Professor Usher quotes Watt in such a way as to indicate that he, too, conceived of the condensing chamber as Watt's greatest contribution. Marshall McLuhan might say that Watt and Professor Usher were victims to "lineal" or "sequential" thought, a habit which McLuhan attributes to the way type is arranged on a page. That is, they apparently thought of a steam engine as a conversion process, in which water and heat are converted by a sequence of events into usable power.

"Today, in the electric age," McLuhan observes, "we feel as free to invent nonlineal logics as we do to make nonlineal Euclidean geometries." Today, too, a student may learn that "the crucial contribution made by Watt to the development of the steam engine," as the author of a caption to a diagram in *Scientific American* puts it, was the flyball governor. For, as the caption writer notes, although the flyball governor went out of use with the steam engine, it "has won renewed significance . . . as a symbol and demonstration of the feedback principle that underlies all automatic control systems." It took us quite awhile to appreciate this because as it happened the man who brought the Industrial Revolution here was also a lineal thinker.

Chapter Nineteen

". . . AND TO SERVE HIS SECRETS"

When our people were fed out of a common store and labored jointly together . . . the most honest among them would hardly take so much true paines in a weeke, as now for themselves they will doe in a day.

—JOHN SMITH, speaking of the Pilgrims

1.

SAMUEL SLATER was born in 1786, eighteen years after the date generally stipulated as the start of the Industrial Revolution, eight years before the American Revolution and twenty-one years prior to the outbreak of the French Revolution. The sequence would warm the imagination of any industrial spy worth his fee. For the first event brought to realization a highly transportable piece of information of great commercial value, the second created a ready market for it and the third drove up the price astronomically. The information was embodied in the cotton yarn spinning mill devised by Sir Richard Arkwright and placed under a letter patent in 1769. The Arkwright Mill, using water power in place of men and animals, and containable under a single roof, was able to turn out an abundance of cotton at a cost so low that British manufacturers were able to underprice anything made by older methods in the principal markets of the world.

The second event, the American Revolution, created a market for the information. The colonies, once they were released from the suppressive forages of British troops and agents with orders to root out any threat of independent colonial technology, began actively to seek release also from dependence on British manufacturing. Bounties were paid to inventors who devised textile machines, although they fell far short of the Arkwright model. Moses Brown, a converted Quaker and retired merchant of Providence, Rhode Island, had invested especially heavily in various devices, none of which, working singly or in combination, enabled him to exploit the market he felt was potentially larger than even the British knew.

The third event, the French Revolution, threatened a large market for Britain's output, thus increasing its dependence on the American market. This in turn caused the British Government to take extraordinary security measures, including rigorous enforcement of laws which forbade textile craftsmen to visit North America and prohibited anyone from taking out of Britain parts, models, specifications or anything else that might prove helpful to a waiting American mechanic.

Ingenious efforts were made to break the blockade, notably an attempt by the American minister to France. By means still unknown, he enlisted agents who purchased and dismantled parts of Arkwright machinery in England and sent the pieces to the U.S. Paris legation. From there, they were transshipped in boxes labeled "glassware" or as replacement parts for farm implements. Nearly every shipment was intercepted by British agents between Paris and the coast, or on the high seas by the British Navy.

All persons leaving England were thoroughly searched by customs and Navy officials before boarding their ships, and watched alertly while on board. Inevitably, the surveillance drove up the value of the information. There is no evidence, however, that Slater was thinking along these lines when, at age fourteen, he signed on as an apprentice to Jedediah Strutt, Arkwright's backer and partner. Considering, though, the smooth execution of his coup, he might as well have been.

2.

Strutt had asked the elder Slater for the services of his oldest son; but William Slater, a timber merchant and neighbor of Strutt's, recommended Samuel instead on account of the boy's evident interest in things mechanical. A year after Samuel left home, however, his father died, leaving the boy to sign a new indenture of his own. He thus contracted to "learn his art with" Strutt, "in the manner of an apprentice to serve from the date of these presents unto the full end and term of six years and a half . . . to be fully compleat and ended, during which term the said apprentice to his master faithfully shall serve his secrets. . . ."

It must be said for Slater that he kept his bargain with Strutt if not the one imposed upon him by England herself. As Arnold Welles notes in a short but thoroughgoing account of Slater's exploit:

> During the early days of his term the boy became so engrossed in the business that he would go for six months without seeing his family, despite the fact that they lived only a mile away, and he would frequently spend his only free day, Sunday, experimenting alone on machinery. In those days, mill owners had to build all their own machinery and Slater acquired valuable experience in its design, as well as operation, and in the process of spinning yarn. Even before completing his term of indenture, he was made superintendent of Strutt's new hosiery mill.

If a passage had been written in that tone about Robert Aries, it might have sounded ironically sinister. Young Slater, however, was concerned principally with avenues to owning and running his own mill. After Arkwright's patents expired, factories containing a number of improvements multiplied so rapidly that he saw little hope of being able to gather together the capital he would need to catch up. "His attention," Welles writes, "had been drawn to the United States by an article in a Philadelphia paper saying that a bounty of £100 had been granted by the Pennsylvania legislature to a man who had designed a textile machine. Young Slater made up his mind that he would go to the United States and introduce the Arkwright methods there."

And he did: by the only method that in late 1789 was feasible. Passing himself off as a farmer, he carried with him so well hidden that it was not discovered, one piece of printed matter. That was his indenture for use as a credential in finding a job. In his head, however, so firmly imprinted in his memory that it endured a 61-day voyage, weeks spent working for a yarn and cloth maker in New York, a period of negotiation with the man who was to back him, and long months devoted to articulating what he knew in iron and wood, he carried the working specifications for a modern cotton mill. It was in effect the Industrial Revolution itself that he had committed to memory, and carried like a yoghurt culture to a waiting bowl of hot milk.

3.

In December of 1789, Moses Brown received at his home in Providence, Rhode Island, the following letter:

> Sir,
>
> A few days ago I was informed that you wanted a manager of *cotton spinning*, etc., in which business I flatter myself that I can give the greatest satisfaction, in making machinery, making good yarn, either for *stockings* or *twist*, as any that is made in England; as I have had opportunity, and an oversight of Sir Richard Arkwright's works, and in Mr. Strutt's mill upwards of eight years. If you are not provided for, I should be glad to serve you; though I am in the New York manufactory, and have been for three weeks since I arrived from England. But we have but one card, two machines, two spinning jennies, which I think are not worth using. My encouragement is pretty good, but [I] should much rather have the care of perpetual carding and spinning. If you please to drop a line respecting the amount of encouragement you wish to give, by favor of Captain Brown, you will much oblige, sir, your most obedient humble servant.
>
> Samuel Slater
>
> N.B. Please direct to me at No. 37, Golden Hill, New York.

The Captain Brown to whom Slater referred sailed a packet between Providence and New York, and during a chance meeting told Slater of Moses Brown's interest in textile manufacturing. In today's business world Captain Brown would have been thought something of an innocent for not having arranged the meeting himself and claimed a finder's fee. Moses Brown, moreover, would have been thought by the enthusiasm of his response to have misappropriated his reputation for shrewdness. He and his associates, he confessed, were "destitute of persons acquainted with water-frame spinning" and offered Slater, sight unseen, all the profits from successful operation of their machinery over and above interest on the capital invested and depreciation charges. And then:

> If the present situation does not come up to what thou wishes, and, from thy knowledge of the business, can be ascertained of the advantages of the mills, so as to induce thee to come and work ours, and have the *credit* as well as the advantage of perfecting the first water-mill in America, we should be glad to engage thy care so long as they can be made profitable to both, and we can agree.

The exchange itself, to be sure, urges against qualifying Slater as the first American industrial spy. He was no mere broker. He clearly meant to work at making his information commercially valuable to himself. He did, too, although perhaps more than he bargained for.

Slater's first thought upon seeing the assortment of contraptions that Brown had gathered, was to go home. He was only twenty-one, he may have reckoned, and had paid for his folly. Brown, though, appears to have been that breed of businessman who combines a sharp eye for talent with the abilities of a salesman. He prevailed upon him to stay. "Thee said thee could make machinery," he challenged, "why not do it?" Slater agreed to give it a try, if Brown would supply a trusted mechanic to make the machinery from his design. In support of the old adage, "the last man in closes the door," Slater insisted that the mechanic be put under bond to prevent him from either disclosing the nature of the work, or copying it. The condition recognized a fact which has persisted to plague modern corporations. It may be that as much information is lost through subcontractors that a company is forced to share with a competitor as through the activities of spies.

Slater was put up by Oziel Wilkinson, an ironmaster whose daughter he eventually married. During the early part of the first winter, he worked at improving Moses Brown's old machinery in the hope of being able to salvage it. When that became clearly futile, he began to design from scratch, calling on his memory for the mathematical tables by which to compute the variations in speeds of different parts of the Arkwright machine. The struggles and disappointments he contended with through the summer and into the next winter would, if made into a movie script, bring sniffles from critics who would accuse the scenarist of falsifying history for the sake of dramatic impact. Even after he got the mill running in the following winter, he had to go out and break the ice every morning to get the water wheel spinning. This affected his health for the rest of his life. Though Slater lived to be sixty-seven, Moses Brown survived him.

4.

Since he had kept his bargain with Strutt, and moreover had not infringed on existing patents, Slater's qualifications as an industrial spy depend largely on his having betrayed England; or, at least, England's wishes at the time. Ideological sons and daughters of John Calvin, however, would be among the first to concede that this alone would not be enough. Calvin was caught up on a dilemma which impales U.S. courts and legislatures yet today, although on stumpier and blunter horns. That was, how to favor law and order while sanctifying the Reformation; or, as in our case, how to protect the security of political society while paying service to the evident benefits of revolution. Calvin's answer was simple: All revolutionaries were to be treated as instruments of the devil until they succeeded. Then they were to be regarded as divine instruments for punishment and change.

There can be little doubt of Samuel Slater's standing in Calvin's order of things. "By the time he died in 1835," Welles records, "Slater had become generally recognized as the country's leading textile industrialist. In addition to his cotton and woolen manufactures, he had founded a bank and a textile-machinery factory and had helped promote several turnpikes, including a road from Providence to Pawtucket and another from Worcester, Mass. to Norwich, Conn."

At Slater's death, Moses Brown estimated Slater's estate at $1.2 million, and at a time, as the saying goes, that a dollar was a dollar. He and his partners, Brown's cousin Smith Brown, and his son-in-law William Almy, had extended the full use of their personal capital and energies, which is about all an entrepreneur could do in those days before the advent of the limited-liability and immortal corporation. They secured the help of the Government in Washington to raise tariffs on imports from Britain, and even got Alexander Hamilton to give them a plug in his Report on Manufactures.

Yet there was nothing they could do about the fact that by the end of the War of 1812 in the area comprised of Rhode Island, Massachusetts and Connecticut alone there were 165 mills, and that many of them had been started by former employees of Slater who had gone into business for themselves. Nor could they have prevented the fact that by the year Slater died, Almy, Brown, though enormously profitable, had only a fraction of the well fractionated $4.7 million annual market in manufactured cotton goods.

These competitors were in no meaningful sense spies; they hadn't as much as broken legal injunctions against copying Slater's machines. But even before the War of 1812, more groundwork had been laid for the first genuine industrial spies. One was the patent law signed by George Washington in 1789; the other was the grant of a corporation charter by the State of New York in 1811.

Chapter Twenty

THE YANKEE DOCTRINE HAS ITS DAY

The patent system added the fuel of interest to the fire of genius.

—Abraham Lincoln

I do not think America is a good place in which to be a genius.

—Samuel Butler

1.

At the time of the Industrial Revolution, the only British corporation to speak of was Britain herself. "Speculation, dishonesty, and financial excesses," Adolph Berle has noted, "caused the South Sea Bubble crash in 1720, and so discredited the corporation as an institution that for nearly one hundred years thereafter it was virtually outlawed in the English-speaking world." The framers of the Constitution, therefore, had enterprises in mind no larger than the Arkwright-size factories in England when they decided to take a leaf from the mother country, and "To promote the Progress of Science and useful Arts, by securing for limited Times to Authors and Inventors the exclusive Right to their respective Writings and Discoveries."

The first patent law, signed by George Washington on April 10, 1789, required that the applicant for a patent pay a small fee and provide specifications and models enough to "enable a workman or other person skilled in the art or manufacture whereof it was a branch" to make and use it. The Secretary of State, then Thomas Jefferson, and two fellow cabinet members, were to sit as a patent board and to determine if the invention was "sufficiently useful and important" to warrant a letter patent.

"It is a matter of tradition," a Government historian wrote nearly a century later,

> handed down to us from generation to generation, by those who love to speak of Mr. Jefferson and his virtues and eccentricities, that when an application for a patent was made under the first act, he would summon Mr. Henry Knox, of Massachusetts, who was Secretary of War, and Mr. Edmund Randolph of Virginia, who was Attorney General, these officials being designated by the act, with the Secretary of State a tribunal to examine and grant patents; and that these three distinguished officials would examine the application critically, scrutinizing each point of the specifications carefully and rigorously. The result of this examination was that during the first year a majority of the applications failed to pass the ordeal, and only three patents were granted.

Jefferson clearly was not the man for this job. He was himself a mathematician, astronomer, architect and inventor. In addition to such conveniences as an adjustable reading lamp, a pedometer, a stool that could be folded up to make a walking stick, and the swivel chair (which his political enemies said he devised in order to be able to look in all directions at once), he also contrived a machine for treating hemp and an improvement in the mold board of the plough that significantly affected the nation's agricultural development and won him a decoration from the French Institute. Yet it appears not to have occurred to him to obtain a patent on any of these or his many other inventions, or to put them to commercial use.

A lesser man would have perceived what Jefferson did not, that men who lacked his gifts and occupations might see dreams of riches in the invention of a Hula Hoop. In their second year the board issued thirty-three patents, and in the third only eleven. Public pressure forced the Congress, over Jefferson's objections, to take an entirely different tack. From 1793 to 1836, the word "useful" was construed in the administration of the act to mean nothing more than the opposite of hurtful, or pernicious. For forty-three years, all any inventor had to do to get a patent was to pay a small fee and register his submissions, much as authors obtain copyrights. Jefferson feared that the change would lead to a "promiscuous creation of monopolies," which he thought to be, in any art or industry, against the theory of popular government and pernicious in its effects. This fear was not borne out, though, until long after the law had been reformed.

2.

Senator John Ruggles of Maine, who in 1836 mounted the campaign for reform, observed that the number of lawsuits that sprang up were "onerous to the courts, ruinous to the parties, and injurious to society." What's more, he said,

> . . . it is not uncommon for persons to copy patented machines in the model room; and having made some slight immaterial alterations, then apply in the next room for patents. . . . Thus prepared, they go forth on a retailing expedition selling out their patent rights for states, counties, and townships to those who have no means at hand of detecting the imposition, and who find, when it is too late, that they have purchased what the vendors had no right to sell. . . . This speculation in patent rights has become a regular business, and several hundred thousand dollars, it is estimated, are paid annually for void patents. . . .

Apart from the Federal Government itself, states, counties and townships were at that time the only U.S. corporations of any size or consequence. Thus a patent huckster might be able to sell the same patent to one entrepreneur each in several hundred localities.

The patent law reform of 1836 set out requirements that in principle have obtained since. It re-established the practice of examining inventions, this time against a "*new* and useful" standard. The relation between Sam Slater and Moses Brown, the unpropertied inventor and the uninventing capitalist, now becomes instituted as a recognized distinction, alongside the division between capital and labor. Negotiable titles to invention join titles to capital as means of production.

Titles to invention, to be sure, disappear. Once the invention, a machine, say, is articulated, sold and successfully used it passes over into capital. The right to use of the possession after a while passes into the public domain, and it is only the wealth it has created that may be passed on to one's sons, and their sons, and so forth. However, the nature of the relation is such that each transaction may leave two capitalists standing where only one stood before.

Among the first to recognize the opportunity inherent in that phenomenon was a new kind of information broker, who flourished briefly during the flicker of time between "Home on the Range" and "Hog Butcher to the World" America. Perhaps the most successful of them was Henry Gerner, "Capt. Engineers" and editor of the monthly *Patent Right Gazette,* founded in 1871. A handsomely printed, outsized newspaper of good stock, it eventually reached a circulation of many thousands.

3.

Captain Gerner grew prosperous simply by recognizing before inventors did that they were moving into a seller's market. "Our mission concerns all," he proclaimed. "It is to promote civilization through the most patent means—those which dot the path of progress through ages viz. *new and useful inventions.*" Despite sluggards in the ranks, he asserted,

> . . . the truths of science have nevertheless forced themselves into the obscure crevices of inertia. . . . We shall try to dispel the idea prevalent that inventors are visionary enthusiasts and impractical men, and show that the true inventor is always an honorable, enlightened and benevolent person, disclosing to the world some of the wonderful phenomena of Nature's mysteries for common benefit.

The way he proposed to do this, of course, was to act as broker between inventors, the patent office (flat fee $25, including a year's subscription, models and drawings extra) and "capitalists" (usual commission 15 per cent). "Genius needs capital, but capital is morbid without genius," he warned.

The *Gazette* was principally a catalogue of newly patented inventions, described in straightforward sketches and captions, ranging in gravity from "The Novelty Necktie Retainer" through "Improved Portable Russian Steam Bathing Apparatus" to "An Improvement in Steam Engine Governors." This fare was surrounded by news from the world of science ("Prof. Tyndall recently said that the shock from a single Leyden jar was very unpleasant, but a heavier discharge such as he once received from a battery of fifteen jars, is painless; he felt nothing but was simply extinguished for a sensible period of time."), of literature ("The late Napoleon has ruined his bookseller with his dry and heavy 'Life of Caesar.' "), together with Humors of the Day ("Clergymen, like brakemen, do a lot of coupling."), along with an occasional excursion into the social sciences ("It is gratifying to see that we are receiving an excellent, and perhaps to some extent a better class of immigrants. Out of the 101,015—in the first quarter of 1871—there were 17,845 English, 4,613 Scotch, 30,814 Germans, 5,727 Swedes").

Captain Gerner's correspondence column ran heavily to suggestion. ("W.P.N.—St. Louis, Mo. We wrote you in the middle of March, informing you that we had a bonafide offer for your patent of $15,000 . . . We haven't heard from you yet.") He did not want to leave the impression, though, that he was on the take. ("To Alex. R.S., S.I., New York:—Your invention for 'quelling a riot in a city' is new, but certainly not useful or allowable. A Patent would not be granted for 'your invention.' We believe 'Clubs to be Trumps' on such occasions.") In truth, he was something of an inventor himself. On Sunday, July 30, 1871, the ferryboat *Westfield,* plying between New York City and Staten Island, blew up, killing nearly 100 persons and maiming another 100. The *New York Herald* three days later contained a letter from Gerner:

> About four years ago a gentleman living on Staten Island, who took an interest in my steam boilers, exerted himself to have one (constructed under patents issued to me by the United States Government) placed in the ill-fated ferryboat Westfield. I examined at that time the now-exploded boiler, and offered my opinion "that it ought to be removed at once." No alteration was made, however, in the Westfield until last Sunday, when the boiler saw fit to remove itself.
>
> When on a steamer about to start, although I do not set an undue value on my life, I always try to take the least risk possible, by getting as far from the boiler as circumstances will permit. Once started, I prefer, especially on a cold day, to be as near the boiler as I conveniently can. All risk of an explosion is then virtually at an end. . . .

Gerner's classified columns contained advertisements for an assortment of services to inventors: "Incrustations prevented by Winans' Boiler Powder," "Philosophical, Medical and Optical Instruments," "Provost's New Battery and Barjou's New Galvanic Fluid," as well as pattern and model makers, law blanks and the like. It would, of course, have been the ideal place to advertise for a private investigator interested in patent work. But none appeared in any issue for the year

1871. This would indicate that there was not yet much work available in the patent field, for private detectives in those days were far from shy of advertising their services. A newspaper of that era carried this ad, signed by Allan Pinkerton:

> Corporations or individuals desirous of ascertaining the feelings of their employees, and whether they are likely to engage in strikes or in joining any secret labor organizations with a view of compelling terms from corporations or employers . . . can obtain a detective suitable to associate with their employees and obtain this information.

4.

A half century earlier there were no corporations to speak of, nor much call for Pinkerton's kind of work. In fact, until 1811, with a few rule-proving exceptions, private corporations were unknown in the United States. During the first half of the nineteenth century, individual partnerships or other forms of business organizations that must be reconstituted every time a principal dies were the nation's largest repository and generator of capital. When New York began tentatively to issue charters, the authorities and investors, being offspring of the Enlightenment, tended to be literal-minded in their regard for these new creatures of the state. It takes a wrench of the mind to regard something which claims to be corporeal as being also immortal, to have a life of its own no matter who owns or runs it, and able through issuance of shares to multiply indefinitely, amoeba-like.

Here we will find it useful once again to turn to a dissent by Mr. Justice Brandeis. Eighteen years after the appearance of "The Right to Privacy" in the *Harvard Law Review,* Brandeis was retained by the State of Oregon to argue before the Supreme Court the merits of a law prohibiting the employment of women in industrial work for more than ten hours a day. *Muller vs. Oregon* has, on that account, come to be recognized as one of the reasons majority opinions from the Court are so much more instructive as to the human condition than they were in the earlier part of this century.

Dean Louis H. Pollak of the Yale Law School has remarked that the brief Brandeis filed was "a revolutionary departure from a style of advocacy which had contented itself with a relentless recital of the legal abstractions judges had offered in other more or less comparable cases." For Brandeis prevailed, "by filing a brief that laid before the

Court, in painstaking detail, all the relevant considerations of public health and industrial practice that underlay the ten-hour law."

In the years that followed the *Muller* case, Dean Pollak says, the "Brandeis Brief" became "an indispensable instrument of constitutional adjudication, forcing lawyers—in time, even judges—to address themselves directly to the concrete public issues in dispute." The style of advocacy is shown to good advantage in Brandeis' dissent in *Liggett Co. vs. Lee,* which came to the Court four years after *Olmstead.*

The case involved the Florida Anti-Chain Store Law, specifically a provision which imposed heavier license taxes on vendors with stores in more than one county than upon those whose stores were all grouped in the same county. The majority held that a county line did not offer a reasonable basis for classification of a generally imposed state tax. Brandeis agreed that the tax might be discriminatory, but not on that account alone constitutionally objectionable.

Brandeis argued that if the plaintiff thought the "compensation demanded for the corporate privilege" too high, it could move. On the other hand, "a review of the legislation of the several States by which all restraints on corporate size and activity were removed, and a consideration of the economic and social effects of such removal, will help to an understanding of the Anti-Chain store laws. . . ."

"The prevalence of the corporation in America has led men of this generation," Brandeis wrote, "to act, at times, as if the privilege of doing business in corporate form were inherent in the citizen; and has led them to accept the evils attendant upon the free and unrestricted use of the corporate mechanism as if these evils were the inescapable price of civilized life and, hence, to be borne with resignation." But Brandeis argues:

> Throughout the greater part of our history a different view prevailed. Although the value of this instrumentality in commerce and industry was fully recognized, incorporation for business was commonly denied long after it had been freely granted for religious, educational and charitable purposes. It was denied because of fear. Fear of encroachment upon the liberties and opportunities of the individual. Fear of the subjection of labor to capital. Fear of monopoly. Fear that the absorption of capital by corporations, and their perpetual life, might bring evils similar to those which attended mortmain. There was a sense of some insidious menace inherent in large

> aggregations of capital, particularly when held by corporations. So, at first, the corporate privilege was granted sparingly; and only when the grant seemed necessary in order to procure for the community some specific benefit otherwise unattainable. The later enactment of general incorporation laws does not signify that the apprehension of corporate domination had been overcome. The desire for business expansion created an irresistible demand for more charters; and it was believed that under general laws embodying safeguards of universal application the scandals and favoritism incident to special incorporation could be avoided. The general laws, which long embodied severe restrictions upon size and upon the scope of corporate activity, were, in part, an expression of the desire for equality of opportunity.

After 1830, manufacturing and mining companies in the East were generally constituted as common stock corporations. Whatever fears native organisms might have harbored, they were overcome by the corporation's ability, as Adolph Berle points out, to "get things done." In the days before air and water pollution, city slums, side effects and brake failures became all the rage, Thomas Jefferson was looked upon as something of a pessimist for having believed that it would take a thousand years to civilize and populate the region of the nation *east* of the Mississippi. He could not have foreseen, of course, what use the corporation would make of mechanical invention, nor could he have known its appetite for labor.

The early corporations were the English heirs, so to speak, of Latin ancestors. They assumed all the formal prerogatives of the guild city, including a pronounced tendency toward monopoly, demanding the same protection that England had given its entrepreneurs, all without interference from anything bearing the force of a divinely inspired royal conscience. And they did get things done. Between 1820 and 1860, manufacturing capital in the United States multiplied decade after decade from $150 million to an even $1 billion. Yet, in the 1850's, iron works commonly paid dividends of 40 per cent and some ranged as high as 100 per cent on invested capital.

5.

Not until Reconstruction, though, in the aftermath of the Fourteenth Amendment, did the corporation come into its own. I know of no legal ground more treacherous for the layman to attempt to negotiate; one's best hope in attempting to reach the point salient to these speculations is to hop from bog to bog. The point of departure is the Fourth and Fifth Amendments. In 1857, Chief Justice Taney held in the Dred Scott case, as summarized in the Annotated Constitution published by the Government Printing Office, that the Negro:

> . . . was ineligible to attain United States citizenship either from a State or by virtue of birth in the United States, even as a free man descended from a Negro residing as a free man in one of the States at the date of ratification of the Constitution. That basic document did not contemplate the possibility of Negro citizenship. By the Fourteenth Amendment this deficiency of the original Constitution was cured.

We may take that much as, if not settled, reflecting at least a respectable body of opinion concerning the Fourteenth Amendment. Then, to return to Dean Pollak, "There ensued one of the most extraordinary chapters in American legal history—a chapter which is still not fully explored or understood." Dean Pollak (*The Constitution and the Supreme Court, A Documentary History*) quotes from an article, "The 'Conspiracy' Theory of the Fourteenth Amendment" by Professor Howard J. Graham, setting out "the facts known as of 1938":

> In an argument before the Supreme Court of the United States in 1882 Roscoe Conkling, a former member of the Joint Congressional Committee which in 1866 drafted the Fourteenth Amendment, produced for the first time the manuscript journal of the Committee, and by means of extensive quotations and pointed comment conveyed the impression that he and his colleagues in drafting the due process and equal protection clauses intentionally used the word "person" in order to include corporations. "At the time the Fourteenth Amendment was ratified," he declared, "individuals and joint stock companies were appealing for congressional and administrative protection against invidious and discriminating state and local taxes. . . . The unmistakable inference was that the joint committee had taken cognizance of these appeals and had drafted its text with particular regard for corporations.

Professor Graham then refers to a tax case involving the Southern Pacific Railroad in which Chief Justice Waite announced: "The court does not wish to hear arguments on the question whether the provision in the Fourteenth Amendment to the Constitution, which forbids a State to deny to any person within its jurisdiction, the equal protection of the laws, applies to these corporations. We are all of the opinion it does." Professor Graham commented:

> It is literally true therefore that Roscoe Conkling's argument sounded the death-knell of the narrow "Negro-race theory" of the Fourteenth Amendment expounded by Justice Miller in the Slaughter-House cases. By doing this it cleared the way for the modern development of due process of law and the corresponding expansion of the Court's discretionary powers over social and economic legislation. Viewed in perspective, the argument is one of the landmarks in American constitutional history, an important turning point in our social and economic development.

And in the security industry.

6.

For more than half a century after the Civil War, Pinkerton was invoked by workers and union organizers as a generic noun, like Coke or zipper, to denote, besides the original, any number of imitations. Among the Populists of 1892 who wrote into their platform a resolution to abolish all Pinkertons, a mention of Pinkertonism carried with it about the same effect as Stalinism had on the Republican National Convention of 1948. Long after the advent of "labor statesmanship" there were a number of labor leaders who bore vivid recollections of Pinkertons in skulls still scarred with mementoes of encounters with them. A former cowboy who had worked twenty-two years for Pinkerton described his experience in a book entitled: *Two Evil Isms—Anarchism and Pinkertonism.*

Pinkerton's now supports a public relations man whose belief it is that between 1850 and 1908, when the branch of the Justice Department now known as the FBI was formed, Pinkerton's National Detective Agency was the only organized law enforcement agency operating on a national basis to fight crime. For having foiled a plot to assassinate Lincoln, Pinkerton was made the first chief of the U.S. Secret Service. His reputation was not made, however, until labor, too, sought to incorporate. "History," Malcolm Muggeridge has pronounced, "is the propaganda of the victors." Thus accounts of the bloody labor wars of the nineteenth and early twentieth centuries seem to be losing in color and detail in favor of chirpier renditions, as in this paragraph from a high school textbook:

> After all, the great corporations were powerful in their own right, and, conscious of common interests, many industries were forming associations for the battle against unionism. Singly or together they possessed the means to protect their property during strikes and to keep it in operation. This warfare required armies. Men of vision, like Allan Pinkerton, the founder of the great detective agency, answered the call. In 1866, the Pinkertons first hired out guards to employers to protect their property during industrial disturbance. The business grew with such rapidity that within twenty-five years the Pinkertons had multiplied their offices, increased their forces, furnished men for more than seventy strikes, and had gone into *preventative work* [emphasis mine]. The profits in selling protection were so great that competitors multiplied. Each had its arsenals of weapons and ammunition and recruited its forces in large part from the vicious and criminal classes of the population. By 1900 the pattern was set for a new century.

Not quite. Nelson C. Gridley, in a paper read on October 6, 1888, before the Patent Law Association of Chicago, suggests of the nineteenth century that "the typical man is the inventor." He adds, with the wryness that perhaps in those days passed for black humor:

> As a class, inventors are looked upon as enthusiasts, fanatics, seekers after will-of-the-wisp theories, until some day the public wakes up to the fact that one out of the million has immortalized himself, and conferred incalculable benefits on the human race. Then, if it cannot crush him or deprive him of the results of his labors, it bows down to him, pours gold into his pockets, erects statues to his memory, and complacently absorbs his glory under the grand title of our "National Genius."

Samuel Morse died in 1871, nine years after California passed the first wiretap law, a prohibition against interception of telegrams. Joseph Glidden got a patent for barbed wire in 1874. In 1876, Alexander Graham Bell received a patent for the telephone. After that came Edison, Ford, Diesel and numerous others. The year 1880, a patent office historian writes cheerfully, "inaugurates one of the greatest decades of invention of all time. The trolley car, the incandescent light, the automobile, the cash register, the dynamo, the pneumatic tire, smokeless powder, transparent film, electrical welding, the cyanide process, the steam turbine, and the electric furnace are all invented or introduced during the next ten years." And in 1895, the Illinois legislature forbade newspapers to tap one another's telephones. *Now* the pattern is set for the new century. The dominant figure of that pattern was woven into the American experience, however, out of an invention that was not patentable or copyrightable, nor was it held by anyone as a trade secret.

Chapter Twenty-One

AN END OF INNOCENCE

A person asked Diogenes in mockery, "How comes it to pass that philosophers are the followers of rich men, and not rich men of philosophers?" To which Diogenes answered soberly and yet sharply, "Because the one sort knows what they have need of, and the other does not."

1.

A PSYCHIATRIST, writing in the magazine *Science*, has defined neurosis as the incapacity to accommodate experience, and to act upon it. As Scott Buchanan has said of corporations, "habits of feeling, action and even thought are established and accumulated unawares. They may cause frustration and disorder similar to those complexes which cause hysteria in individuals." Even old-fashioned biologists looked upon health, the capacity to survive, as inhering in the capacity to adapt to novel circumstances. Rapid and extensive decomposition of the knowledge of one's environment into unformed heaps of information may, however, be permanently disordering.

Few of us enjoy that capacity which someone said describes Newton's genius. We are not, that is to say, equipped to hold a great many events in our heads simultaneously and to juggle them until we hit upon a relation of forces, or of cause and effect, that will exhibit some comprehensible order. We are inclined, therefore, to foreclose on possibilities. For most of us would consider it to be a hell worse than that to which Sisyphus was committed, to have to work for very long on a problem that we have been given no reason to suppose has a solution.

Imagine, for example, being locked in a prison cell and being told by the warden that in order to gain back your freedom and communion with ordinary society, you must construct a universe in such a way as to compose the differences between the Newtonian and Cartesian universes. It must also exhibit a characteristic visualized by the warden in a bad dream. As he recalls it vaguely, in this dream world energy was equivalent to mass multiplied by the speed of light, multiplied by itself.

Had we not been made acquainted in any way with Einstein's general theories, we should likely, most of us, at first panic; and then begin to occupy our thoughts with ways to make life in the prison cell bearable. Similarly if we were to confine ourselves to the categories contained in the system of double-entry bookkeeping described in the fifteenth century by Luca Pacioli, we would be unable to take on with much feeling of authority problems which corporations of any size today dispose of routinely.

For illustration, here is a simple problem taken from a set of readings having to do with the methods by which great corporations today order their awareness. A newsboy buys papers at two cents and sells them at five cents; he receives a one-cent allowance on unsold papers. He finds by experience he has, as an average, ten customers a day, appearing at random; that is, he has no regular customers and one person passing is as likely to buy as the next. Ought he to buy fewer, more or the same number of newspapers? While we are able to conceive of numerous considerations, far more than those enumerated in the problem, that might enter into a solution, we haven't the means by which to articulate so much as the factors enumerated, except one by one. We are inclined therefore to handle as much as we can, as "practical," and to assign the rest to the "theoretical." The moment we do, however, we commit ourselves, as do most newsboys, to trial and error.

We may try six, eight, ten or twelve newspapers to see what happens. We have to try each number for a long enough period of time to give us some experience with each; until, that is, we have achieved, as the system technologists say, the "right mix," given our newsstand location, number of customers, and so forth. If we try each of the five possibilities, from eight to twelve papers, we may lose money on some of them as compared to the profits we realize when we hit the "right" number.

After each experiment, moreover, we are none the wiser about the relationship of the elements in our mix. Suppose that someone builds an office building near the newsstand, and we come to be patronized by a dozen or fifteen or twenty customers at random. Having no way to calculate the effects of this change, we start our experiments all over again. Suppose further that, seeing the traffic come by our corner, another newsboy opens a stand across the street from ours. We haven't the means, either, of reckoning this factor into our calculations. We might say that we have found ourselves in an information explosion.

If we do decide to experiment, we start at eight copies, because common sense tells us that eight copies of the newspaper we sell will cost us less out of pocket. The profits we might gain by buying more are unrealized, while any losses we suffer through experimentation, we suffer here and now.

Thus common sense indicates further that if we can come into a position of control over the market, that is, make it expensive in time or money for our customers to go elsewhere for their papers, we would be safer getting the kid across the street to agree to a higher price for the number of papers we are, between us, making available. Here again, we are faced with a calculation—how much will the market bear?—but we can vary it quickly within a day's time. If the first few customers won't pay, we can decrease the price, minimizing the chance of having papers left at the end of the day that we would take by varying the size of our orders.

We might further, being in a position of market control, induce the publisher, who wants to reach our customers so that he can sell advertising, to reduce his price to us; or at least take our leftover copies as returns, thus at least minimizing our risks, and perhaps improving our profits.

Suppose now, though, that a city ordinance labels our agreement with the other newsboy a conspiracy, and tells us that if we don't break it up, we may be fined heavily or even be sent to jail. Common sense would indicate that we band together all the newsboys to form a trade association, the purpose of which is to induce the city council, by whatever means the officers we select choose to employ, to pass a law permitting newsboys to obtain licenses. We, of course, will not make much of the fact in public that the license will carry the same effect as a legally enforced franchise. We have become men of our times, the times being the first thirty years of this century.

2.

Innovations caused by the informing capacity of the human intelligence at the rate and on the scale experienced by the patent office in the 1880's induces in one not only a livelier sense of what one can do, but also of what can be done to one. The trick in staying healthy is to keep premonitions of the latter from getting the upper hand, thus causing that condition described by Jackie Mason: "Was I self-conscious? Listen. When I saw a team go into a huddle at a football game, I *knew* they were talking about *me*."

Men of affairs, whether entrepreneurs or politicians, are perhaps less given than others to frustration and hysteria, and not alone, as it is widely imagined, because they are in position to direct innovation and contain it within their own capacities. They have, as a rule, never interested themselves much in expressions of the form, *A* is *B*, as in "Man is a Rational Animal . . . etc., and therefore."

Like a great many inventors of the nineteenth century, businessmen were occupied principally with statements of the form, "If *a* or *b* or *c* . . . , then, etc." as in "Sure, Isabella, but let's say for the sake of argument the world *isn't* flat." They were preoccupied, in short, with consequences of action, and with methods for reckoning what they didn't know by what they did, such as the effect of a steel wage settlement on auto sales, preferably in advance of a competitor or other stock market investors.

The great virtue and strength of this habit of thought is that it promotes, as I hear it expressed among aspiring and recent college graduates, "*awareness!*" The disorder that Buchanan describes occurs when awareness exceeds the ability of the aware to inform its awarenesses. When this occurs, the aware being may become a victim of the disorder that gave Sinclair Lewis opportunity to focus his own disordered indignation. The condition strikes with particular sharpness at beings who are aware also that their competitors are as aware as they. So as to expropriate it from clinical use, but not with the license of cocktail party badinage, I'll avail myself of the definition contained in Webster's *Third New International Dictionary:*

> par-a-noia/ . . . a tendency on the part of individuals or a group toward suspiciousness or distrustfulness of others that is based not on objective reality but on a need to defend the ego against unconscious impulses, that uses projection as a mechanism of defense, and that often takes the form of a compensatory megalomania.

3.

In 1900, the Sherman Anti-Trust Act had been on the books for a decade. Courts and legislatures, though by now comfortably conversant with the corporate person, were confused as to how to apply or to enforce the law. Orville Hitchcock Platt, Senator from Connecticut, doubted that

> . . . all competition is beneficent to the country and that every advance in price is an injury to the country. Unrestricted competition is brutal warfare, and injurious to the whole country. The great corporations of this country, the great monopolies of this country are every one of them built up on the graves of weaker competitors that have been forced to their death by remorseless competition.

Finley Peter Dunne had Mr. Dooley sum up Theodore Roosevelt's first message to Congress this way: " 'Th' trusts,' says he, 'are heejous monsthers built up be th' inlightened interprise iv th' men that have done so much to advance progress in our beloved counthry,' he says. 'On wan hand I wud stamp thim undther fut; on th' other not so fast.' "

Thus the corporations were able for more than a decade after the Sherman Act to go on buying and selling state legislatures as if they were family retainers, digging, burrowing and drilling into the entire North American continent south of the Canadian border as if it were a private truck farm, and holding foreigners, legions of whom were coming from Europe to work for them, in roughly the same regard they might have for natives who dive for coins tossed overboard in exotic ports. All the same, peace of mind seemed to elude them.

By 1905, when the Supreme Court took the first genuinely effective swipe at the trusts, Pinkerton's forces were numbered as armies. His imitators and competitors were also numerous. Then the monopolies, now at a size where no one man, nor a dozen men, even if they thought they could trust one another, could keep an eye on everything, found themselves under gentle siege by the White House. They reacted as if the President and the muckrakers had given labor and the public a dispensation to visit special indignities on the person and property of the corporations.

In 1909, the Burns International Detective Agency entered the enforcement rolls. In 1913, Irving M. Dogle formed Globe Detective Service. He became, as an annual report of recent vintage observed, "one of the first 'private eyes' in the Philadelphia area." But

> He was not satisfied to spend his time tracing missing persons, keeping suspicious individuals under surveillance, and cooper-

> ating with police in apprehending wanted criminals. The times were unsettled. Socialist and radical labor activities kept employers in a state of alarm. Greater industrial security at the plant level was imperative. Mr. Dogle seized this opportunity to render a signal service to industry by furnishing needed investigative services.

Growing even more rigid and uncommunicative, the giant corporations imparted to the public some of the same emotion their executives and directors seem to have felt.

In 1914, Walter Lippmann commented:

> There is in America today a distinct prejudice in favor of those who make the accusations. . . . The sense of conspiracy and secret scheming which transpire is almost uncanny. "Big business," and its ruthless tentacles, have become the material for the feverish fantasy of illiterate thousands thrown out of kilter by the rack and strain of modern life. It is possible to work yourself into a state where the world seems a conspiracy and your daily going is beset with an alert and tingling sense of labyrinthine evil. Everything askew—all the frictions of life are readily ascribed to a deliberate evil intelligence, and men like Morgan and Rockefeller take on attributes of omnipotence, that ten minutes of cold sanity would reduce to a barbarous myth. I know a socialist who seriously believes that the study of eugenics is a Wall Street scheme for sterilizing working-class leaders. . . . Not once but twenty times have I been told confidentially of a nation-wide scheme by financiers to suppress every radical and progressive periodical. . . . I remember how often Lincoln Steffens used to deplore the frightened literalness with which some of his articles were taken. One day in the country he and I were walking the railroad tracks. The ties, of course, are not well spaced for an ordinary stride, and I complained about it. "You see," said Mr. Steffens with mock obviousness, "Morgan controls the New Haven and he prefers to make the people ride."

Anyone who grew up even slightly disadvantaged during the Great Depression knows something of this closed-in feeling. School teachers, periodic announcements from the world of science, and the movies, especially the movies, attested that the world was crawling with possibilities. At an age at which John D. Rockefeller had perhaps been moistening his eyes on oil wells, progeny of the Depression sat in darkened movie houses being shown the goodies of this world by Carole Lombard from the top of a Fifth Avenue bus. At home they might learn that the only thing holding up realization of these possibilities was Big Business. There were dozens of variations on the story that Forbisher Cartels was preventing the introduction of a self-generating electric light bulb for fear of destroying the profits of the Apex Edison Utility Combine.

Hollywood, under the circumstances, performed the service it does so well, keeping a candle flickering for long-departed national heroes. Who can forget the inventor of the light bulb, a white-haired Spencer Tracy—he was, as it happened, an aging Mickey Rooney—come at last to his just desserts: apple pie with a slice of cheddar cheese? Or Don Ameche's "Come here, Watson, I need you?" The answer is anyone not afflicted with insomnia and an addiction to the Late Late Show. At the time, though, they were the last mementoes, the reminiscence impregnated still with the possibility, of the inventor as hero-entrepreneur. In truth, the inventor had pretty much gone the same way as John Moses Browning, the great gun designer and one of the last inventors to qualify even part-way as an entrepreneur.

Chapter Twenty-Two

HAPPENINGS

Oh, let us never, never doubt
What nobody is sure about.

—Hilaire Belloc

1.

In keeping with a common practice, Browning was in 1899 being supported by the Winchester Firearms Company while he tinkered toward the invention of a self-loading semiautomatic shotgun. After putting the final touches on his work, he delivered it to Winchester's president, T. G. Bennett. Upon receiving the prototype, Winchester's engineers went to work drawing up specifications, and its lawyers, reputed to be among the best in the patent field, began work on definitions for a patent application. The lawyers, though paid by Winchester, worked ostensibly for Browning, expecting him in turn to sell his rights to Winchester for a lump sum payment. So they did their customarily thorough job, as did the engineers. After receiving his gun back several times for minor improvements, Browning wrote to Bennett complaining, "Our experience has been that a gun gets worse treatment in a draughtsman's office than in a duck hunter's camp."

In high pique, Browning was determined to strike back. He insisted that instead of the usual lump sum, Winchester pay him royalties on sales instead. He knew, of course, that Winchester had always stood fast against paying royalties to any inventor. In the authorized version that has come down through generations of Winchester management, Bennett brooded awhile before deciding to stand by company policy. Browning, too, stuck by his guns. He picked up the papers and sold them, outright, to Winchester's principal competitor, Remington Arms Company, airtight patents and all.

It would be pleasant to be able to report that Bennett lived to regret his decision, but he didn't. The reason he didn't has to do with the phenomenon reported on a half-century later by the University of

Michigan Survey Center. The Center noted that in the first half of this century, 90 per cent of the increment in this nation's Gross National Product had arisen from investment not in tangibles, such as plant and equipment, but in education, organization, design and the myriad activities that find shelter under the vast umbrella labeled Research and Development. In short, the corporation began to acquire two more attributes of the medieval guild, proprietorship of skills and invention, and a guild, or trade, mark.

2.

When Theodore Roosevelt and the muckrakers made "trust" as in "trust-busting" into a dirty word, they eventually put Commercial Investment Trust to a good deal of trouble and expense: The cost of changing all of the signs and letterheads by which a corporation identifies itself, and then of telling the world that it is doing business at the same old stand but under a new sign; the trouble of having to explain to those who ask, "What was your name before it was CIT Corp?" That was, of course, before the days of the 52 or 48 per cent Federal tax on corporate earnings obligated the Government in effect to match the petitioning corporation's cost of changing its name.

At a dinner in celebration of his installation as editor in chief of Time, Inc., Hedley Donovan observed that, "In 1964 this company stands or falls not by our financial reports, not even by what we print in our publications, but by what is lodged in people's minds after they read our publications. That is what we are all about." So that we don't misread the intent of the remark, I should point out that it was reported by Andrew Heiskell, Chairman of the Board of Time, Inc., in an address to the New York Society of Security Analysts, as elaboration on his own observation:

> I want to talk about an asset that may be buried deep down near the bottom of a mythical schedule of our assets. It probably would appear something like this: "Indefinable something—Value $1." Not a particularly impressive entry. Certainly in itself nothing to borrow money against. Nonetheless, in my opinion, this particular entry represents what could well be the most important single asset we possess.

This realization comes more easily to publishers of magazines than it does, say, to the printer. This is because publishers are accustomed to it by work and conviction, by selling advertising, and by endeavoring to influence readers. Manufacturers of "things" are not accustomed to thinking of the things they make or the things they make them with as if they were events, as if to be no more than information articulated in a certain way, because they traditionally have not had to. Considered as events, assets like real estate, plant and equipment, and even cash, fluctuate, grow and decay, in relation to the events around them, but they do not vanish in the way that yesterday's newspaper vanishes.

Finding the names and devising devices to suit 26,000 new products a year has itself become something of an industry in the postwar years. Computer technology has helped by reeling off all of the possible combinations of words and initials that a management or market research team ought to consider. Computers are used also to help to find new names for corporations, as when Cities Service became CITGO. Numerous others, though, seem to have been made by the human mind unaided, such as American Brake Shoe Company to Abex.

Not all have been made so abruptly, so that one day one is dealing with United Oil Products, and the next with UOP. Haloid became Haloid-Xerox before coming finally to be Xerox Corp. Cowles Magazines, Inc., rushed the process a bit: within a period of twenty-four months it went to becoming Cowles Magazines and Broadcasting, Inc., and then (at this writing) Cowles Communications, Inc. These changes accompanied a sequence of events in which Cowles first went public and then obtained a listing on the New York Stock Exchange. A change of name may help a stock perform better, as when American Brake Shoe became Abex, by giving investors a dimmer idea of the business the company has gone into since last heard from.

Neither the cost of lodging these names in the public mind, nor an estimate of how much would be exacted for the purchase of their use, is reflected normally in a corporation's capital assets. Nor does the Internal Revenue Service regard them as capital investments, except under special circumstances. If a magazine, for example, were to sell popular features as separate assets, and then sell its name and good will independently, the buyer of the name would be assumed to have bought a capital asset. Thus it is assumed that one might buy, say, General Electric Co., and for an extra dollar the former owners would throw in the name.

3.

Until the end of the War of 1939–45, 90 per cent of shotgun buyers, many of whom swore by the name Winchester, could not be dissuaded from their faith in pump action and double-barrelled models. At the time Remington introduced John Moses Browning's new gun, a Winchester salesman making his rounds would likely have considered himself remiss in his duties as husband, father and breadwinner had he not capitalized on the name Winchester and the conservative leanings of hunters to hint that the new Remington Autoloader wasn't all that it was cracked up to be.

If that was true then, it was even more true after the Congress, in 1905, extended the protection of patents to trademarks. To illustrate: Several years ago, a firm with an address in Ohio purchased space in several magazines to advertise a device it called a Bu-Nab. A Bu-Nab consists of two pieces of tubing, about three inches long and perhaps a quarter of an inch in diameter, coated with a silvery substance and held together at their ends by two small pieces of plastic. It resembles one of those small pieces of business visible in trade magazines photographs intended to treat the reader to an inside view of a computer. Each Bu-Nab was sent in a clear plastic, snap-open box, together with a small sheet of instructions assuring the recipient that his Bu-Nab was made from the finest materials and would, with reasonable care, give years of service. The user was cautioned, moreover, to keep his Bu-Nab away from excessive heat.

The advertising made no secret of the fact that in the meaning of the patent law a Bu-Nab came as close to being useless as any material object that occupies space can come. That was its principal attraction. Conceivably once it was shown that Bu-Nabs were in demand, the manufacturer might be encouraged to apply for a patent on a new machine used in making Bu-Nabs, or even on replacement parts. Prior to 1905, he would have had to take his chances, though, on his investment in the name Bu-Nab. Like those hucksters in the free-for-all days of the patent laws, anyone might trump up some claim to having used the name, then bring the original user into court to prove that he was in fact, the first user of the name, and that he had been using it actively. This would have left the Bu-Nab maker vulnerable either to lengthy and pesky litigation, or frequent settlements with claimants.

The 1905 law protected trade names, as embodied in a specific typography and design, that were registered with the patent office and used for five years. After that the trademarks would be incontestable; no other product, no matter how useless, could be sold as a Bu-Nab, except perhaps in Monaco. This gave substance enough to trademarks to encourage corporations to spend money in promoting and advertising them as if to be an investment. These expenditures in turn gave salesmen and distributors something they could lean on, and upon which to depend in making investments of their own in stores, warehouses, trucks and the like. Thus an inventor who hoped to go into business for himself would need more than a "pushing man," as Captain Gerner used to say, with money; he also needed "distribution."

As it happened, Winchester prospered without a semiautomatic shotgun until 1954. Returning veterans of the Second World and Korean Wars, having become accustomed to the use of semiautomatic weapons, began to show more interest in Remington's shotgun, which had over the years been improved under a series of patents. Two Winchester engineers who had worked on developing a semiautomatic embracing a different principle than that used in the Remington gun got some help from the protagonist of another movie, "Carbine Williams," released in 1950. Marshall Williams, as we may recall, was imprisoned in 1920, at the age of twenty, on a conviction of having shot and killed a deputy sheriff trying to raid a still he was operating in Goodwin, North Carolina.

While in prison he began to work, furtively at first, but later with the help and approval of a warden, devoted in his own way to the cause of rehabilitation, on the weapon which led to the invention of the Carbine, a semiautomatic rifle used with great success in the war, alongside the Browning Automatic Rifle. In the forties, Winchester retained Williams for a fee, plus royalty, on the shotgun problem. He delivered in time for Winchester to catch the trend toward semiautomatic shotguns.

4.

Our laws, as we might expect, are being strained for having been drafted by men who thought they lived in a world not entirely of the mind. In the summer of 1966, Donald F. Turner, Assistant Attorney General and head of the Antitrust Division, proposed that the Government subsidize research on the effectiveness and safety of consumer products and publicize the results. The proposal threatens no use of Government power to interfere in the market, or with the conduct of corporations, contains no threat of competition from the Government, and suggests no use of enforcement measures.

It would seem to suggest, in fact, no more than is being done by the Food and Drug Administration and other agencies involved with public health and welfare on a larger scale. It is only after examining Mr. Turner's reasoning that we come to know what threat it poses to business, why it should have come from the head of the Antitrust Division, and why it should have been addressed to a symposium on advertising in a meeting of the Federal Bar Association.

Through advertising, Mr. Turner reasoned, corporations create consumer preferences which enable them to charge "high monopolistic prices" for their products. In point of fact, he contended, consumer goods manufacturers who spent heavily on advertising "tended to earn profit rates which were 50 per cent higher than those which did not undertake a significant effort" of advertising. To Mr. Turner's way of thinking, these high profits "represent monopoly rewards." This comes about, he said, because the consumer, with neither time nor the means to test the quality, safety or other merits among competing products, responds by purchasing "an established brand rather than a cheaper but unknown product." Hence: "the phenomenon of unbranded products which sell at prices substantially below those of heavily advertised products, even where there is little real difference between them."

He suggested as an example the fact that the four largest companies account for 90 per cent of the sales of detergents sold in consumer size packages, but only 47 per cent of sales to businesses and institutions whose purchasing agents are paid to know how to get the most for their employers' money. Mr. Turner proposed, therefore, that the Government on its own initiative, or by contract with a private agency, such as Consumers Union, which publishes *Consumer Reports,* do for the public what purchasing agents do for large corporations.

5.

Admission of trademarks to patent protection contributed heavily to the security of corporations, but it was still not enough. Until around 1915, the courts were willing also to treat trade secrets as if they were property. This was in the days before a corporation would invest $250,000 in a study of its operations by a management consultant, and several times that for marketing surveys, "design engineering," art work on soap wrappers, psychological depth studies, radio ratings and story ideas. It was also pre-Xerox and pre-recording tape. In order to lay hold of a customer list or the map of an oil field the thief would have to take the list or the map physically off the premises. The principal concern, in full circle from the Middle Ages, was the brewer's art: the skill and process for making compounds, the cellophane and plastic that were turning a gunpowder maker into a chemical giant, and would make other firms prosperous on soda pop, lotions and medicines.

Some of these compounds and processes were patentable, but many were not. The great fear was that an employee would walk off with the secrets. Still, employees moved around much less than they have in recent years. To deal with the occasional loss of a trade secret by a defecting worker, the courts reached back into Common Law as interpreted in the nineteenth century by a British magistrate in *Lumley vs. Gye.* Lumley was an impresario who had invested heavily, to the extent of purchasing a theater in London's West End, in the talents of Johanna Wagner, an opera singer. When Miss Wagner went to work for Gye instead, the court held that making her go back to Lumley smacked of the indenture system, but they prohibited her from going to work for Gye.

Inevitably, however, cases came to be more complicated. Courts tried as best words would allow them to define a trade secret so that it might answer to the requirements of a definition of property. As a result, the literature is full of definitions, none of which has seemed satisfactory to any significant number of courts over a period of time long enough to warrant reliance upon it. As a member of the Corporate Lawyer Institute has written: "Trade secret seems to imply the existence of some sort of property and suggests that a trade secret ought to be definable as such. In fact, however, this is but rarely the case. Instead, judicial protection of trade secrets usually involves protection against acts by one's competitors which the court deems contrary to good business morals rather than protection of a specific property."

The problem was formulated as well as it has ever been by Mr. Justice Holmes in 1917. Walter E. Masland, a former employee of du Pont, intended to manufacture "artificial leather." Du Pont wanted him enjoined against using or disclosing secret processes du Pont had developed for making artificial leather. Masland said he intended to use only processes known to the trade; but du Pont was also unwilling to have him depose what these were in the taking of proofs. Holmes sent the matter back to trial for hearing by a judge who would "in his discretion reveal them," as it became necessary to the case. He then noted:

"The word 'property' as applied to trade-marks and trade secrets, is an unanalyzed expression of certain secondary consequences of the primary fact that the law makes some rudimentary requirements of good faith. . . . The property may be denied but the confidence cannot be."

There was one additional protection the courts would provide, but it was slow in coming. Until *Standard Parts vs. Peck,* decided in 1924, an employee who had not agreed in advance to assign his rights to inventions could claim title to any save those he was hired explicitly to create. Even if he invented something that had to do with the employer's business, such as a venetian blind in a window shade factory, his employer could claim no more than a shopright—in effect, a nonassignable license to use the invention—but the worker retained title, including the right to assign the invention to other licensees. In *Standard Parts,* the court said "that the inventive skill of one employed at a stated compensation to develop a process and a machinery to secure a certain result for the benefit of the employer is the property of the employer and not the employee." This decision is today assumed to mean that employees enter into "an implied contract to assign" rights to their inventions to their employers.

There the trade secret stood while in the first thirty years of this century the business community added to its rolls Madison Avenue, management consultants, more drug and chemical companies, Radio Corporation of America, the Columbia Broadcasting System, International Business Machines Corporation, Bell Laboratories, the Gallup Poll, and most of the periodicals now prominent nationally and in the trades. Before pressing on, however, it will be useful to know something about The Method.

Chapter Twenty-Three

THE METHOD

The complete exposition of the Newtonian theory and its applications to explain both the permanent stability and periodic variations which are found in the solar system are largely the work of two Frenchmen—Lagrange and Laplace.

—William C. and Margaret Dampier

1.

"All the business of war," Arthur Wellesley, Duke of Wellington, believed, "and indeed all the business of life, is to endeavor to find out what you don't know by what you do; that's what I called 'guessing what was at the other side of the hill.'" If that is indeed the case, then things might have gone much worse for Lord Wellington had Napoleon I taken into battle his contemporary and fellow countryman, Pierre Simon, Marquis de Laplace. Things might have gone much differently for us, too, in war and peace, had we failed to avail ourselves of knowledge Laplace thought belonged among the little that we know for sure. That is, *how* to find out what is at the other side of the hill.

"It is truth very certain," Descartes asserted, "that, when it is not in our power to determine what is true, we ought to follow what is most probable." From where he stood on Descartes' shoulders, Laplace felt able to assert that, "However arbitrary the elements of the planets may be, there exists some very remarkable relations between them, which may throw light on their origin." Having successfully exposed that relation, and a theory about its origin, Laplace asserted further that:

> *All* events, even those which on account of their insignificance do not seem to follow the great laws of nature, are a result of it, just as necessarily as the evolutions of the sun.

Therefore:

> Given for one instant an intelligence which could comprehend all the forces by which nature is animated and the respective situations of the beings who compose it—an intelligence sufficiently vast to submit these data to analysis—it would embrace in the same formula the movements of the greatest bodies of the universe and those of the lightest atom; for it, nothing would be uncertain and the future, as the past, would be present to its eyes.

That none of us, not even men of genius, possesses this intelligence, ought stop us, Laplace says, from trying to learn by analysis what we don't know by what we do. By analysis he did not mean the activity signified by this definition from a standard dictionary: "1: separation or breaking up of a whole into its fundamental elements or component parts ('his problem defied analysis')." He meant, as defined in *Mathematics Dictionary* (James and James): "The exposition of the principles involved; a listing, in mathematical language, of the data given in the statement of the problem, other related data, the end sought, and the steps to be taken."

"Strictly speaking," he wrote, "nearly all our knowledge is problematical." If we choose a *set* of events, and observe them as of a network over a period of time, as if they constituted in themselves a model universe, these events, like births and deaths in a given population, will "exhibit some very remarkable relations." These relations may be expressed in mathematical terms and made calculable. So, therefore, may be the next event in the sequence, to a greater or lesser degree of certainty, depending upon how much data we possess about the model universe. As one of his demonstrations, Laplace constructed an actuarial table, using much the same principles used for that purpose today.

The "calculus of probabilities," Laplace believed to be no more than the "calculus of common sense." So it would seem today. The Method is taken as much for granted as the statistical methods involved in actuarial tables, polls, surveys, television ratings and market tests, by means of which native organisms as well as corporations reckon with their environment. Through them we know with more or less certainty the cost of living generally, the condition of the economy, whether it's a good time to look for a new job, whether the incidence of a disease is such as to require special measures, and much else occult and familiar.

It seems to me no more than just that whatever is erected in place of the old Brooklyn Navy Yard ought to be named for Laplace, in honor of his contribution to the form of cost analysis which converted the yard from what it was into a piece of available real estate.

To refer to the calculus of probabilities as the calculus of common sense, though, is much like observing in a discussion of the Reformation that there was nothing unusual in Martin Luther's having in 1517 nailed ninety-five theses to the door of the castle church in Wittenberg. "Any scholar," G. R. Elton notes, "who wishes to defend any proposition of law or doctrine could invite learned debate by putting forth such theses, and church doors were the customary place for medieval publicity." Laplace's common sense stands in about the relation to the modern world as Luther's did to Sam Slater's England, and Thomas Paine's to his world, but they are different.

2.

To illustrate, we need only restate the newsboy problem: A newsboy buys papers at two cents and sells them at five cents; he receives a one-cent allowance on unsold papers. He finds by experience he has, as an average, ten customers a day, appearing at random; that is, he has no regular customers and one person passing is as likely to buy as the next. Under these circumstances, the Poisson law may be expected to describe the number of customers arriving. The chances that m customers will arrive on a given day is given by:

$$P(m) = \frac{e^{-10}10^m}{m!}$$

Suppose the newsboy buys k papers and m customers appear. If m is equal to or less than k, m papers are sold at a total profit of $4m-k$; if m is greater than k, k papers are sold at a total profit of $3k$. The newsboy's expected profit is:

$$E_k = \sum_{m=0}^{k} (4m - k)P(m) + \sum_{m=k+1}^{\infty} 3kP(m)$$

The chance he will be able to serve all the customers who will pass by is:

$$S_k = \sum_{m=0}^{k} P(m)$$

The accompanying figures depict how the newsboy's profit depends on the number of papers he buys, *k*, and how his ability to service customers depends on the papers he takes.

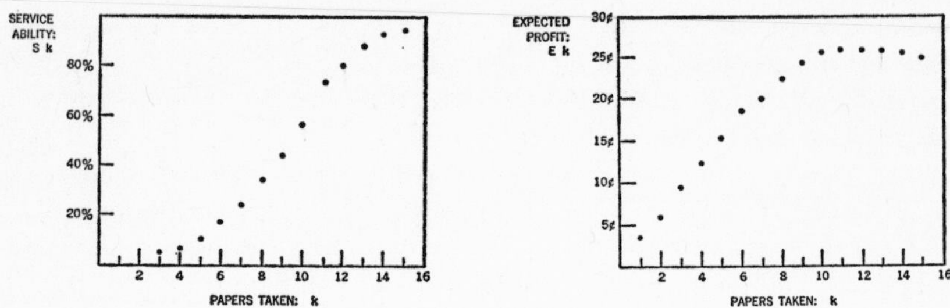

Because of chance variations in the number of customers available, if the newsboy buys ten papers every day, he will not average the expected three cents per paper or thirty cents per day and will meet the available demand less than 60 per cent of the time. In fact, he can make a little more profit by buying not ten, but twelve papers daily; if he buys fifteen daily, he can make the same total profit on the average while meeting the available demand 95 per cent of the time.

For those who did well in mathematics, the solution may hold some interest. For the rest of us, it will serve to demonstrate that the operations are sufficiently formidable to discourage their regular employment by the governing bodies of corporations, let alone by newsboys. The mathematics involved, though, are perhaps the least of the obstacles to its use.

Laplace's form of common sense requires adoption of a habit of thought that remains disconcerting to numerous Anglo-Saxon physicists, let alone men of affairs. In treating of a network, and not what the network describes, the mind has to become accustomed to looking at objects not as if they *are*, but *as if* they are. The value of Laplace's habit of thought, therefore, is hard to get across to a man who, say, has just invested $3 million for the construction of a steam turbine, even if it was with borrowed money. This is a barrier that some businessmen crossed if with only a part of their minds, after 1922, when radio became a prime advertising medium and helped to break down the distinction in their thinking which Daniel Boorstin of the University of Chicago has characterized as between event and pseudo-event. The chapter in which he discusses this development is headed: "Is the Psuedo-Event Real?"

"There was a time," he remarks, "when the reader of an unexciting newspaper would remark, 'How dull the world is today!' Nowadays he says, 'What a dull newspaper!'" He takes as an example of a pseudo-event one offered by Edward L. Bernays, a pioneer in, as Bernays labeled the science, "consent engineering." The owner of a hotel asked a public relations counsel how to increase the hotel's prestige, so as to improve its business.

> In less sophisticated times, the answer might have been to hire a new chef, to improve the plumbing, to paint the rooms, or to install a crystal chandelier in the lobby. The public relations counsel's technique is more indirect. He proposes that the management stage a celebration of the hotel's thirtieth anniversary. A committee is formed, including a prominent banker, a leading society matron, a well-known lawyer, an influential preacher, and an "event" is planned (say a banquet). . . .

Analytically speaking, events are not real or unreal except as consequences of other events. Advertising men, like confidence men, know this as if by nature. Take, for example, the following paragraph from *Gray Matter*, a publication of Gray Advertising Agency.

> Advertising unhampered by mental blocks could change indigenous attitudes. Supposedly, deodorants would have no appeal in cultures where body odors are regarded as less offensive than here. Yet there was a time when we in the United States were not so sensitive to body odors until advertising made us conscious of B.O.

Is B.O. a pseudo-event? Not to the president of whoever it is makes Lifebuoy soap, nor to whoever buys it; nor for that matter to all those who felt more than half-safe for having bought whatever it was made *that* slogan into a household phrase. Nor again, those who owe their weekly paychecks to B.O.

Advertising men possess a livelier awareness of the Laplacian network because they make a good part of their living observing the consequences of the "unreal." Also many of them are inclined to calculate relations as they are defined in whatever they understand to be Freud's model. This is again a work of genius in which energies and forces, and the events of *id* and *ego,* are posited, but not accessible to examination, nor excisable by surgery. Like God and conscience, they have to be reckoned by their effects.

In Freud's terms, it would be useless to distinguish between need and desire. If someone is left nude and shuddering in the cold, his desires are customarily occupied with food, clothing and shelter; the necessities, as we say. What is the point, then, in calling these desires needs, and other needs desires? It is an easy leap, if you don't look closely, from that simple point to saying that all expressed desires are also needs. Thus, a few years ago when tailfins became used by social commentators as the symbol of waste, advertising men took out ads to ask, in effect, what are luxuries and what are necessities? And left it at that.

A system should not be held to account for the employment made of it, however, any more than we can blame Luca Pacioli for the old-fashioned entrepreneurial habit of looking upon labor as being no more than a cost item. Having combed our minds free of Newton's "solid, massy, hard" objects, and emboldened by the calculus of probabilities to plunge into any problem, we would, before the last great war, still have been left to deal with two practical limitations upon our newly discovered capacities.

3.

Let's say we construct a model universe consisting of all persons who watch television for at least one hour between the hours of seven and nine P.M. By means of analysis drawn from the calculus of probabilities, we draw up and sell estimates of how many persons in the universe watched the educational channel offerings as opposed to, say, *Gunsmoke.* Now suppose, however, that someone cares deeply enough to invest the enormous sums that would be required to take an actual census of all television viewers in a single evening. The cost would have to include internal checks, together with security measures to guard against the introduction of "noise" or distortions by potential opponents of the census. And suppose that the census showed results greatly at variance with those reported the same evening by a standard rating service. Today, the investment would not have been wasted, except to the purpose of discrediting the ratings. Before 1947 or thereabouts it might have been.

The information from the television census would be unwelcome to a rating service only if it challenged the supposition Laplace made of "very remarkable relations" among events in a network; that is to say, the very basis for statistical sampling. This it could not do. Thus, no new information is unwelcome. On the contrary, any new information is manageable, and therefore practical, if not in an existing model, then to some model we may require at some time in the future. It only adds to our experience, and therefore may make future guesses less problematical.

A case in point: when Dr. Abraham Carp, director of selection for the Peace Corps, was asked by a member of the House subcommittee investigating invasions of privacy to make some accounting for the types of questions contained in the Minnesota Multiphasic Personality Inventory, he explained that:

> . . . the developers of the test identified 566 items which they thought would be potentially useful in differentiating between people with various psychiatric problems and those who are normal.
>
> In the scales that have been developed to date, only 371 items have turned out to in fact be useful in differentiating between psychiatric normals and abnormals. The other items are in there primarily for research purposes, to lead to the development of future scales which may in fact be useful. . . .

Thus Dr. Carp could assign the two uses of the test to management risk-reduction and an inventory of research for future application. In like manner, the proprietor of a rating service could only express his gratitude at having the results of the census, and assure everyone that by taking them into account, his rating would be even more accurate than in the past.

Before the 1940's, however, the storage of new information would have been severely limited by space and time: the space for the filing cabinets, shelves, card file drawers, or whatever, in which to store it, but even more critically by the time which elapses between the point at which the need for the information is established, and a decision using it is made.

4.

In order to inform operations vastly more complicated than a single newsstand, a model would have required the work of researchers, space for storage of information and a multitude of skilled mathematicians. The model might scarcely have begun to take shape before the need for it had passed.

Thus corporations had to make do with double-entry, Euclidean, linear, Newtonian habits of thought to constitute their experience, to conjure up their environment, to calculate the consequences of their actions, and to keep track of things. And no one would have suggested that they were "persons" except in the sense of the "legal fiction" taught of even in high school civics classes. We may now turn to the consequences of that state of mind, and how The Method came into its own.

Chapter Twenty-Four

THE SYSTEM COMES TO LIFE

To Mr. Henry Ford, who is planning to spend a hundred million dollars on our education. Would that we had as much to spend on his.

—KENNETH BURKE, dedication of an article published in *The New Republic,* 1930

1.

ON OCTOBER 29, 1929, there occurred an event so traumatic in the lives of the great American industrial corporations that only thirty-five years later, a trice in the life of an immortal being, the New York Stock Exchange had officially expunged it from conscious memory. A *Fact Book* issued by the Exchange in 1963 commemorates the start of the Great Depression with this item, whole and entire: "Oct 29, 1929 First and only 16-million share day—16,410,030 shares." After Black Tuesday, not much was to be seen of the Newton-Slater-Holmes world. It was held together by two conceptions that might have been plausible but only in the absence of great corporations. These conceptions were first, that the market was all the sensor and governor that a natural feedback mechanism like the economy of the nation required to regulate itself and remain healthy. This may have been true, except that no one had the opportunity then, or has had one since, to see a demonstration of a market economy free of administration of critical prices by one corporate body or another.

The second conception was that competition would work the same wonders in the political and economic order as it had in the order of nature described by Charles Darwin. It appears to have escaped the popular consensus that when a businessman spoke of the economic lessons to be perceived in Darwin and in the social commentators who extrapolated his theory for employment in the economic world, he was talking as most of us do when we discuss the theory of evolution; that is, not about process, but about history; not about competition in the future, but in the past. The winner's circle is already occupied.

Knowing of John D. Rockefeller's eye for risks on the downside, it seems to me highly unlikely that he would have invested $75 million in a great university, including a triumphant chapel, if it had occurred to him that the ultimate survivor might turn out to be Chinese, or some made-to-order mutation. I doubt, in fact, that it occurred to him even once that the ultimate survivor might turn out to be something he couldn't recognize in a mirror. But after the Great Crash, the jobless and bewildered began to gain a more vivid knowledge of what is meant by suvival of the fittest. They became aware also of the corollary to Darwin's theory which biologists today strain to get across to us.

It is the belief that anything, literally *anything*, is possible. This awareness was reinforced at the time by the back-to-the-drawing-board sense of possibilities that rises from the ashes of failed experiments. One possibility that occurred to many persons all at once is that the nation might do better without private business corporations. Thus, the security industry prospered as did few other industries, principally on the strength of Red scares, labor battles and the siege mentality induced in business by "that man in the White House."

2.

I take it on competent authority that Franklin Roosevelt believed, as Jefferson had believed, that the nation had about reached the peak of its economic capacity for the time being, and that most of his efforts were directed toward distributing income in a fashion that would prevent Huey Long, or someone like him, from riding to power, with the U.S. Army as his private state militia. In this effort he was helped by the fact that hundreds upon thousands of neighborhood movie theaters, along with millions of radios, had wired the nation into a network which Roosevelt appeared to understand and to know how to use as if by instinct.

Someone has remarked that had it not been for the movies the United States might easily have gone into violent and fatal political convulsions. Perhaps so. There is no telling how many losing breadwinners might have spent their nights out in cell meetings instead of watching Jimmy Stewart or Gary Cooper pull the pomp out from under a carnation-popping Adolphe Menjou or leave Eugene Pallette gaping as he alone could gape, as the hero ran off with the rich man's daughter. There seemed to be some opiate qualities, too, about William Powell and Humphrey Bogart as private detectives, as if they were the last of the entrepreneurs. Maybe the newsreel shots of the poor and FDR gave a boost to the communal feeling peculiar to that time, when even landlords put off collecting the rent for months because there was no one else to whom their flats might be rented.

Radio ought to get some credit, although we may never know how far back Amos 'n Andy, once the highest-rated program in that medium, set back the cause of civil rights. Or for that matter the extent to which nightly commentators retarded the cause of adult education. In all events, Roosevelt used all the new media with great skill to substantiate the benevolent presence of the Federal Government. As, indeed, did the enforcement agencies.

Apart from full-length features about G-Men and T-Men, selected short subjects contained stories from the files of the FBI, which were made into a series entitled "Crime Does Not Pay." J. Edgar Hoover appeared regularly at the end of these skits, under the trademark of the Great Seal of the United States.

Meanwhile, Congress periodically held hearings toward creation of a wiretap policy until room was made for one in Section 605 of the Federal Communications Act of 1934: ". . . and no person not being authorized by the sender shall intercept any communication and divulge or publish the existence, contents, substance, purport, effect, or meaning of such intercepted communications to any person. . . ."

Some doubt has since been expressed by students of these matters as to whether the Congress meant by "no person" to include the Justice Department's Bureau of Investigation. The Department did not think so, evidently. O. John Rogge, who served as Assistant U.S. Attorney General, has recorded that the Department "continued to countenance wiretapping in criminal cases of 'extreme importance,' although not in 'minor cases, nor on members of Congress, or officials, or any citizen except where charge of a grave crime had been lodged against him.'" In 1937, the Supreme Court held that "no person" includes Federal law officers, and that "any person" means the Federal courts. Thus, by invoking the so-called "Weeks rule," which makes evidence illegally obtained inadmissible, wiretap evidence is not permitted in Federal courts. In subsequent refinements, the Court determined that if information was gathered which led to the arrest of some person not a party to the conversation, he could not successfully object. Also, evidence obtained by listening to only one end of the conversation was held to be admissible.

These indications of security consciousness may have been necessary because like everyone else the antisocial elements in society were getting organized. Their exploits were numerous, and made to seem even more numerous by movies which, by condemnation, gave them a certain cachet and vividness, glory and a lively presence in the environment. The impression was reinforced by a press that in the provinces seemed to be dominantly Hearst. It was all very nervous-making to a nation of citizens who had been assured that all they had to fear was fear itself.

Roosevelt's use of the media, and his easy way with movie moguls (who controlled their environments as if they contained nothing more than backlot stage sets) gave hint that he had at least a tactical politician's grasp of the next great step in the march of systems science. The concept, together with all of its implications, was not yet fully understood even by those at Bell Labs and other points of meditation where men were in the thirties occupied with the behavior of circuits used in telephonic and wireless communication.

3.

Some years ago, after Dr. Frank Stanton (he holds a Ph.D. in psychology), president of the Columbia Broadcasting System, had appeared before a Senate Committee investigating violence in television shows, I wrote in *Commonweal:*

> . . . when a particularly noxious example of an "action" show was tossed at [Dr. Stanton], he remarked that the action shows seemed to be in the downtrend and he, according to the Times report, "applauded" the trend. The account made him sound as if he were no more than an interested spectator, a willing servant of uptrends and downtrends. He was, in short, a study in power without responsibility. How can you fight a thing like that?

That was before I fully understood the feedback principle, and Dr. Stanton's responsibility to it. He is, as I now realize, a governor, or thermostat, as it were, in a highly complicated servomechanism. The circuit consists of a sample taken from the environment or market, which is expressed as the rating, broadcasters, advertising agencies, client sponsors, a verification sample, which is to say sales figure, stock market prices, writers, producers, actors and actresses, their agents, published critics, the Federal Communications Commission and the Congress.

The energy regulated in an automatic control system, whether a steam engine, a thermostat or a newt, may be expressed in different ways. In the CBS network and in the system of which that network is a part, the flow of energy is expressed in units of dollars. It is a simple system in that all components within it agree to accept the dollar measurement of energy, and to accept as binding at least one "signal"—the rating charts. The rating is, therefore, self-verifying in regulating the flow of dollars in the system.

There are a number of other such closed circuits in the system: for example, the comedy writer who writes a script that will gain its sole direct response from whoever indicates the type of laughter a particular joke calls for from a laugh track. If the writer himself punctuates his script with sounds from the laugh track, he may be said to consist of a closed loop within the circuit. If he were to be paid according to the response his work received from the laugh track, he would almost invariably be among the top paid writers, which would prove the efficacy of the system.

Similarly, there is no economically feasible way to determine with certitude if the sales figures are a feedback from the circuit into which a television show is programmed, or from some other circuit into which the corporation is plugged. In this, however, television ratings are no different from the statistics upon which, for example, the Federal Reserve Board acts to change the discount rate.

Henry Ford I had some notion of the feedback principle as far back as 1930, perhaps from an intimation that may have come to him as he watched an assembly line. He was sure he had the key to the economic puzzle. His message was, in effect, "Consume and ye shall receive." This infuriated Kenneth Burke, the poet and critic.

"We realize now," Burke wrote in *The New Republic,* "that culture resides in *prosperity,* that production can only follow *consumption,* that the maximum possible consumption is made possible by the maximum possible *waste,* and therefore that *culture depends upon a maximum of waste.* (At least until there is nothing more to waste.)" (The italics are all Burke's.) Burke was also not of one mind with Julius Klein, who has over the years been in and out of the news, most spectacularly in 1966 in connection with the Senate's inquiry into the money affairs of Senator Thomas Dodd of Connecticut.

Klein had in 1930 pointed out that, "The old Periclean law gave each Athenian the right to own five slaves. It has been calculated that every inhabitant of the United States has today at his disposal the power equivalent of 150 slaves." I see, Burke remarked:

"*We have simply to make sure that the increase in the number of labor-saving devices does not shorten the hours of labor.* Thus when a man is thrown out of work by the introduction of a new machine for the manufacture of a necessary article, we must set him to work manufacturing some article hitherto unnecessary."

4.

As sympathetic as Ford may have been to the feedback principle, he was perhaps not yet ready, as few businessmen were, for John Maynard Keynes. There is some question, I gather, as to whether Keynes' argument, as set out in the *General Theory*, published in 1936, borrowed shamelessly from the Swedish economist, Knut Wicksell. As a polemicist, though, he borrowed from no one. He, like Marshall McLuhan, found poor Euclid an apt foil. "The classical theorists," he wrote, "resemble Euclidean geometers in a non-Euclidean world who, discovering that in experience straight lines apparently parallel often meet, rebuke the lines for not keeping straight—as the only remedy for the unfortunate collisions which are occurring."

Arnold Tustin has paid the systems analyst's tribute to Keynes:

> The periodic booms and slumps in economic activity stands out as a major example of oscillatory behavior due to feedback. In 1935, the economist John Maynard Keynes gave the first adequate and satisfying account of the essential mechanisms on which the general level of economic activity depends. Although Keynes did not use the terminology of control system theory, his account fits precisely the now familiar pattern.

Keynes had a few words, too, for the point from which the New Deal and the economic system was getting the most static: "There is no clear evidence from experience that the investment policy which is socially advantageous coincides with that which is most profitable." This because

> With the separation between ownership and management which prevails today and with the development of organized

> investment markets, a new factor of great importance has entered in, which sometimes facilitates investment but sometimes adds greatly to the instability of the system . . . the Stock Exchange revalues many investments every day and the revaluations give a frequent opportunity to the individual (though not to the community as a whole) to revise his commitments. It is as though a farmer, having tapped his barometer after breakfast, could decide to remove his capital from the farming business between 10 and 11 in the morning and reconsider whether he should return to it later in the week.

Perhaps some, but not all, of what Keynes had to say made him *persona non grata* in the business community. His worst heresy may have been: "The spectacle of modern investment markets has sometimes moved me towards the conclusion that to make the purchase of an investment permanent and indissoluble, like marriage, except by reason of death or other grave cause, might be a useful remedy for our contemporary evils."

Keynes appears to have been received more warmly at the White House than anywhere else. During the early days of the New Deal, the principal use made of The Method in the Federal Government was by the Army in the solution of gunnery problems. In order actively to administer as much of the economy as appeared necessary at the White House, the Government needed skilled administrators, statisticians and economists who were not made to feel insecure by the phrase "Government planning," and who, as they say in the management manuals, would be "receptive to new ideas."

"The economy of a modern nation," Wassily Leontief has remarked, "not unlike the feedback mechanisms . . . must be visualized as a complicated set of interrelated processes. . . . It is not by coincidence that in some advanced phases of his work the modern economist resorts to systems of differential equations similar to those used by the designers of self-regulating machinery."

The New Deal did, in fact, attract an enormous amount of talent, from campuses as well as from the legal profession. It also created another bogy to add to the growing catalog of banes contributing to the general paranoia: the "bu-ro-crat" as he was sometimes called, drawlingly or twangingly on Capitol Hill, or "meddlesome bewrochraht" as he was referred to at the Wall Street Club. Lately he has been known as the "whiz-kid at the Pentagon."

5.

In 1940, Attorney General Robert Jackson effected a return to the absolute ban on wiretapping enforced under the Stone policy of 1924. The following year, in response to a confidential letter from President Roosevelt asking him to approve of wiretapping by the FBI when it seemed to him necessary to the defense of the nation, Jackson reversed himself. In order to carry out the President's wishes while at the same time avoiding a breach of Section 605 as interpreted by the Court, Jackson engineered some bridgework and brought a new corporate person into being. He determined that the Congress had meant to proscribe not interception alone, nor divulgence alone, but the two together: "intercept . . . and divulge." Thus it would be all right for the FBI to wiretap, so long as the eavesdropping agent did not tell anyone what he heard. The problem of how the agent would make his information known to other agents working on a case was solved with similar ease, by regarding the FBI as if it were a "single person."

This of course, raises another problem not endemic to living, breathing organisms. If an FBI agent receives wiretap information from the interceptor of the information, and subsequently leaves the service to become, say, a private security agent, he could presumably divulge the information himself without breaking the law. The same problem would arise, one supposes, with much of the information collected by the FBI but it has, interestingly, never come to the attention of the courts. Like renegade priests and cashiered physicians, veterans of FBI service appear seldom if ever to create litigable issues with the knowledge they possess even after they take up life independent of the corporate person.

But no matter. Something was occurring in the American experience to make Brandeis' opinion in Olmstead into prophecy. Indeed, after Shoeless Joe Jackson disgraced Comiskey Park in 1919, there was some doubt if the Yankee doctrine obtained on the playing field at Briggs Stadium, let alone the corporate board rooms situated elsewhere around Detroit.

It is, of course, possible to accept the reality of nonevents without accepting the antecedents. General Motors, for example, throughout the depression made and touted changes in auto styling each year, while pursuing labor practices characteristic of pre-Newtonian England. In 1937, the La Follette Committee brought out that GM principally, but other "trade associations" as well, had been spying on workers more assiduously than anyone has suggested industrial competitors have spied on one another, then or since. A union official testified that, "I have not been in a gathering big enough to be called a meeting, yet too small to include a company spy." One item indicates, though, why the Burns Detective Agency was not yet qualified to call itself a security agency. One of their men protested that committee investigators had obtained evidence by going through the Burns office wastebaskets.

Strikebreaking, of course, violated the then two-year-old Wagner Labor Relations Act. In January, 1937, the FBI was called in to investigate. Announcement of the Justice Department's interest was made six days after the War Department was called upon to deny allegations that Army and Navy Intelligence and the Department of Justice had given help to an association retained by GM for strikebreaking—this in order to maintain production under Government contracts. The Justice Department announcement also followed by five days an admission from the Navy that it had assigned spies to aircraft factories. Posters of warning began to appear among the public transit ads: "A Slip of the Lip May Sink a Ship," to which someone today might feel compelled to add, "or someone you know."

Chapter Twenty-Five

THE WAR

Probably the battle of Waterloo was won on the playing fields of Eton, but the opening battles of all subsequent wars have been lost there.

—George Orwell

1.

For the conversion of knowledge into a rubble of information, there is nothing to match in efficiency the dislocation caused by a modern war. The process is familiar to anyone who has been conscripted raw, a veritable dishevelment of information, into a military replacement training center. After only a day, two at most, of having been reprogrammed, he feels able to pull unspoken rank on every new arrival, and to taunt the man at the end of the vaccinations line. There were company clerk-typists who may never have recaptured the sweet sensation of power that came with having typed, some hours before posting, the stencils for orders that told who was going to be sent where, or who was getting another stripe and who wasn't.

War also discourages the habit of dwelling too strongly upon physical objects as if they were more real than other events. This not alone because of the newsreel pictures of ancient cities reduced to ruins, but also because of the wrench to one's pre-war habits at hearing that Jeeps still in their crates were shoved into Manila Bay, coupled with the extraordinary mixed sense of apprehension and liberation one gets at dropping a duffel bag full of winter issue into warm Pacific waters.

I suspect General Eisenhower might be dismayed even today to learn how many old-style blouses went to the bottom of a sea in the knowledge that at the other end of the trip the Army would have to supply one of the new "Ike jackets." On the other hand, who can tell how many bright but otherwise unemployable young men were led by this experience to pursue careers in advertising?

Beginning with mobilization, the war also put the seal of duty and necessity on security consciousness, put corporations into an easier frame of mind for hiring investigators, and gave many of the security agents in business for themselves today their early training. While fulfilling their obligations under Government contracts, corporations came to know about security checks, the meaning of "need to know" and hence classification of documents, about how to log and burn them, and incidentally about the hazards of keeping wastebaskets, plus much else that has served them well since.

One tip corporations got from the war is evident in the one-half page of space that IBM purchased in the summer of 1966 in the help-wanted columns of *Editor and Publisher*. The ad solicited the attention of journalists to its need for a service, the description of which was evidently beyond the capability of mere words. The ad was no more specific, that is to say, than to mention that the positions open had to do with "the 20th century's fastest growing major industry: information handling and control." Ordinarily, a member of the audience for which the appeal was intended would think immediately of public relations. This possibility seemed ruled out, though, by the fact that whatever IBM had in mind required "a feel for mathematics" and further by the hint of "a future as promising and fulfilling as that of the data processing field." Whatever the jobs were, or are, must have been important: ". . . every systems advance has proven anew that a data processing system is only as good as the programs developed for its use." The solicitation might have been IBM's way of establishing that it is an equal-opportunity employer, but it seemed to mean business. And in point of fact there is ample precedent for the employment of philosophers in the service of systems science. The late James Newman, the historian of mathematics, noted that:

> In the last war operational analysts were to be found at work in strange places and under strange circumstances. Mathematicians discussed gunnery problems with British soldiers in Burma; chemists did bomb damage assessment with economist colleagues at Princes Risborough, a "secure" headquarters outside London; generals conferred about tank strategy in the Italian campaign with biochemists and lawyers; a famous British zoologist was key man in planning the bombardment of Pantellaria; naval officers took statisticians and entomologists into their confidence regarding submarine losses in the Pacific. . . .

2.

"Operations analysis" was the job description given by Colonel W. Barton Leach of the Army Air Force in 1942 to a group of newly commissioned officers he had assembled. Col. Leach was, by calling, a lawyer, and after the war, a professor of law at Harvard. The group he called together included architects, biologists, civil engineers, economists, geologists, mathematicians and statisticians, plus, to be sure, several lawyers. What these men had in common was an ability which extended beyond that needed merely to perform the mathematical operations to locate the best positions for artillery and radar. Any Newtonian could have done that much. Operations analysts were distinguishable by the capacity to suspend, as if not to make a difference, the distinction common sense makes between knowledge and information.

A case in point is the solution devised by a group of operations analysts who were asked toward the end of the war in Europe to determine which among several German cities they believed might be softest to invasion and occupation by airborne troops. After giving the matter some thought, the analysts asked to be provided with recent obituaries from newspapers published in each of the enumerated cities commemorating soldiers that had fallen in battle.

It might well have occurred to whoever was assigned to get the papers that the analysts were barking up the wrong tree. The newspapers in Nazi Germany were, of course, heavily censored, obituaries included, to prevent them from yielding any information of value to the formation of intelligence estimates. The analysts, though, were not so much interested in the facts contained in the obituaries as they were in learning of the end for which the writers believed the subjects of these notices had given their lives; whether it was, say, "for the greater glory of the Fuehrer," for "the Fatherland," or only that they had been as we were given to say, "killed in action."

By ranking the obituaries according to this factor, they were able to construct a model which yielded a weight for each town according to its dedication to the war and its morale. A town in which newspaper obituaries carried no mention of Fuehrer or Fatherland was supposed, that is, to be the ripest for invasion, and so on down the scale. That the ranking was used successfully is, of course, no verification of the method; some other system might have worked as well or better. Had you made that point under those circumstances, you would also have had to propose another method.

3.

Beardsley Graham, president of Spindletop Research, Inc., is my witness for the statement Col. Leach gave to the first problem he posed. It was, Graham says, "by either luck or rare insight, perfectly balanced between restriction to the topic and freedom of investigation. His complete instructions were: 'Gentlemen, I have only one problem—to put more of my bombs on the target.'"

Common sense might respond with questions such as: How many bombers do we have? How many pilots? What are the weather conditions over the target? What has been our experience with air defense in the target area? Is there any reason to suppose that there have been changes in these defenses? An analytical inquiry might begin, by contrast, with some such question as: What events may be said to comprise a model that is defined by the object of placing missiles on a target by means of manned aircraft? "After a period of self-education," Graham has written, "the analysts recommended new and modified procedures which, along with improved equipment, raised the bombing accuracy by 2,000 per cent." How much of the increase in efficiency was due to improvements in equipment, and how much to the work of the analysts makes little difference, except to judge the work of Leach's particular group. For the improvements, as well as the operations performed, embodied the results of The Method.

Gordon S. Brown and Donald P. Campbell point out that besides operations analysts,

> During World War II great numbers of men were brought together from different fields to pool their abilities for the design of weapons and instruments. As a result, the specialists of engineering and science found themselves talking to one another for the first time in generations. Mechanical engineers exploited techniques of circuit theory borrowed from the communications engineers; aeronautical engineers extended the use of electrical concepts of measurement and of mathematical presentation, mathematicians working with engineers and experimental scientists discovered entirely unsuspected practical uses for forgotten theorems. The enforced collaboration soon

focussed attention on the essential principles that apply to all control systems.

Here and there in industrial systems the work done during the twenties and thirties in circuitry and systems research, energized by large Government expenditures, began to show up in early versions of the machines now used to run oil refineries and bakeries and to help keep us money-honest: Machines that can store and spill out in readily usable form enough information, and make all the calculations necessary to running all of the newsstands in the country, and to tell us, given the input, the correlation between fingerprint whorls, sleeping habits, consumption of Ovaltine and the cephalic index of bombardiers to their accuracy on cloudy days over Monte Cassino.

4.

A short jeep's drive from Manila in 1946, a large, squat quonset hut housed, in the straightforward language of the military, the 56th Machine Records Unit of the Strength Accounting Branch, subsumed at that time under the Adjutant General. He was charged, in this case by General Douglas MacArthur, with keeping track of everybody. The building contained drawers to accommodate punch cards representing every mother's son in the Armed Forces Western Pacific theater, machines to punch out more cards, an International Business Machine through which these cards were put from time to time, a major, two lieutenants, a warrant officer and assorted noncommissioned officers, including a corporal with a high-domed forehead who hailed from Texas and said his name was Smith.

"Said" because it seemed inconceivable that the only man in the entire theater of operations who really understood how those machines worked, and was able, therefore, to make them work, should have been drawing less money than the presiding noncommissioned officer, or master sergeant, of this small segment of the leisure class. The master sergeant perhaps received a better notion of how an "information system" can convert a "fictional" corpus, or corps, into something more clearly resembling native organisms.

At a stipulated time, the machines would inform him through its operatives, also a cluster of corporals, that A Battery of the 123 AA battalion in the field had not sent in its morning reports. A short time beforehand, during the hostilities, these machines had been considered important enough to drag around in vans, like brains contained in the entrails of a fighting machine. It was important to see that A Battery got a dunning letter, BY ORDER OF the Adjutant General for misdemeanors, BY COMMAND OF General MacArthur for serious violations.

Every time a highly classified cable arrived asking where there might be found 17 men with a Military Occupational Specialty corresponding to 405 in the catalog, or how many men would be shipping out under the latest separation date agreement, the information went back through a machine that automatically coded it before it was sent, under a classification that was classified information.

Men came into the unit as privates or pfc's and left after six months wearing three stripes or more. The Army paid its own special kind of tribute to Smith. He was urged to stay on and see that the machines did what they were supposed to do. As I come to think of it now, in the Table of Organization covering the 56th MRU, rankings ascended according to knowledge of what was expected of the unit, and descended according to knowledge of how it got done. This was with the exception of the Warrant Officer, who had not much knowledge either way.

5.

Just as the Depression had begun the incorporation of the Smiths of the world into the great network, the war, through the lessons gained in a common effort, hastened the incorporation of labor. The services maintained a personnel inventory of staggering proportions. Each man had to be quantified, by an intelligence test (The Army General Classification Test was one), by Military Occupational Specialty, by serial number, blood type and other indexes. The corporation learned that the difference between management and labor is not the difference between who works for whom. It is the difference in running a Cartesian network, and being no more than another event in it. It is the difference between "I think, therefore I am" and "I am a member of C Squad, third platoon, F Battery, second battalion, 55th Anti-Aircraft Brigade, therefore I am." Or, put another way, "bosses" is a linear concept; "establishment" is a systems concept.

During the long climb toward the Wagner Act, labor leaders seemed to have been possessed by that inexhaustible belief in the possibility of rehabilitation which is the work of a reformer. Slowly and painfully, although gassed and shot at, with heads aching from thwacks from billy clubs wielded by private and public enforcers of corporate property rights, the workers instructed the great corporations in elementary human relations.

The United Auto Workers in 1947 made as one of their contract demands permission to make regular inspection of GM's books and records. GM, however, suffered a costly strike rather than yield on the point. GM's management argued in effect that the property, though not theirs, was none the less the corporation's and that management by election of the nominal owners (all stockholders) stood in a fiduciary or custodial relationship to it. Privacy of the information in the books was *sine qua non* to management of a corporation, and hence to accountability under that obligation.

This seemed to amount to explicit recognition not obvious in GM's pre-war conduct, that the property was not the management's to do with as it willed, as if it were the management's, but as it might do to make the property more valuable; and under terms of competition administered tacitly by the Department of Justice.

How labor came to be cured in rhetoric, Mayoized, coddled into tolerance of boredom, Muzaked, related to and communicated with must be regarded, though, as a study in the triumph of science over nature, and of the solicitude of well-wishers, from Franklin Roosevelt to the Ribicoff Committee on auto safety, over the seizures of obtuseness which afflict bureaucracies, including those to which Roosevelt and Ribicoff belonged. An observer of this process says we may now rely for continued vitality on Newton's third law of motion, or the theory of "countervailing power." Maybe.

Chapter Twenty-Six

THE TAKEOFF

For years I [have] thought that what was good for our country was good for General Motors, and vice versa.

—CHARLES WILSON

1.

THE EFFECT OF THE WAR of 1939–45 on security consciousness may be likened to that of commercial aviation on the casualty insurance business. What nothing more awesome than the Twentieth Century Limited did for Hollywood in the thirties, the war did for the rest of the world. It implicated the interest and investment of American businessmen in places and persons that had before seemed merely exotic, at most glamorous, and in either event best left to the night-thoughts of oil, copper and shipping companies, and a few bankers.

The war thrust into consciousness new markets, new ways of doing business, and evidence of productive capacity of a magnitude to undermine perhaps the single opinion businessmen shared with Franklin Roosevelt, that there wasn't much more opportunity for substantial increase than had existed in 1929. All the same, while the time elapsed between the last depression and the first postwar year might be about right for converting a frugging high school senior into a Master of Business Administration, the corporate giants had before the war proved to be notoriously slow learners.

It is hard to summon a sense of a world whose men of action had not grown callouses on their inner ears. John D. Rockefeller, Henry Ford and even Ivar Kreuger, the match king, missed the invigorating experience of being a bibbed idiot on a transcontinental flight. I have tried without success, from what one knows of them, to picture any one of them, head clamped in stereophonic earphones, like a tonged ice cube, martini in hand, staring ahead at a nine-inch version of *Thunder-*

ball, while squeezed behind a foldaway tray bearing a protein diet filet neatly trimmed in a plastic dish, and he only a jot among 125 tons of flesh, metal and man-made fibers being hurtled coast to coast.

The security consciousness one feels in those circumstances is not fear of some imminent peril, but rather an enlivened sense that anything is possible. Ford and Rockefeller seem to me to have been the type of men who would have been uncomfortable at having to ride aboard any conveyance in which they could not share their wishes and concerns with the driver. It would, I suspect, have troubled them to be at the mercy of persons and devices to which things might go wrong, but that they had never seen or even heard of; and in which, moreover, in relation to the entire range of possible malfunctions, the man at the wheel is not much better informed than oneself.

At bottom it is the inherent implausibility of the feat being attempted which on first takeoff makes actuarial tables seem like escape reading. This may be why a man who will calmly discuss the next summer's vacation plans with his family while tooling along a turnpike at 60 miles per hour will also, the moment he reaches an airport, dump quarters into an insurance vending machine.

I am told that only 20 per cent of airline passengers do 80 per cent of the flying. I often wonder how many of the 20 per cent would fly if fear of losing their jobs did not defeat prudent common sense. Similarly, we may wonder what commercial airliners would look like today, or to what extent American business would have gotten involved in foreign markets, or what use would have been made of computers, without the impetus of national security measures.

2.

What is to replace in modern man, Walter Lippmann asked in 1929, that belief in the religion of his fathers which he has lost to the "acids of modernity"? Is there any standard which permits him to "put a term upon that pursuit of money, of power and of excitement which has created so much of the turmoil and the squalor and the explosiveness of modern civilization"? What, indeed, was there to so much as rebel against? "The rebel . . . moves in an unreal environment, one might almost say a parasitic environment. He goes forth to destroy Caesar, Mammon, George F. Babbitt and Mrs. Grundy. As he wrestles with these demons he leans upon them. By inversion they offer him much the same kind of support which the conformer enjoys. . . . His energies are focused by his indignation."

Lippmann's observation by no means precludes the possibility that there are real and substantial demons in the world, that they are dangerous, and that they ought to be dealt with. It remarks only upon a fact of life evident to philosophers long before theologians began writing obituaries for God. It is of a piece with the advice Machiavelli, to whom the God of his fathers was a living presence, gave The Prince; that if things seem to be getting out of hand at home, his remedy is to create some external crisis. This is no more than to say that when the "we" to which one is committed by birth or choice seems not to know who or what "we" are, or what "our" business is, we are inclined to rely upon some "they" to focus our energies.

The war established convincingly that there were energies loose in the world of a kind which our pre-war political behavior indicated we thought had gone out with the Vandals and the Goths, that they could be organized to annihilatory effect, and that, if permitted to rattle around loose, would be. We were in addition particularly fortunate in the "they" given us after the war to focus our energies.

3.

The form of organized barbarism embodied first in the Soviet Union and then in Communist China is uniquely subtle and inventive and on that account marvellously malleable. The demon of international Communism has ranged in size from the bane spoofingly regarded in a movie title, *The Russians Are Coming The Russians Are Coming*, all the way up to the creature envisioned by the late Senator Joseph McCarthy, which engulfed clergymen and teachers, not to mention our own State Department and certain quarters in the Pentagon.

This omnipresent "they" was well-suited to exercise of our newly instituted means for ordering our awareness of what was going on about us. These, to be sure, were not always evident. At the time that President Eisenhower confessed that Gary Powers, the pilot of the U-2 shot down over Soviet territory, was a spy, just as Moscow said he was, retirees from the old Office of Strategic Services as well as novices in the Central Intelligence Agency expressed private dismay. The one seemed at a loss to explain how we won the last war, and the other how we would win the next one.

They, of course, knew better. By that time, the division of functions seen sprouting in the 56th Machine Records Unit had become a new force in the systems of checks and balances. There was the President and Congress who knew, or who believed that Secretary of State Dulles knew, what had to be done, and the "industrial-military complex" in President Eisenhower's Farewell Address phrase, who knew how it got done. It appeared that the President proposed and the executive agencies disposed. If it were otherwise, then the U.S. Department of Defense would have had to wait until Secretary Robert McNamara took office before it began to think operationally.

Yet in point of fact, even after Charles Wilson left General Motors to become Secretary of Defense, it was demonstrably possible for President Eisenhower and Wilson, and they in turn with the biggest among the defense industry suppliers, to discuss policy without knowing the difference between the Poisson Law and the Schley Model. In the meantime, the Pentagon operated according to the principles which the War Department had begun to respect on artillery ranges even before the War of 1939–45, and which the experience gained during the war demonstrated was vital for most other purposes. It included, of course, machinery for "reading the other gentleman's mail" that no one, up to and including the President, could dismantle if he wanted to. If the yowls from the Pentagon and State Department didn't stop him from pulling rank, the chances are good he would have ended up in Bethesda Naval Hospital for an extended checkup ordered by his doctors.

I suspect, indeed, that had Secretary McNamara stayed on as President of the Ford Motor Company, he would have been one of the few chief executives in charge of a corporation among *Fortune*'s top 500 who genuinely understood about the Laplacian universe. As it turned out, his principal contribution to the Defense Department has been to bring the principles of operations analysis in from outside, to apply them to the internal environment as well as the external, and to reduce the Department's purchases to the terms of cost analysis.

4.

I emphasize this point not in support of the thesis that there is lurking behind every arras of power some scientist-cuckold of the public will. Nor does it seem to be useful to point yet another finger at the whiz-kids: those intellectuals, a British writer has intimated darkly, who prowl the corridors of the Pentagon like the Jesuits in sixteenth-century Spanish courts. Nor yet do I want to imply that possessors of propertied and political power are victim to "myths" any more than the rest of us. The word "myth" in the recent employment of social commentators has come to occupy a place as a term of convenience. It is a foil, an invention convenient to the common use of dialectical exposition.

I mean only to remark that the assured awareness made possible by the calculus of probabilities converted the security mandate into a mandate by the Government to exact and employ resources we didn't know we had. For under the terms that govern preparation for, as well as the conduct of, modern warfare, few events and scarcely any knowledge may be considered wholly exempt from a place among our security requirements. I haven't any doubt that, given twenty-four hours, any operations analyst worth his consulting fee from the Government could discover a sound explanation for why tapping an Eskimo's telephone call to a stockbroker in New York would be in the interest of national security.

5.

The unspent demand salted away during the war tided the economy over long enough for Washington to have interpreted Russia's designs, translated those designs into policy, and policy in turn into Federal budgets of formidable proportions. As expenditures under these budgets were written into contracts, subcontracts and sub-subcontracts, all industry received persuasive earn-as-you-learn instruction concerning the phenomenon Keynes had in mind when he spoke of the "multiplier effect." It showed up in figures expressing the Gross National Product, the Federal Reserve Board index of production, the Bureau of Labor Statistics index of employment, the Commerce Department series covering business trends, and in profits.

Under the heading of security requirements we find expenditures ranging all the way from an intelligent regard for our continued prosperity, such as the Marshall Plan, to actions which might otherwise have been taken as expressions of a decent regard for our fellow men, such as the huge shipments of wheat to India in 1965 and 1966. Expenditures made under the Marshall Plan exercised a double multiplier effect, by creating demand domestically for capital goods to be shipped to recipient nations, and in the creation of markets for other goods and investments. Substantial amounts of private investment followed the flag, and ultimately took to posting the colors on its own initiative.

The amount and extent of expenditures on research, development and education made under the security mandate would indicate that what we have been watching is not only the decomposition of knowledge into information, but further, the transformation of information into intelligence; again, "information upon which a course of action may safely be based." In the decade 1950 to 1960 alone, public and private corporations were involved in the invention and production of Orlon, the H-bomb, the solar battery, Dacron, color TV, tranquilizers and psychic energizers, commercial computers, silicon, transistors, video tape, polio vaccine, crytron tube, turbo props, polyurethane foam, nuclear submarines, synthetic diamonds, stereophonic recording and playback, jet service, man-made satellites, ICBM's and around-the-world TV.

How much of this innovation is attributable to Government spending is a question that must remain irretrievably moot. The mayors of our largest cities when called upon by a Senate committee could not so much as extrapolate how much Federal money was at that time to be found in their municipal budgets. The more productive question, What would have been the rate and extent of innovation without Government money?, is a matter for no more than speculation. It appears to me unlikely, though, that there are many chief executives of major corporations in the nation who feel able to complain about Government spending without fear of being embarrassed by their own statements of earnings. This fact, in itself, contributes to a state of mind which tends to aggravate paranoia.

Chapter Twenty-Seven

THE INFORMATION EXPLOSION

The current pace of scientific advance gives increasing plausibility to claims of an ultimate capacity to describe and explain—at least in probabilistic terms—most of the phenomena of the real world. The frontiers of human knowledge rapidly recede in the face of the scientist's highly refined perceptions of reality and his careful study of cause and recurrence. The spectre of a world "with no external mysteries in human behavior, but only phenomena that have not yet been adequately observed" may be repelling; nevertheless, we appear to be approaching a "universe codified by statistical rules" in which "the truth is the closest statistical approximation to the observed occurrence of events."

—HAROLD L. KORN*

1.

EUGENE AYRES, writing in *Scientific American,* proposes that the place of automatic control in technology:

> . . . can be seen by considering the unhappy situation of Great Britain. One measure of a country's industrialization is

* The quotations are from Lerner, Introduction to *Evidence and Inference,* 11–13 (Lerner, ed., 1959).

> its capacity for consuming fuel. This capacity depends largely upon the quality of mechanization, which in turn depends upon automatic control. In fuel-consumption capacity Britain's industries have declined steadily, in relation to the rest of the world, ever since 1875. This has happened in spite of her abundant coal resources (until recently) and the fact that she has some of the world's best informed technologists. Her industrial leaders in the main have failed to understand the philosophy of automatic control. In the U.S., by contrast, the intense competition in cost, yield and quality had driven us steadily toward more and more automatization.

A wise Frenchwoman once said that we ought to take seriously what we do, but not our doing it. She had the advantage, however, of not having been programmed into an all-encompassing feedback system. Not all of the evidence that we *have* been is confined to the business and television pages, news stories about the cost of living and health of the economy, books like *On Thermonuclear War,* or the wheels of tape and consoles of flashing lights one sees in the mind's eye when approaching a bank teller or an airlines reservations counter. A look at the buildings and houses erected since 1947 are a further sign. The buildings, some of them, look as tentative in conception and construction as a child's Erector Set model. They are, in short, articulated forms of information.

Further indication is to be found in the quality of some of the products that come pouring out every year, the purposes to which we put film, tape and paper, the behavior of our young and our contemporaries toward the old, as well as evidences so much taken for granted as to be second nature—like the turnover in automobiles every two years, the rapid changes in fashions, and not only in women's dresses. How many new cigarette brand names hit the market in the thirties? How many new toys raged through the market? How many new drugs? How often did refrigerators and washing machines turn over? And so on.

For further demonstration, as well as for evidence of good analytical thinking, one may find on the sports pages of *The New York Times* these days advertisements like the following: "Corporate Management Information System Project Leader. . . . Responsibilities include the direction of a team to research the information needs of corporate and general management, for the purpose of planning and controlling business operations." Perhaps the most compelling evidence of all, though, occurred in the summer of 1966, when influential leaders in the business community, having watched stock prices plunge through several of the "floors" posited by one chart theory or another, importuned the President to *raise* taxes. Thus had Lord Keynes succeeded where George III failed.

It need not follow, though, as Ayres suggests, that in employing operations research and computer technology, a management need understand the philosophy underlying them. The point may be illustrated with the help of a case cited by Cyril C. Herrmann and John F. Magee in *Harvard Business Review*. It concerns a company carrying an inventory of a large number of finished items which had trouble maintaining sound and balanced stock levels:

> Despite careful attention and continued modification of reorder points in the light of experience, the stock of many individual items turned out to be either too high for sales or inadequate to meet demand. The problem was solved by a physical chemist who first collected data on the variables, such as size and frequency of order, length of production and delivery time, etc.; then set up an assumed system, which he tried out against extreme sale situations, continually changing its characteristics slightly until it met the necessary conditions—all on paper . . . and thus was able to determine a workable system without cost of installation and risk of possible failure.

The physical chemist has here performed an exercise in operations research. Edward C. Bursk and John P. Chapman, editor and executive editor of *Harvard Business Review*, explain in the introduction to the volume in which the exercise appears that "Operations research (popularly known as O.R.), when its methods are fully understood, helps a manager to single out the critical issues which require executive appraisal and analysis, and provides him with factual bases to support his executive judgment." "Fully understood" by whom? In the case in point, the company may have been said to have thought operationally, or in a word preferred by many of those concerned with such matters, analytically; but not necessarily the company's management.

Suppose now that, encouraged by this application of O.R., the management chooses to call in a management engineer to see if the same sort of thinking cannot be applied to production, marketing, use of personnel and all the other variables managers are paid to know how to vary. The consultant does his work, part of which is to recommend purchase of devices that will, among other things, give management a running account of the variables included in the physical chemist's "model" of the company's operations. These devices, arrayed under the heading of computer technology, will moreover make automatic corrections in routinely correctable variables. With these, the company may be said to be thinking analytically, while the understanding of the philosophy of automatic control may remain only in the heads of the chemist and the consultants.

2.

Ayres, in his comment concerning the British lag in adopting automatic control, may have had in mind an attribute endemic to industrial leaders which, though it appears to result from an understanding of the philosophy of automatic control, in reality answers to nothing more sophisticated than the double-entry ledger system. In the terms of this system, analytically speaking, any adjustment in the inventory of variables which causes operating revenues to rise, and operating expenditures to descend, ought to be encouraged. I can perhaps best illustrate, in keeping with the subject matter, with the help of a probabilistic fable.

I assume that most of us have been drawn, if only by the reading of a newspaper, into the occasional controversy surrounding publication of statistics on crime. It is alleged frequently that reporting techniques vary from one police department to the next, that domestic quarrels and family violence are lumped in with street muggings and so forth, so that the reckoning the consolidated figures give us of our environment is misleading. Philadelphia, for example, once underwent a 70 per cent jump in major crimes, but the "crime wave" was later shown to be the result of a new policy of reporting complaints.

We may easily suppose that a phenomenon of this proportion might catch the attention of a foundation—let's call it the Dusenberg Foundation—and that the foundation might, in consequence, underwrite an attempt to establish a new and more meaningful crime reporting index. The project would begin, of course, with the assignment of a group of sociologists to the task of finding out whether such an index is at all feasible. It might occur to the researchers to look for variations among city neighborhoods that would yield a reliable indication of relative crime-proneness. To this end, they might conceive it to be useful to look for variations in observance of "everyday law" such as violations of anti-littering ordinances, dog-licensing regulations, and stoplight violations.

Stoplight violations might prove to be an especially fruitful area for investigations. The information conveyed by a traffic light is "intelligence," "information" as defined in a Navy manual, "upon which a course of action may safely be based" only if we assume that the significance of the various colors is accepted as if it were common knowledge in the community, and is consistently acted upon. However, let us assume that the research team discovers statistically significant variations among a group of neighborhoods under study over a short period of time. For working purposes, the researchers wish to extrapolate this data to form the basis for a national test.

In order to test for crime-proneness on a national scale they cast about and then determine on an index relating incidence of stoplight violations to mean income, church attendance, car ownership per capita and age distribution. For convenience, the team labels this "raw index" the LSD, the Light-Signal Denial, Index. Before going on to test the validity of the LSD, they calculate that it would do no harm to turn the results of their preliminary researchers over to the National Association of Public Security comprising all the police chiefs in the nation, in order to get the association's thinking about the project.

It happens that the Public Information Officer for NAPS has after many years convinced its officers of the necessity to keep him informed. And like many persons in his position, he seldom has the opportunity to give the reporters with whom he deals a good story, and at the same time to perform a public service. He therefore visits the wire services and newspapers, giving each a Xeroxed copy of the report, together with a summary.

He knows the report won't be read, but it gives heft to the authority of the summary, and confidence to a reporter writing under deadline pressure. The editors are glad to see him, because they know at least what he is up to. The more operations-minded this nation becomes, and the more ingenious become those who make their living relating other people and objects to the public, the harder it becomes for a newspaper editor to discern where the propaganda net leaves off, and where it is hooked in. How is he to know that the sincere-looking visitor who wants to tell the story of the National Hangnail Foundation's fight to reduce the nine billion man-hours lost annually to hangnails in reality works for the Nail-Clipper Manufacturers of America, which is in turn controlled by General Grooming, Inc.?

Every newspaper in the nation wishes, of course, to compare its own LSD with that of other cities, and most are gratified to learn that the highest, or most hazardous, LSD's are to be found in New York City. Within a week, hundreds of newspaper editorials will have deplored one of two things, either the moral decay that is undermining the spiritual values of our nation, or the moral bankruptcy that permits the nation to tolerate conditions such as are to be found in the high LSD neighborhoods.

After some inter-agency squabbling in Washington, it is agreed that the Department of Urban Affairs should contract with the study group to provide a model for compilation and reporting of LSD figures, and to issue an LSD index monthly. After this is done, a leading oil company, as a public service, offers Xeroxed copies to customers who ask for them. Large trucking companies, having inventoried their accident rate, ask for copies to be delivered regularly to their Traffic Flow Control Departments.

The LSD computation comes eventually to show up in insurance charges against automobile owners in high LSD neighborhoods, as well as truckers who regularly make deliveries in these neighborhoods. These are reflected in higher charges for deliveries to the neighborhoods, and then again in prices. At each stage, of course, there is a little extra for sales and enforcement, or as in the case of the store-owners paying the higher delivery fees, a pittance in anticipation of the prices at wholesale he has been led to expect as a result of the "LSD Scandal" through his reading of the *Merchant's Digest Newsletter*.

At this juncture, one of the major publishing companies, a sizable factor in "the knowledge industry," decides to issue a combined LSD and POT (Pilferage Out of Trucks) Index and to sell it, along with some feature material, as a weekly newsletter, *Inside Trucking*. The day that the first issue is mailed, *This Is It!*, "the magazine for people who care," carries under signature of a member of the original LSD team, an "as told to" story about the LSD hoax. The research team, on going back for the second phase of its study, had discovered, it appears, that LSD variations were attributable almost entirely to the random incidence of oscillatory myopia, a hitherto unrecognized phenomenon whereby some persons are seized by brief flashes of nearsightedness. Nearly everyone afflicted with this disturbance had, however, been inclined to shrug it off, attributing the seizures to advancing age, weather conditions, the egg rolls they ate, or the liverishness persisting from the night before.

As a result, ophthalmologists had not had enough cases called to their attention to have collected data on its incidence. The Dusenberg Foundation sample had been taken over a period of time so short as to be useless for obtaining a notion of the distribution of this phenomenon. It was discovered only because an optometrist having received a number of complaints about his work had mentioned it to a prescribing physician. After the exposé appears, the executive secretary of the Trucker's association chooses as his topic for an address to warehouse operators, "The Information Explosion."

Now the problem is this. Let us say you are the chairman of the executive committee of a large manufacturer of either electrical equipment and appliances, or of optical components and accessories. In checking with your advanced systems engineering division, in the former case, you discover that the cerise SAF-T-LITE you have been selling to NASA for use as a night lamp on the moon has been discovered also to penetrate to a nearsighted person with unvarying consistency. Tests made upon a dozen persons afflicted with oscillatory myopia show conclusively that they receive the same signal during a seizure as when their eyesight is normal.

At the optical company, you learn that the TRANQUILLENS developed under a Government contract as defractor eyepieces for defense against laser beams, which were thought to be useless for other purposes, turn out otherwise. They are able to convert light energy within a certain wattage range, which includes the range of all wattages employed in every stoplight manufactured, into a beam that exhibits the same characteristics as the SAF-T-LITE. Naturally, your inquiries in either case are made under high-priority security conditions; this for several reasons, including the possibility that a competitor might have missed the magazine exposé.

You make an inquiry as to how many stoplights there are in the country. No one, as it happens, knows, except everyone knows there is one hell of a lot. All of them are bought and maintained by public bodies, i.e., a market with ready cash and, relative to penetration of a consumer market, low sales cost. Of course, once the security wraps are off, airlines will want to inquire about your product, auto manufacturers might even be willing to pay a little extra over the cost of this year's tail lights in order to get safety mileage out of it.

3.

The first question is this: Assuming the price of the TRANQUILLENS and the SAF-T-LITE to be the same, does it make a difference which one gains the market? Second, assuming that whichever one you make costs more than the other, should you give up the market? If your answer to the first is "no" and to the second "yes" you should stick to whatever you're doing for a living, but at all costs avoid seeking a career in business. If your answers are the reverse of those, you may be coming down with the same *malaise* that Drucker perceived in some corporations. It is a disorder long familiar to students of the Federal Government. There, it exhibits itself in the raillery and mock scandal to be found in old copies of the *Congressional Record*. On pages referred to in the index under headings having to do with foreign aid or defense and space appropriations, one may find members of the Congress amusing their colleagues with stories of waste and extravagance and discoveries of allocations for studies of such exotica as the mating habits of rare insects.

As another symptom of the same disorder, an Administration official has told me of the impossibility of trying to get a particular executive department to support the promise a cabinet member had made to a committee of Congress that his department would stop certain investigative practices. "The men who really run that department have been there most of their working lives. Cabinet Secretaries come and Cabinet Secretaries go. When the men down the line receive an order, they figure 'What does he know?' and they get the word around that the heat is on—for a while. And then they go back to doing what they were doing."

These are symptoms of "dissociation." The pertinent part of the definition in *Webster's New World Dictionary* is: "the process in which a group of mental activities breaks away from the main stream of consciousness and functions as a separate unit." When found in any governing body of a public or private corporation, it is almost always an indication of imperfect feedback.

Chapter Twenty-Eight

FEEDBACK

It had long been recognized that the corporation, an artificial entity, had some human or at least anthropoid characteristics, in addition to paying taxes unwillingly. In 1827 an English lawyer, Howel Walsh, conceded this entity a body and a head, "a throat to swallow the rights of the community, and a stomach to digest them!" But, he asked at the Tralee Assize, "whoever yet discovered in the anatomy of any corporation, either bowels, or a heart?"

—Irving Brant

1.

Let us imagine that someone popped a contraband potion into our morning coffee, and we are wafted off to the headquarters of the National Broadcasting System. Here we find Dr. Robert Paleoff with A. R. Nielsen on his carpet. "Nielsen," he is saying, "it occurs to me that we are in the position of a mining company that pays the miners, but gets the raw material free. I want the persons whom you interview from now on to get fair value for the information they give you. And forget everything you've learned about wheedling answers out of people." If the company's clients didn't put it out of business, it would be because someone else got the president to quit before news of his aberration became common knowledge.

Now Paleoff calls in his own staff. "Gentlemen," he begins—in the movies and hence in dreams, all pronouncements of this sort begin with a portentous "Gentlemen"—"Mr. Justice Brandeis once said, 'The general rule of law is, that the noblest of human productions—knowledge, truths ascertained, conceptions, and ideas—become, after voluntary communication to others, free as the air to common use.' It appears to me that we have gotten into the habit of treating these noblest of productions as if they were slugs for a vending machine. This is a hell of a way for a man or corporation to spend his life.

"From now on, I want you fellows when you conceive of a program to think of our purpose as this: To find out and to make as clear as we can what men would do if they knew what they were doing. This may involve a salary cut of say eighty to ninety per cent, but you'll be pleased to know, it's across the board." These instructions are, of course, leaked by a situation comedy producer to the newspapers. The lead editorial in the following morning's *New York Daily News,* which hits the street early the same evening but just after the announcement of Paleoff's retirement, starts out, "Who the hell does Paleoff think he is, trying to tell us . . . etc."

The value of the thermostatic job which remains after these kinds of occurrences are ruled out is a trifle hard to explain. Thus, during the 1950's, the apostles of professional management had some trouble articulating why it is we should take seriously what *they* do. In addition to not being the corporation's owner, the management does not customarily create the innovations the corporation makes either of substance or in marketing tactics. The advanced systems division creates the goods, and an advertising agency opens a place for it in our environment. At about the time the New York Stock Exchange began to extol the virtues of "people's capitalism" it became fashionable among the philosophers of management to define "professional management" as "getting things done through people" and its value to the community as the adjudication of the conflicting claims made on the goods of this world by stockholders, worker and consumer.

The catechism had scarcely caught on before it began to puff and wheeze under the weight of common experience. What's more, "getting things done through people" offends the democratic sensibilities of persons through whom things are getting done. No one likes to be manipulated, least of all those who are. And the "balance of interests" doctrine isn't of much use anyway in highly cyclical industries where production cutbacks always leave a reminder of which of the three groups, stockholders, worker and consumer, goes over the side first when the boat begins to leak.

2.

There is no doubt, however, that managers take seriously their doing whatever it is they do, and that they also take seriously the judgment of the owners of the corporations they run. That isn't quite the same, though, as taking seriously what the corporation does. For the observations Lord Keynes made in 1935 are even more appropriate today to the stock market than they were then. In order to judge how seriously the owners take what the corporation does, one need only listen to a "story" being related by an analyst for a brokerage house to a large customer. We should also be asked to believe that these owners can take seriously at one time more events and considerations than seems humanly possible.

Consider for a moment the number and kinds of events, political, theological, sociological, psychological, chemical, that would enter into an investment decision concerning such events as the introduction of birth control pills, the Public Health Service Report on smoking and cancer, Medicare and aid to education programs; or, for that matter, to the growth of publicly owned companies that provide private investigators, electronic alarm devices, polygraph tests, personnel investigators, uniformed security details and the like. In truth, no one is expected to take all of these matters seriously; indeed, it might prove fatal to try.

For the test of a story is its salability. Keynes likened investing in the stock market to the activity of judging a beauty contest. The idea, he said, was not to choose the most beautiful girl, but one the other judges would think to be most beautiful. "We have reached the third degree where we devote our intelligence to anticipating what average opinion expects the average opinion to be." Many investors rely on charts, which are highly probabilistic models showing investor behavior in respect to certain stocks. They do not, of course, indicate anything about the so-called "fundamentals" underlying these stocks.

It is precisely because there are so many elements in a stock's performance that the fundamentals, the information contained in balance sheets, had to be separated out for independent description, part of the necessary exposition in the story. In recent years, the most salable stories derived from a "concept," like the agricultural concept. This concept flourished when it became apparent that the Federal Government was beginning to regard as vital and feasible the feeding and agricultural development of the hungry nations of the world. The concept suggested several possibilities among sulphur and potash producers, farm equipment manufacturers, railroads, shipping and others.

In general the best concepts are those which represent the most ingenuity, such as a concept under which the buyer obtains "leverage" and "participation" in the "farm concept" through an investment in West Virginia Turnpike Bonds. Everyone has from time to time heard of the "ground floor" concept. In a highly speculative bull market, where goodly amounts of money can be made trading in well-known securities, the ground floor concept is more likely to have to do with innovations under development or being introduced by existing companies than with new companies.

This inclination recognizes the fact that innovations are more likely to come from the research facilities of IBM or Xerox, say, than from small companies, and that in any event the cost of introducing and gaining acceptance for new products, and gaining a market, is beyond the means of most small operators.

The judgment of a company's future performance, in sum, involves consideration of a great many events, some "real" and some "pseudo." Managements of publicly owned companies are well aware of this. They are judged to a great extent by their own stockholders according to the performance of their companies in the stock market, and that performance may be important to the availability and cost of capital they may need from time to time. They must necessarily, therefore, think to a great extent in much the same terms by which their performance will be judged.

Among most of those who own corporations on any given day, the key word is "performance." It may be argued that in order to implant a trademark in the public mind, and to perform well, a corporation must also provide a needed service or product. That is true, but "good" and "needed" are not necessarily interchangeable, nor does the need always exist before the product. It makes a considerable difference whether one defines good and needed as in the eye of the maker, or in terms of feedback. It often makes a difference, too, in the amount of sleep an executive gets.

3.

An intimation at least of the philosophy of automatic control is critical to a performance-oriented, as they say, company. It is vital to any hope of profitable conversation with customers of the size of the Department of Defense and the National Aeronautics and Space Agency. It also helps toward an understanding of the Securities and Exchange Commission's efforts to adjust to the world of information feedback. On May 24, 1966, members of the Commission met with members of the Financial Analysts Conference to discuss inside information as it pertains to SEC disclosure regulations. A privately circulated memorandum records what happened:

> Insider information is now clearly defined to be that which is used for internal corporate purposes, as opposed to that usually given out to the public to allow general investment judgments to be made. Tests as to whether information is inside information are: whether the information would likely have an impact on the market price of the securities, whether it is of a specific nature such as a dividend increase, acquisition of assets or an ore discovery as opposed to the background and statistical type of information that a securities analyst generally gets, whether the information in question is used by the analysts for their own end, and whether the information in question would have real impact on the judgment of a prudent investor.

Note that the definition has to do entirely with the consequences of information, its impact and uses, and does not attempt to classify insider information as opposed to outsider information in terms of kinds of information. It is, in short, a good analytical statement. Of course, every securities analyst wishes to avoid having to pay damages as a result of trading on inside information. However, try to conceive of some unpublished information gathered from a company in which he then chooses to invest, which would also not have impact on the judgment of a prudent investor.

Knowledge of analytical methods may come in handy to a performance-oriented company, like knowledge of how to make a fire with two sticks. In the absence of skilled workers and machines, a soft drink bottler in Venezuela, for instance, got a line on his competitor's share of the market by paying rubbish collectors piece rates for the discarded bottle caps they brought in, together with a report on where they were collected. From observation of success in such modest uses, a company may be encouraged to go on to others. For example, the Sentry Life Insurance Company attempted, and at last report succeeded, in singling out high-risk young drivers by administering a "temper test" or "attitude" examination. In return for taking the test, those who passed obtained a 15 per cent discount. At this point, however, dissociation begins to set in, and it is apparent in the way some corporations treat their employees. In the course of setting up the books, as it were, operations research may reveal overlooked assets, like the 1,000 shares of Haloid Corp. stock grandfather piled with some papers in the attic; it may also expose huge losses in inventory, the number of man-hours lost through alcoholism, now-and-then coffee breaks and Asian flu, a costly rate of credit delinquencies, a frightening ratio of "noise" to "signal" in communications between management, purchasing and marketing, or almost anything.

Much of the same information might be turned up by an old-fashioned efficiency expert, but not in quite the same way. The information obtained in operations research is customarily presented in the form of ratios: inventory losses expressed in terms of sales volume, credit delinquencies to accounts receivable, losses in man-hours, and the like. These ratios may be expressed in turn in ways that indicate a course of action not available to common sense: perhaps that free flu shots, free coffee and buns at a stipulated hour, and rehabilitation for alcoholics may be more effective and point to better performance than disciplinary rules and firings.

The results of analysis might at the same time indicate the need for a better credit and personnel inventory, hence the need for the Minnesota Multiphasic Psychological Personality Inventory and for the services of men like Norman Jaspan, security agent, to keep an eye on the stockroom, as well as perhaps on the coffee wagon man while he is doling out the free doughnuts. This process contributes in turn eventually to dissociation among men who value their privacy more highly than do most of those who are being watched.

I turn here to Professor William M. Beaney, professor of politics at Princeton University, as a witness and not because I believe he qualifies as a case in point:

> This is a society now in which everyone wants to ask more and more questions of everyone else and I am afraid that I am a member of an academic band, so-called social scientists, which has helped bring this about. That is in studying human behavior, if you are to get behind theory, you have to have some data, you want hard facts, and how you get those, is either by observing the way individuals and groups act, or you ask them questions to see what they can tell you about the way they act, and their motivation and so on.

Hear now the complaint of Leonard E. Schwartz, writing in the *American Behavioral Scientist:*

> Project Camelot . . . was one of the biggest social science research projects in modern times. Conducted by the Special Operations Research Office of the U.S. Army, its primary mission was to determine the potential for social revolution within a given country. . . . Project Camelot was proceeding well until June, 1965, when Ralph Dungan, American Ambassador to Chile, wired a cable to the State Department protesting strongly the type of questions being asked of prominent Chileans by researchers from SORO. This protest turned into a *cause célèbre* involving the State Department and the Department of Defense among others. . . . Many felt that the manner of suspension was certainly lacking in taste if not in judgment.

4.

Dissociation in a Cartesian environment contributes greatly to security consciousness. An executive who is not performance-oriented may not be at all disturbed over the $1.5 million suit filed by A. C. Nielsen Company against Rex Sparger. Sparger once made his living as an investigator for the House subcommittee that looked into the manner in which TV ratings are constructed and sold. Sparger conceded that while pursuing researches for a book, "How to Rig TV Ratings for Fun and Profit," he in some way got hold of a list of the homes Nielsen uses as its sample for gathering the information used in ratings that can determine who in show business or advertising works next year, and at what.

Woody Allen once ascribed his wealth to an uncle who, having invented the concept of the royalty, received a royalty on every royalty paid. The very fact that A. C. Nielsen believes a single use of its sampling list to be worth $1.5 million indicates that the French Academy of Science ought to put in a bid for royalties for past contributions to ratings methods made by former members. In all events, Sparger sent questionnaires to 58 homes (Nielsen's suit alleged) with $3 enclosed. The questionnaires asked those who received them to record their impressions of the commercials that punctuated "An Evening with Carol Channing" televised on February 18, 1966, over CBS.

For returning the questionnaire, the recipient was to receive an additional $5. Thus, it might have seemed in numerous board and conference rooms around New York that millions of people were watching Miss Channing instead of someone or something else. Mr. Sparger said he had also intended to give the Bob Hope Christmas Special a boost by calling up a Nielsen sampling with the news that someone they knew would appear on the show.

A *New York Times* reporter asked Arthur Nielsen, Jr., president of the firm, whether he planned to make changes in the sample. Mr. Nielsen said he didn't know. "We want to find out if Sparger really had 275 homes. We think we've got a good security system." As events developed later, it appeared that Miss Channing's husband paid $4,000 to Sparger for some research work. It had not been clearly established, though, whether there was any relation between that event and Sparger's research for his book, but the very prospect dampened hope for an unalloyed opinion from the courts as to how much Nielsen's principal asset is worth. The matter was settled with Sparger's agreement not to make further disparaging remarks about the Nielsen ratings.

Another matter about which a non-performance-oriented corporation does not have to scratch its head is how much it *doesn't* know beyond what it can find out in the customary course of business. The assertion "We don't yet know enough" from psychologists and educators sometimes infuriates parents seeking guidance. This is of course because their children are programmed into a real-time sequence, so that events which occur to them at an early age become irrevocably a part of the event known as their child. Performance-oriented businessmen sometimes get intimations of the same kind of frustration in the course of making a market test.

First, the researcher has to select his test market. The *Wall Street Journal* says that General Foods

> . . . considers availability of mass media for advertising, overall stability of the economy, the ratio of food chain stores to independent outlets, geographical location and how closely the city approximates the national population mix in age, sex, income, family size, ethnic and religious groupings, education and so on. (Some cities come fairly close to duplicating the national mix; Syracuse, N.Y., and Columbus, Ohio, for example.)

Then there is the hazard that a test will be "jammed" by a competitor. This refers to the practice of rushing a competing new product into a test market with much hoopla, just as your competitor is introducing his.

"A Chicago food company executive," the *Journal* reports, "recalls that one coffee company put its premium grade coffee in a fancy canister, raised the price a few cents and tried it out in one large city. A rival firm promptly copied the canister design, filled it with its cheapest grade coffee, cut the price and put it out in the same city. The executive questions that any kind of reliable results could be obtained from testing under such conditions." Having allowed for that risk, the tester may learn at some expense how much what he doesn't know can hurt him. He may, for example, discover in the course of a $500,000 test that because of the high Mormon population, Salt Lake is no place to test a new brand of coffee.

Or he may discover, as Chock Full O'Nuts Corporation did, that frozen doughnuts may be a hit in a test in 100 supermarkets but when allowed to thaw slightly, as they will in nationwide distribution, they don't taste the same. A successfully tested cookie when put out to low-volume delicatessens exhibited an unexpected trait. After sitting on a shelf for a while the cookies tasted like soap. Or it may be that the research model did not have enough information in it. "A specialty soap," the *Journal* records, "successfully tested, flopped in the national market after the manufacturer built a plant especially to produce it; the loss ran into millions of dollars."

5.

The contribution made by dissociative security consciousness to defective feedback may be illustrated by the controversy surrounding the "freedom of information" bill signed in 1966 by President Johnson. The bill purports to make more information available from the Executive Branch. The President noted in signing the bill that a "free flow of information is essential to a democratic society."

If one wishes to know the effect of such a measure, though, the man to talk to is not the man who signs it but the men who led the support of the bill, and those who have the most to lose by its passage. A principal supporter of this bill was Kenneth David, professor of law at the University of Chicago. He said: "Government men will find new excuses for withholding information under terms of this bill at least until they get judicial interpretations to the contrary." He thought it a "monstrosity of draftsmanship" and urged that it be vetoed and the job begun again.

In this connection, as in many others, it is worth quoting at some length from the pages of the *Wall Street Journal:*

> In their crusade for "the people's right to know," however, journalistic organizations have been handicapped by a surprisingly widespread acceptance of Government secrecy. There has never been any quarrel, of course, about the wraps that surround the Pentagon's war plans or the Central Intelligence Agency's personnel roster or the Internal Revenue Service's individual income tax returns. But Congress has received a whole series of demands that various information about individuals and businesses be kept locked up, lest citizens be embarrassed or competitors discover each other's secrets. The escape clauses in the "freedom of information" bill have resulted.
>
> Among those alarmed by the bill's original language was the Western Oil and Gas association. Its producer members feared that snooping lease brokers would be able to see their oil well data filed with Federal agencies. So the bill's drafters obligingly inserted loophole No. 9, permitting Federal secrecy about "geological and geophysical information and data (including maps) concerning wells."
>
> The U.S. Chamber of Commerce testified vigorously in favor of the information bill. But later it sent Congress a second-thoughts letter on behalf of the Association of American Railroads, concerning accident reports that railroads must file with the Interstate Commerce Commission. Railroads don't want "unconscionable" lawyers searching these now-secret files for names of injured people who might be persuaded to sue, the letter said. While lawmakers authorized no specific secrecy for these files, the ICC might be able to invoke loophole No. 7, which protects "investigatory files compiled for law enforcement purposes."
>
> Also trapped by the disclosure vs. secrecy dilemma was the National Association of Broadcasters. The NAB loyally joined other news media in urging Congress to pull down "barriers to a free flow of information from Government to the American people." But it also asked for continued secrecy of data filed by broadcasters with the Federal Communications Commission. The bill covers this point in loophole No. 4, protecting "trade

> secrets and commercial or financial information obtained from any person. . . ."

And so on through a roster of reasons why some part of the information can't be made available. A Justice Department official seemed to express the relief of functionaries in executive agencies: "I suppose very little in the way of additional disclosure would result from this bill."

6.

There has never been a time when the patent office has not been overworked to the point of causing a delay, uncomfortable to inventors, between the time an application is filed and the time the application is ruled upon. During this period, applications together with sketches and descriptions or innovations were, until September, 1965, available to examination by the public. Apart from giving competitors an opportunity to see what was coming, this practice also permitted a corporation to gather the names of innovators employed by other corporations.

It was perhaps inevitable, therefore, that the patent office should have closed its files of applications, as it was that a publishing company should have within a few months thereafter announced to the trade an encyclopedia of all patent assignments in the file within a few weeks of the time it was closed, at $90 per volume; and, of course, that a Japanese company should have put in an order for 31 copies, sight unseen. *The New York Times* records that:

> The text is arranged alphabetically by company, from ACF Industries, Inc., to Zenith Radio Corporation. Under each company heading the inventor's name appears alphabetically. As there are often two or more inventors to an application, they are listed separately. The number of assignments ranges from one for Allied Research Associates to 3,150 for the General Electric Company.
>
> In the back is an alphabetical list of inventors, with the company to which each has assigned patents.

If I were to learn that a set of the galley proofs was not available in the elephantine information retrieval system kept in Moscow, or wherever in Russia it is kept, I should be as alarmed as Sherlock Holmes was to learn that the hound hadn't barked in *Silver Blaze.*

7.

That information has value has always been apparent, but not in the same way as it is apparent in an information feedback system. Inevitably, movie and television producers have been more aware of the value of information conceived in this way than are most others. That is why they pay Samuel W. Tannenbaum, the surviving partner of Johnson and Tannenbaum, $50 to $100 to go through his stock of nine to ten million index cards. Over the years, he has watched for and recorded every traceable mention in print of titles of books, plays, television shows, movies and radio broadcasts. The value of this cache may be estimated from a remark attributed by the *Wall Street Journal* to a movie executive: "You tell me the title and I'll tell you how much it will gross." WSJ quotes James Nicholson, president of American International Pictures, as estimating that a title determines as much as 70 per cent of a movie's gross.

"This being the case, the movie and TV companies make every effort to insure that no one steals their titles, and that the titles they choose haven't been inadvertently stolen from someone else, which would make them vulnerable to lawsuits. As a result, title searching has become a thriving business." Indeed, at one network checking and keeping abreast of titles cost $60,000 per year. Since the network only began to maintain its own title clipping and filing system in recent years, it will never be entirely free of dependence upon Mr. Tannenbaum's services.

Lessons like this are seldom lost on large corporations. From *Automatic Data Processing Newsletter* came news in May, 1966, that IBM has entered a new business: the sale of computer-prepared market research reports to U.S. industry. The reports will be compiled automatically from two electronic data banks through a technique IBM calls "information sharing." Information sharing sounds like the neighborly thing to do, except that each of the "custom market profiles" IBM undertook to sell are priced from roughly $3,500 to $10,000. The value that inheres in this information lies of course in what IBM has done to convert it from "raw data" into a salable product. What, then, is the means of production?

When Sam Slater set up his mill he was inclined, naturally, to look upon the mill as his means of production. Similarly, when "pushing men," as Capt. Gerner put it, purchased the rights to inventions, they supposed the machine or product described in the patent papers to be a form of capital, as it indeed was. Moreover, a single invention with routine improvements over the years might have earned enough to care for its owner, his heirs, and their heirs, giving them further opportunity to branch out. That might still be true of an invention here and there.

Until fairly recently, it might have taken a good deal more than theorizing to have persuaded a businessman that a substantial investment in heavy machinery and an existing product can be undone, willy-nilly, and before he can do anything to stop it, by an idea that may have popped into the head of someone tossing in his sleep. It was too much for him to believe that a psychologist's report, or a designer's doodlings, or a pile of notebooks in a laboratory, or a set of statistics drawn up by a company he never heard of might cost him a substantial share of his market. He remained committed, in short, to a narrow range of information, largely confined to facts about his plant, his product and what he knew of existing markets.

But when innovations occur of the variety and at the rate they occurred during the 1950's and 1960's, he will have begun to recognize a phenomenon that happened to farmers, perhaps, before it did to manufacturers. Farmers have had long experience, going back at least to the thirties, in looking upon the informing capacity of human intelligence as the means of production. An agricultural economist, Professor Theodore Schultz of the University of Chicago, points to the implications of that fact:

> Although it is obvious that people acquire useful skills and knowledge, it is not obvious that these skills and knowledge are a form of capital, that this capital is in substantial part a product of deliberate investment, that it has grown in Western societies at a much faster rate than conventional (non-human) capital, and that its growth may well be the most distinctive feature of the economic system.
>
> . . . It has been widely observed that increases in national output have been large, compared with the increases of land, man-hours, and physical reproducible capital. Investment in human capital is probably the major explanation for this difference.
>
> *Much of what we call consumption constitutes investment in human capital* [italics mine]. Direct expenditures on education, health and internal migration to take advantage of better job opportunities are clear examples. . . .
>
> Laborers have become capitalists not from a diffusion of the

> ownership of corporation stocks, as folklore would have it, but from the acquisition of knowledge and skill that have economic value.

Having recognized that piece of intelligence, we may find it easier to look upon some products as events—articulated forms of information—and to adopt the Cartesian habit of thought, at least to the extent of agreeing that if an event makes real money, it's real. A comptroller of a corporation is helped along to this view of the world upon discovering that his corporation has spent more in any given year on advertising and promotion plus research and development than the company would get were it to sell all the real estate, plant and equipment it owned.

All the same, Peter Drucker, who knows about these matters, observed during a lecture at Stanford University that while managers had more facts at their fingertips than ever, they still lacked effective controls over "the constant drift toward the irrelevant and unproductive" in human organization. He noted the "gross abuse" of computers as "a tool for grinding out huge quantities of totally meaningless data" and added that the mere fact "that we can quantify something is no reason for measuring it."

Drucker's experience indicated that:

> . . . ninety per cent of the volume of a business is usually represented by two to five per cent of its products . . . practically all the innovations in a research laboratory, no matter how large, come out of the work of a very small percentage of the research people. And invariably 80 per cent of a company's distributors move, at best, 20 per cent of its output, while 10 per cent or fewer of the distributors move two-thirds to three-quarters of total sales.
>
> This, unfortunately, very few managers know. The traditional information systems, especially accounting, conceal rather than highlight this fact. . . . [For this reason] managers are inclined to allocate their time and energy according to the sheer number of decisions reaching their desks—not by their importance. . . . We tend—as people with a new tool kit always do—to go to work where it is easy . . . a new approach, a new technology, a new set of tools should always be put to work on the difficult, rather than the easy, on the things the old tools could not do at all rather than on the

> things they did passably well. It should give new power rather than be frittered away in improvements.

Corporations, public and private, hoard information and innovation as if it were gold, not only from innovators, but also from ordinary citizens, then render what they can as coin, and keep the change. It is in their nature. This habit points, though, to a question which nagged several of the Congressmen who were attempting in the 89th session to draft new patent and copyright legislation, but who are not yet themselves quite attuned to information feedback thinking. The question is why anyone who is not among a corporation's population of stockholders and employees should take seriously its doing something, as opposed to someone else's doing it. This is at bottom the question being asked by critics of the Federal Government's policy toward patents on inventions created by Government expenditure.

Chapter Twenty-Nine

"THE GOVERNMENT IS NO GENTLEMAN"

Never give a sucker an even break, and never smarten up a chump.

—W. C. Fields

1.

The Federal Government in fiscal 1966 spent under contract to corporations and other institutions all but about $3.5 billion of some $15.5 billion in Federal expenditures for research and development. There is no longer much question of the relation between the individuals who team up to do the actual inventing toward which these public funds are directed, and the corporate persons of which they are, as it were, the employed substance. By exercise of shoprights and by adoption of employment contracts, private corporations have assured themselves the benefits, as if to private property, of the inventions created with Government money but on their premises.

What's more, in 1952 Congress added to the "new and useful" test a third test. It is that the invention also must not be "obvious . . . to a person having ordinary skill in the art." Lawyers have argued that the Congress meant to make even slight improvements patentable if the improvement isn't obvious. They propose that an improvement can be said to be not obvious if a competitor copies it, if it meets commercial acceptance, or if persons skilled in the art testify that it filled a long-felt need they had not been able to satisfy.

The Supreme Court, however, said the invention still had to be proved substantially new and different. For instance, Graham Plow, Inc., secured a patent for a device that absorbed shock and reduced the hazard of damage to farm plows in rocky soil. Deere & Co. copied it, asserting that it was an obvious improvement. Lawyers for Graham took the position that it was obviously not obvious by the mere fact that Deere copied the improvement. But the Supreme Court, affirming a lower court, said the device "presents no operative mechanical distinctions, much less nonobvious differences."

The *Wall Street Journal* reported:

> A restrictive approach in the granting of new patents generally favors large corporations, according to some patent-law experts. Typically, large companies with extensive research facilities produce innovations substantially different in structure from products already on the market. On the other hand, individual inventors and small companies frequently come up with innovations that are little different structurally from already patented items, although some produce markedly different results.

What then of the relation between Government as the source of capital, and the private persons, the corporations, which it employs to make inventions? Should private contractors be made to stand in the same relation to the Government as John Moses Browning to the Winchester Arms Co.? Ought, that is, as Senator Russell Long of Louisiana has proposed, "all information uses, processes, patents and developments [obtained through public expenditures] be freely available to the general public"?

The answer would not appear to be as clearcut as it may seem, one way or the other. Suppose that a woman retains a dress designer. She does not expect to receive payment for the future revenues made possible by the experience the dress designer obtains while making her dresses. Suppose that in making the dresses, the dress designer gets some notions that enter into other dresses she makes. Or suppose she sells basically the same design to a large garment maker. Should the original customer be thought of as the owner to the rights? Is she entitled to royalties?

Suppose that the dress designer employs workers in her shop. Singly or together they create the design to meet the demands of the customer. What is their relation to the design and any money it may earn? As difficult as these questions are, in a way, they become even more difficult when we add to the list of considerations the question of what is the most "socially desirable" policy, apart from the socially desirable end of doing justice.

2.

It appears that, unlike Browning, corporations who are not assured in advance that they will retain rights to their inventions balk at reporting more about what they have discovered through using their patron's funds than they are compelled by their agreement to reveal. Team research is likely to "throw off" proprietary information that has commercial value outside the requirements which prompted the Government contract. Corporations are naturally reluctant to part with this incidental intelligence by overdivulging themselves to Government scientists. This feeling is enlivened by the fact that in regard to proprietary information, the Government is no gentleman.

The Pentagon is not itself the most security-worthy customer with whom a contractor has to deal: first, because the Government may not be prevented from infringing a patent, and second, because a Government contractor may not be sued for damages or royalties for manufacturing a patented item for the Government. The suit has to be brought against the Government. A Government worker may be fined and sent to jail if he misappropriates a trade secret, but that doesn't do much for the firm that lost control over the use of the information. Raymond Harris, a lawyer in the Office of General Counsel of the National Aeronautics and Space Administration, explains a contractor's relationship with the Government this way:

> Suppose the Government buys an item of supply either in the open market or by having the item developed. There is no requirement in the contract for the furnishing of drawings and none are furnished. The Government, after it obtains possession of the item, assigns an engineer and a draftsman to take it apart, measure it and test it, and to determine by analysis exactly how, and from what materials, it is made. The draftsman then prepares a complete set of drawings suitable for use in manufacturing the item, and these are attached, as the specifications, to an invitation for bids. The firm which either sold the item to, or manufactured the items for the Government, objects. Does it have any legal recourse? My answer is "No," assuming there are no patents covering the product.

And even if there were patents, the Government might hold itself liable for damages, but may not be stopped from infringements.

This process is known in Government circles as "reverse engineering." Harris says it is not extensively used, because it is too costly, too time-consuming and unreliable. "It is probably indulged in by industry to a much greater extent than it is in Government."

The keeper of the Government's conscience in these matters is the Comptroller General. He has the power to disapprove any payment made by a Government official which he considers to be contrary to law, and he uses that power, as Harris puts it, to make a "gentleman out of the Government." He used it to good effect in 1960 and 1961, when he held that, as Harris summarizes it,

> . . . where the Government had obtained technical data from the Gayston Corporation under conditions wherein the Government had agreed not to use the data without the consent of the Gayston Corporation and was further obligated to maintain the confidential character of the data, it could not issue an invitation for bids to the general public based on this data, but must procure the item disclosed from the Gayston Corporation. The Comptroller General required that the invitation for bids be cancelled.

Federal agencies are given wide leeway in deciding if a contracting corporation should be given assurance that it will enjoy the commercial rights to anything it may turn up while using Government funds, before or after the Government has had a chance to look at the invention. Policy differs from agency to agency, and in the case of the Commerce Department, within the Department itself. In an effort to formulate a consistent policy toward patents, President John F. Kennedy in 1963 issued a memorandum. A bill offered by Senator John McClellan of Arkansas drew its inspiration from the Kennedy memorandum. The bill was described by the *Congressional Quarterly* this way:

> Both the contractor and the Government would retain "irrevocable, nonexclusive, nontransferable, royalty-free license." The Government would take title at the time of contracting when the contract (1) was to "create, develop or improve products, processes or methods" intended for commercial use by the general public or required by the Government for such use (such as improved fertilizers, materials handling equipment for certain agricultural industries and civil defense equip-

> ment); (2) concerned the "public health, welfare or safety" (drugs, medical instruments, prosthetic devices, water desalination, air safety, weather modification and control); (3) was in a scientific or technological field in which there had been little work outside that supported by Government funds; (4) concerned services for operation of a federally owned research or production facility or for coordinating and directing the research of others. The contractor could take title or get an exclusive license, upon contracting, if (1) the agency head felt the public interest would be served or (2) the contract required the use of knowledge and skills in an area in which the contractor had acquired technical competence in a non-governmental position. But the agency head could recapture Government rights, if, upon seeing the invention, he felt it would be in the public interest to do so. The agency head could also require a contractor who had title to an invention or discovery to license others after showing that (1) the contractor had not brought the invention to practical application or (2) that such licensing would benefit the public.

However, to Senator Long, letting contractors have the rights amounts to handing over a monopoly, an unfair advantage for a company at Government expense and unjustified costs to the public when it goes to buy the finished product of service resulting from the discovery or invention. He has consistently urged a bill that would, except under certain conditions, give the United States "exclusive right and title" to inventions discovered in research under Government contract or lease, and also to inventions made by Government employees while doing official work or using Government facilities. The contracting agency might be permitted to waive these rights if the Federal Government's share were less than half the total spent on making the invention.

The debate was left unresolved, which is to say effectively in the direction of the Kennedy memorandum. While it was on it drew the heated expression characteristic of debate in which the participants are speaking as if in two separate worlds. After reading the eighth of a series of drafts attempted by the patent advisory council to interpret the Kennedy memorandum, Senator Lee Metcalf of Montana told the Senate that it had been "prepared by the representatives of special interests" in the Commerce Department and the Office of Science and

Chapter Thirty

BUGS

Them that asks no questions isn't told
a lie.
Watch the wall, my darling, while the
Gentlemen go by!
Five and twenty ponies
Trotting through the dark—
Brandy for the Parson,
'Baccy for the Clerk;
Laces for a lady, letters for a spy;
Watch the wall, my darling, while the
Gentlemen go by!

—*A Smuggler's Song*

1.

ALMOST ANYONE can think of a way to get on someone's premises to plant a bug. Two guises that are mentioned most frequently by security agents are the telephone man and the cleaning man. As a telephone man, the bug man carries along with him the equipment he is likely to need anyway. He stops at the building superintendent's office and says he's got to get in to make an adjustment on a telephone. Given the key, he goes out and has a copy made. This enables him to spend as much time in the apartment as he needs, and also to get back in to remove the bug. The cleaning-man guise is best brought off by actually getting a job with a company holding a cleaning contract for a number of office buildings. Most maintenance companies are usually looking for any able-bodied help they can get, and with no security problems to speak of themselves, don't usually ask many questions.

There are dissertations in state and Federal statute books and regulations that argue why one *should* not install an eavesdropping device. But not with great force. Congress appears indisposed to tidy up national policy on eavesdropping. This disturbs some in the legal profession who believe that, like "intercept" and "divulge," law and order are inseparable. Others appear to believe that a modicum of disorder makes the wiretap laws resemble a minefield of unexploded judicial interpretations, and thereby makes it sufficiently hazardous to discourage indiscriminate practice, especially by Government agents. Some thought has been given in the Senate to the possibility of licensing merchandisers of investigative accessories, or of requiring registration of purchasers. The idea has been dropped, though, as being ineffective as well as unenforceable. Bugs are made up from materials found commonly in hardware stores and in radio shops. Strewn about in a workshop, the components are no more sinister than lumber and nails.

State law is an even patchier work. Six states authorize wiretapping by police officers. Five of these require court authority. Thirty-three states prohibit wiretapping. Eleven have no laws. Twenty-four states follow the common law practice, rather than the Weeks rule, and permit wiretap evidence to be used in their courts, even though it may have been obtained illegally. In 1952, the United States Supreme Court held, in effect, that Section 605 of the Federal Communications Act does not presume by implication to bar the use of wiretap evidence in state courts. Meanwhile, like all laws and regulations that are hard to enforce and are meant principally to warn and to educate, those against eavesdropping and wiretapping add to the worries of the tempted amateur, but not to those of the professional. Recognizing as much, the State of New York has, since 1957, made it worth a private detective's license to so much as possess equipment that could be used as evidence of an intention to eavesdrop, or to hire the services of a professional eavesdropper. These provisions were added onto the New York State laws which made it a felony to actually use devices to listen in on a conversation into which the auditor has not been invited.

2.

The effect of this new prohibition has been to take bread out of the mouth of, among other members of the Association of Licensed Detectives of New York, George Perl, who does business as Advance Detective Agency at 30 Church Street in lower Manhattan. A visitor to Perl's office took note of the formidable recording hardware on his desk. Perl explained that he had hooked a direct connection from his telephone line into the recorder so as to be able to record reports from his agents in the field. He said he relied on the permissiveness of New York Telephone Company repairmen who have occasion from time to time to check Perl's wires for outside taps, or to make some modification in his wiring.

Other than that, he maintained, he has been, since 1961, unable to procure the services of eavesdroppers from whom he could once purchase information without jeopardizing his own license or standing in the community. "Four or five" licensed detectives, he said, continue to run the risk, but for the most part business that might involve eavesdropping has shifted into the hands of "unlicensed individuals." The law drove his former eavesdropping specialist, whom we could not trace down, into the business of making and selling equipment on a form of leaseback arrangement. Perl says the leaseback man charges $1,000 for equipment put together into a system to fit the specifications of a particular job; this on the understanding that he will buy the entire system back for $500 once it has served its purpose. As for Perl: "I wanted to bug a shipping room just to see what the shipping boss was saying to his clerks and to anybody else who was coming into the place, but I can't even do a simple thing like that."

Because of the 1961 law, Perl has lost, he claimed, twelve to fifteen retainers, which could mean as much as $50,000 in gross income. The income to the four or five licensed detectives who still engage in, or hire, eavesdropping has risen to become, he said, "astronomical"—which to Perl means $100,000 annually. We would have to assume, however, that the law has also driven up the price of a reliable drop, so that if the investigator subcontracts the work, the cost might run as high as one-half of the total fee for an assignment. The picture may not be as black, though, as Perl paints it. For while laws of this sort make scarcer and more valuable the services of a few, they do little to reassure the businessman who believes for some reason that he is being bugged, or ought to be.

3.

Thus, numerous licensed agencies have made a good business out of debugging. For as little as $125 a day, or as much as $2,000 for a complete job, the client may have his office gone over and decontaminated. Depending upon the client's means and the nature of his suspicions, the exterminator may give the office a once-over with instruments devised to sense a transmitter in the area, or he may use instruments together with sight inspection employing several helpers. To judge from the comments of a sampling of debuggers, it would appear that these inspections seldom turn up anything. Moreover, like the morning's Wassermann certificate to the day's second customer in a brothel, they also seldom leave the client free of his suspicions. Some order checks more regularly than they see their dentists. Debugging, therefore, produces a higher volume of business for the numerous experts willing to compete in the larger but safer company of technicians.

Robert Huerta, an ace debugger, says that from time to time he finds spent bugs—bugs in which the power supply has been exhausted—which means, of course, that he was called in too late to do much good. Huerta achieved some notoriety among debuggers when in January, 1965, he located a bug that had been planted in the Florida home of Lewis S. Rosenstiel, President of Schenley industries. The purpose of the bug was never established, although Mr. Rosenstiel had some strong suspicions.

"American business history," he told a Senate committee, "is replete with instances of legitimate corporations being plundered by corporate takeover artists to the detriment of shareholders and employees alike. In some instances this illegitimate attack on American business may be managed by a foreign raider under more favorable tax and antitrust laws than the raided American business."

In short, Rosenstiel appeared to believe that a corporation pirate was listening in on conversations he held with his business associates in connection with a tender offer Schenley was planning.

To order a debugging is not without some peril in itself. Few security agents are as cheeky to duly constituted enforcement agents as is Archie Goodwin, Nero Wolfe's helper. In real life licensed detectives like to make themselves as helpful as possible to the law, as if to put some goodwill in the bank against the day they might be found under the eaves themselves. A New York lawyer contends that debuggers, whether they find anything or not, "run to the Feds to tell them there's a guy who thinks somebody may be listening in on him."

Debugging requests frequently arise out of a construction the client has put upon the many stories he has read and heard concerning bugged martini olives and the like. From as much as an outsider can learn about the common practice in this line of work, the professional bugger varies his equipment according to the job, frequently trusting to the reliability of wires, well-powered and sometimes chunky equipment, including sizable microphones. He does not create, or pay much attention to, the fashions in gadgetry to which amateurs are attracted. He is inclined to look upon the promotion of the bugged martini olive and the martini olive jammer as gimmickry calculated to sell "investigative accessories," or to dramatize the eavesdropping phenomenon for narrow political motives.

It should be noted, though, that the courts have decided business corporations do not share in the personal traits invested in the FBI. If an employee of a private business taps a wire on orders from an official of the corporation, he may not divulge what he has learned to the official without running a serious risk with penalties called for by Section 605. A few states are even more hardened on this count. In California, which has always frowned heavily on all forms of eavesdropping, the president and foreman of a small plastic company, MC Corporation, were arrested on the allegation that the president had instructed the foreman to bug a competitor.

The charge, felonious conspiracy, specified that the foreman had placed a microphone in a window frame over the desk of the president of Bott's Line, Inc., which makes Botts Dotts, small plastic discs intended for use in dividing traffic lanes on California freeways. The president of Botts Line said that his company had been losing business on competitive bids. When a workman discovered the microphone while, it was reported, pulling up geraniums, Botts's men kept watch until, they said, they saw the foreman draw up with a truck containing a receiver. The lawyer for the arrested man said it was "sort of a counterespionage matter" but did not elaborate. The son of the Botts president said, "We thought Dad had lost his touch."

4.

We are thus left, as we often are, to conjure with a reflection of Walter Lippmann's, written many years ago:

> . . . the average American will condemn in an alderman what in his partner he would consider reason for opening a bottle of champagne. In literal truth the politician is attacked for displaying the morality of his constituents. You might, if you didn't understand the current revolution, consider that hypocrisy. It isn't; it is one of the hopeful signs of the age. For it

> means that unconsciously men regard some of the interests of life as too important for the intrusion of commercial ethics.

That, to be sure, was written at a time when central heating was still expensive, and security was something one obtained from a quilted blanket on a cold night.

Chapter Thirty-One

BROADS

And Joshua saved Rahab the harlot alive, and her father's household, and all that she had; and she dwelleth in Israel even unto this day; because she hid the messengers which Joshua sent to spy out Jericho.

—*Old Testament*

Cherchons la femme.

—ALEXANDRE DUMAS
Les Mohicans de Paris

1.

THE FRENCH might have been kinder to future history teachers as well as to their own reputation for gallantry had they permitted Margaretha Geertruida Zelle to live and write her own memoirs. We might have been deprived, though, of the legend that when she appeared to face her maker at the Caserne de Vincennes on October 18, 1917, she wore nothing but a fur coat which at the last moment she threw open to reveal herself to her executioners. What's more, generations of male adolescents would have been deprived of the secret fascination generated by the account of one who saw the "Eye of the Morning" dance. "To witness this spectacle," he wrote, "was to receive the impression that one had actually been present at the metamorphosis of a serpent taking a woman's form."

If the truth ever catches up with the wheezes about Mata Hari, we may credit the Nineteenth Amendment to the Constitution and books like *The Feminine Mystique.* For the wish to be treated as equals has brought out in many women qualities that make it hard for men of any age to put much stock in, or to be much intrigued by, legends of their capacity for perpetrating genuinely spine-shivering evil. Even so, I am as certain as I am that the Bank of England will rise tomorrow that if Carrie Nation incarnate had been sent to report on the activities in Vietnam, she would, within six hours of her first beat, have become the subject of flattering stories about how she got it. They would circulate among male journalists at the Caravel bar in Saigon, even if at the expense of some poor Viet Cong officer's reputation for devotion to the Seventh Commandment.

Of course, every private investigator heeds Virgil's warning—"Varium et mutabile semper Femina"—and thus never uses women as eavesdropping devices, so to speak. Not, that is, in the manner that Ralph Nader suspected girls were used in order to check on, as Agent Vincent Gillen put it, "his marital status, his women, boys, etc." Besides, not even the eleven states that have no wiretap laws look down with any lenient hope of reform on pimps or anyone who lives off the proceeds of prostitution. And even if they did, in order to reach where the action is, the girl bug might have to cross a state line, then leaving the investigator to contemplate in his own bed the penalty clauses of the Mann Act.

These facts may help to keep the use of women agents within the bounds of prudence, but they do little to reassure the genuinely security conscious. The testimony of the ages suggests that a woman employed in a temporary and casual affair invites treatment as a non-person; the shared intimacies of the night in Fort Wayne seem at the moment as if to be all part of a monologue. It isn't until later that the conventioneer starts to reflect on just what it is he did say, and to fret about it. He worries, too, about finding himself in the same situation again, and the anxiety only grows deeper following the next time he does. His anxieties are prey to, and part of, the tales which have sprung to credence concerning the use of women in industrial espionage.

Anyone may reconstruct these tales for himself. Take the standard repertoire, together with the several variations, of stories beginning with the farmer's daughter, ranging through all those that make the rounds among eighth-grade students and those told daily in whatever passes these days for a smoker. Make the protagonist a private investigator trying to make off with a plausible-sounding, but highly sophisticated, trade secret. With a little ingenuity, you, too, can let on that there is more going on in the world than meets the eye of the poor clod who pours his feelings out over a telephone. My favorite was represented to me as having been part of a genuine case that reached the courts, thereby protecting the source from the embarrassment of attribution.

The anonymous investigator in this tale had learned—using, of course, methods of his own—that a ravishing stewardess for a foreign airline was also the carrier during her frequent journeys to the United States of contraband chemical substances. The agent confronted her, so the story goes, with his information, thereby blackmailing her into agreeing to take part in a scheme involving the sort of "compromising situation" prevalent under New York State's pre-1966 divorce laws. The victim was to be a production executive who knew how to make something that the investigator's client firm did not. The staging and execution was a triumph of dramatic direction, and the event commemorated on a reel of tape. Upon being confronted with the evidence, the executive asked for time to think it over, and then asked if he might have a copy of the tape.

His request was granted. (The question "Why?" only furrowed the brow of my source.) As promised, the victim returned the tape along with another. The extra tape was of the conversation, containing many mirthful remarks, between the executive and his wife as he told her of the whole scheme in some detail, including an ungallant, comic-opera description of his night with the stewardess. This suggested to the investigator that he had better try another tack. He kept track of the executive's wife for a week, and discovered, *sacrebleu!*, that she was enjoying a dalliance with her husband's boss. She, upon being confronted with the evidence, exhibited the anger and distrust of the self-sacrificing wife betrayed. Her remarks were to the effect, "Yes, and the s.o.b."—meaning the boss—"still hasn't kept the promise of the deal that he made to Bertram two years ago."

Of course, Bertram paid the agent to find out who he was working for so that the two principals could make their own deal, which they did. As a result the consumer may now choose between two examples of the things Bertram knew how to make, and we are no longer at the end of a leash held by a monopolist. The moral, I suppose, is that if you want someone to sell out, quote your price before going to the expense of hiring a security agent.

We ought not, before going on to more substantial matters, neglect the unfaithful wife. In this vein, many of *Playboy's* Ribald Classics may serve as basic material. To Counter-Industrial Espionage Agent Harvey G. Wolfe, as reported in *The Nation*, goes the credit for this one. The owner of a large construction company came to Wolfe with a common problem. One of his competitors had been underbidding him with uncanny consistency. For two months, a top Wolfe agent checked out every suspect in the client's office. He gained knowledge of many things, but no clue as to who was leaking the client's bids to his competitor. So Wolfe wired the client's house for sound. You may take it from there. I hasten to say that I have no reason to doubt Wolfe's veracity, nor the means or inclination to visit every construction company headquartered in California in an effort to obtain more detail.

2.

Having dispensed with the lore, we may now consider some of the ways women *are* employed in security matters. The Sunday supplement *This Week* for February 6, 1966, gave an authentic-sounding account of an interview with a woman, identified only in a general way by her personal and physical qualities, who earned her keep by taking assignments to pose as a factory or office worker in order to gain the confidence of other employees, and thereby information to provide peace of mind to client managements. The report had a comfortingly chirpy sound to it, as if it might have been about a girl CIA agent posing as an airline stewardess in order to travel to exotic places, there to defend the American Way of Life.

Of the 1,800 private detectives licensed in New York State, only a smattering are women. Even so, every agency gets assignments that women can execute more easily and at less risk than men. The most obvious is suggested by the fact that in most corporations the only person to gain the presence of the No. 1 man more often than the No. 2 man is the No. 1 man's secretary. She types his letters and memoranda, monitors his calls, coming and going, frequently fills out his expense account and with practice can eavesdrop without seeming to. For precisely these reasons, a security agent might find it easier to plant a No. 2 man in an office than plant a secretary where he wants her. Security-minded executives, a phrase that has grown close to being a redundancy, select their secretaries with great care. Attempted bribery of an existing secretary carries a risk that is beyond calculation. Moreover, secretaries seldom resign and take other jobs, leaving their positions open, at precisely the times private investigators are trying to install a plant.

I have been led to suppose, however, that the most trusted secretaries may be sources of intelligence almost equal to that of a detective agency's plant. I once had occasion to telephone an executive of a large corporation in Pittsburgh. His secretary said, regretfully, that the man I was trying to reach had "stepped out of town." I have been told by competent authority that in all of its ambiguity, hers was the perfect response. More commonly, a secretary says, as if basking in reflected glamour, "I'm sorry, but he's in Paris." This sort of response can alert a competitor, or someone who is doing some thinking on behalf of a competitor, to hazards and opportunities he had not known existed. Why Paris? Is it a deal with "X"? Is he thinking of investments there? And so forth.

Common experience would indicate the perils that result from permitting a secretary to believe that she is paid to exercise feminine intuition, or whatever passes in her mind as her own discretion. Thus: The management of a corporation that sells information services thought to create a public market for its stock. The president of the company entered into negotiations with a brokerage firm that was to organize the underwriting of the issue.

The president set as his rock bottom selling price a figure that represented seventeen times the earnings per share it was estimated the company would show by the end of the year. As the negotiations pressed on, a partner in one of the brokerage houses that had been enlisted for the underwriting telephoned the company president's office at a time that he knew the president would not be in. He asked the secretary what she thought her boss' estimate might be of a firm in the same line of business that was already publicly owned. He was thinking of investing in it, he said, and wanted Mr. Worthmore's opinion for his own use. The secretary volunteered that she thought Mr. Worthmore would say that the company was worth no more than ten times earnings. "Good," the brokerage partner said, "In that case, when he comes in, will you ask him why the hell we should pay seventeen times earnings for his stock?"

3.

With all of the sordid stories making the rounds, it seems inconceivable that companies which lease out temporary secretarial help can make money. A possible consequence of hiring temporary help was brought home to an editor of a magazine. A reporter brought him a story which said that a well-known corporation was about to test-market a low-priced version of its leading product. The company, on seeing the item, complained to the advertising department of the magazine, which in turn complained to the editor. The corporation was not ready to announce the new line, principally because its directors were about to issue two shares of new stock for one of the old, and did not want to introduce extraneous matters liable to confuse investors or the Securities and Exchange Commission.

The story lead came to the editor's desk in this fashion: The reporter's wife had signed on with a temporary help agency, and was assigned to a motivations research firm. The firm was, in turn, preparing a presentation to the company's advertising agency in a bid for work connected with introduction of the product. The executive to whom the reporter's wife was assigned had meticulously written pertinent parts of the presentation in pencil and foolscap and given it to her to type, which she did. He, of course, had no further use for the handwritten composition, so she took it to her husband to ask if there might not be a story there. He thought there was, and so did the editor. Thus began and ended their careers in industrial espionage.

Women agents are most effective in offices, stores, shipping rooms and factories to investigate inventory losses and bookkeeping irregularities. The retailing business, especially, is notorious for competitive espionage, outright piracy of fashion designs and working methods, as well as for the size of its inventory shortages. A talented investigator can appear as if to be a slightly dowdy, put upon but cheerful working girl, who blushes ever so slightly upon being made privy to the gossip that permeates that world in which typists, filing clerks, bookkeepers and others among "service personnel" spend half of their waking hours. Where the turnover of workers is relatively high or includes a good deal of temporary help, a woman agent can take a backroom job, write her report, and slip out with no one except a culprit, or several, being any the wiser. Among the things she may learn is how buyers respond to management pressures to reduce inventory shortages.

4.

We owe to Richard Rosenthal of *Women's Wear Daily* a buyer's own description of this phenomenon. "Some efficiency expert or someone from Harvard Business School must have told the board chairman that the key to eternal bliss is a low shortage," the buyer explains. "I'm not saying it isn't important, but the way they're nudging us about shortages—well, sometimes it's like volume and markup hardly count." And so the buyer arranges to lower his shortage. By fiddling with the customary discount permitted for advertising, and a complicated system of remarking price tags and vouchers, he can manipulate to create the impression that he is reducing shortages. Among the other tricks he uses: "I found a source for some stuff I used to throw away, like damaged customer returns the vendors won't take. Let's say it's snagged hosiery or old shoes shoplifters leave on the floor. I don't buy that stuff so we'll use it as an example. Well, this guy who exports junk to Ghana or somewhere pays me cash. I mark the junk down to nothing for the record, and take the money upstairs and ring it up as a sale. That's kitty and it's honest."

The buyer gains nothing for himself. But the girls in the receiving room, whose cooperation the buyer requires in order to bring off the price tag manipulation, receive some "candy" once in a while from the buyer.

Similarly, the president of a fair-sized security agency relates how girls in the accounting department of a major supplier, as if for a favor, helped small retailers by shuffling billing dates in the file to give cash-short producers the money they needed to keep their creditors happy. To a security agent, this sort of manipulation is indistinguishable from theft. As Norman Jaspan, a security agent who conducts his business as a "management engineer," told the Retail Controllers Group of Maryland: "The need to know what is going on is highlighted by the findings of some of our management surveys. In more than 50 per cent of the cases, with no prior indication of dishonesty—inventory manipulation, falsification of records, kickbacks and other forms of dishonesty have been uncovered." He noted solemnly that "dishonesty is dangerous and can infect the bloodstream of an honest employee."

There are more employment opportunities for women in the security industry today than ever before. They are used to pose as door-to-door salesladies in order to check on workers who have called in sick. Expense account audits frequently take male agents into restaurants and nightclubs where in order to be inconspicuous they need someone to escort. As we have mentioned, women acting as cleaning ladies can uncover wads of information. Not Mata Haris, precisely, nor even Rahabs.

Chapter Thirty-Two

BRIBERY

Loyalty and ethics have their price, and International Latex has paid it.

—Remark attributed to the defendant in *B. F. Goodrich vs. Donald Wohlgemuth*

Too poor for a bribe, and too proud to importune;
He had not the method of making a fortune.

—Thomas Gray, on his own character

1.

Nearly everyone possesses some trust, for the betrayal of which someone, somewhere, is willing to pay. This fact in itself may induce a touch of paranoia in the chief executive of a large corporation, and inhibit his communications with others who work for it. There is also the problem of the man who doesn't know the value of the information he possesses, and who may just give it away. A bribe is not, in any case, easy to define. I will take it here to mean an emolument for a service that ought not be rendered. I use the old-fashioned word emolument because in the business world, no less than in the world of politics, education and the professions, a bribe may take any one of a number of forms.

An example of a run-of-the-mill bribe was described in the earlier and separately published of the two Harvard Business School reports. The words are those of "an oil company executive."

"When I was out of town last month, I was told by a local banker that one of their customers, in answer to 'Why don't you hire a geologist?' said: 'Why should I? I have five company geologists from five companies on a $500-a-month part-time payroll. Any one of them would cost twice as much if I had him full time.' Actually, the guy had geologists from five different companies reporting to him on the activities of their companies."

A corporation may easily contribute to bribery as if inadvertently, when it "rents" outside consultants. It would be impractical, as well as bad form, for a client to try to learn where a consultant gets information; for where he gets it is as much his stock in trade as the information itself. Thus the clients of Robert Aries were able to share in his knowledge without having, as he had, to bribe employees of chemical and pharmaceutical companies.

By an inversion of circumstances, a bribe may purchase silence, as well as information, and the payment may consist of not doing something, as in blackmail. I have often puzzled if this is what Samuel Dash had in mind at the time he wrote this intriguing aside into his pioneer work, *The Eavesdroppers:*

> I counted on certain law enforcement contacts, including the Chicago Crime Commission, to recruit an investigator for the study. No one could suggest a candidate. Finally a law school professor came up with the name of a man who appeared to be the answer to our needs. He had been an investigator in the Chicago area since 1913, doing much of his work for the federal government. He had also been a private wiretapper and manufacturer of wiretap devices. However, after working a few weeks, he submitted a report indicating he was unable to obtain the information we sought. In view of his background this was nonsense.
>
> It was clear he had been persuaded not to carry out his assignment or had been frightened away. There was one clue in his report. Although he professed no knowledge of the information we sought, there were two questions which he answered fully. One of these questions concerned illegal activity on the part of telephone company employees in aiding wiretappers and the role the telephone company played in preventing such action. Our investigator set forth at length the official telephone company rules. . . . The other question completely answered by the investigator was one requesting the name of someone connected with the telephone company in Chicago who could be contacted for further interviewing. The investigator's typewritten answer gave the names of a special agent in

> the Chicago telephone company, his business address, office telephone number, home address and home telephone number.

There are a number of questions the answer to which cannot be verified by an outsider. One of them is the allegation by competent authority that it would be impossible to install a sustained tap on a telephone without the paid cooperation of a telephone company employee. As Dash suggests, the telephone company is unresponsive to any suggestion of the possibility. However, in June, 1966, the Senate subcommittee on administrative practices heard testimony from a former special agent for New York Bell Telephone that he had been, in effect, blackmailed by the Internal Revenue Service for failing to cooperate in investigations of handbook operators in Brooklyn and other places on Long Island.

The agent, William Hussey, claimed that he was discharged after more than forty years of service with the Company, that he and his wife were tailed and harassed for eight months, that as many as twenty taps had been placed on his home phone at one time, and that he was indicted for income tax evasion. While he attributed this to his lack of cooperation, the IRS evidently supposed that Hussey was "playing footsie" with handbook operators. The bookies, it appears, hire telephone company men part time to keep them informed of police taps. Hussey, however, calculates that he was fired because "the big brass are mortally afraid of the regulatory agencies. They'd throw four vice presidents out the window if any agency told them to."

Even so, Hussey alleges, the phone company observes the ancient rule, all things in moderation. A superior of his was dismissed, he said, for being overzealous in his cooperation with authorities. In that case, he said, the Long Island supervisor had set up a wiretap school for young police officers to teach them how to install reliable taps. There was no mention of tuition, so we may never know if the school was being operated *pro bono publico.* It may be worth noting here the testimony given the same day by Bernard Spindel, a private security agent turned electronic technician and James Hoffa's personal specialist. After noting that court orders permitting wiretaps on a lawyer's conversations with his clients were an everyday occurrence, he said that many police officers install devices on bookies' lines at their own expense in order to learn what the daily take is and what the policeman's cut should be.

Hussey's initial encounter with the IRS deserves a more permanent place in the annals of collisions between agents of bureaucracies. When he was called in for questioning, Hussey said, on his 1961 tax return, an agent remarked: "You know, you're in a position to make a lot of money." The agent was referring, of course, to Hussey's work supervising the phone taps on bookmakers. "I thought he was just giving me the needle," Hussey testified. "So I said, 'If I was going to be a thief I'd rather be in here. It would be a lot more lucrative.' So right off the bat we didn't see eye to eye."

2.

To qualify as a bribe a transaction ought to enumerate in some detail the service expected and be specific about the price. For that reason it is hard to classify some practices which seem to teeter near bribery. One of the richest sources of information to any company are its suppliers and subcontractors, many of whom also do business with competitors. Individual salesmen for the supplier or "sub" gather and prudently dole out information in the hope of cementing relations or getting some extra business. That would seem to be no more bribery than it is *noblesse oblige*. Also, whether a job offer constitutes an attempt to bribe would depend greatly on the circumstances. Let us suppose, for example, that Eugene Andrew Mayfield had used his head.

Mayfield, you may recall, was the fellow back in Chapter 14 who fell into the hands of the FBI while trying to sell to the Colgate Company the budget embodying Procter and Gamble's plans for trying to get us to use Crest toothpaste. Had he spent less of his time watching spy movies, and more of it posing hypothetical questions to a lawyer, he might have brought it off, too. This would have left him not only richer, but still able to write indignant letters to newspapers about corruption in Government without having to fear responses starting with "let's look at Mayfield's record."

Mayfield had every advantage going for him. The principal edge, which he blew, was that the possessor of the information was in the same state and within walking distance of the likeliest customer. He did not have to use so much as the bus or subway, much less the telephone or the mails, to promote his scheme. His chief problem was to find a way to copy the budget without removing it from P & G's premises, or misappropriating any of its property, such as paper used in an office copying machine. In most offices, this can be overcome by telling the office manager that you have something personal you would like to copy on the office Xerox, and by offering to pay for the use. This sort of request is disarming and plausible, because the cost of getting material copied by an outside service runs usually twenty-five cents a page; sometimes less, but never as cheaply as the few cents per copy charged to a regular business user.

Having made the copy and paid for the materials, Mayfield would have been free in his choice. He could not do with it as he wished, of course, any more than the purchaser of a book is permitted to represent the order of words contained in it as his own; but it was his in the sense that he cannot have been said to have stolen anything tangible. His next problem was to find a way to gain an interview with someone at Colgate who was in, and of, a capacity to understand the value of his information, and could be relied on to get a decision concerning its purchase without needing a diagram.

It is at this point that a little tact, intelligent forethought and attention to detail can convert a bribe into a routine business transaction. Whether to deal directly or through an intermediary is a question that rests on where the purchaser and seller would be left standing in case either blew open the transaction. In purchasing the services of policemen or telephone company employees, it would seem to be no more than prudent to follow Ulmont Cumming's example and deal through a third party, a broker whom the purchaser and seller have more reason to trust than they do to trust one another. However, if the seller knows of no reliable agency through which he can deal, it is always best to deal directly.

3.

A common mistake made by buyers and sellers alike is to suppose that candor will somehow relieve them of any damage to their reputation or of any other onus that the offer or acceptance of a bribe might entail. In reality, the contrary is more often the result. I can best illustrate with an experience.

A freelance public relations consultant for a large corporation wanted to sell me the story of how his client's investment in India, which included installation of some new and dramatically technical machinery, had caused a province there to prosper and to change the customs and outlooks of thousands of people. The story seemed to me well worth considering, and so I asked him for more material that might help me to reach a decision as to whether to assign someone to it. He said he would get it posthaste, and then: "Your end could come to five figures." I must have looked puzzled, because he quickly added: "I don't mean in money, of course. I was thinking, perhaps of leaving a white Jaguar in front of your door with a key in the ignition."

I have seen many potentially good stories lost in this fashion, but never quite as bluntly. Candor cost this man all chance to obtain what he might have been able to gain for the price of a lunch. He could always have gotten the client to pay for the car as if to give it to me and given it to his wife, instead. His reputation would have been intact. Mine might have suffered, but that's the chance one takes. As it turned out, he got the free lunch.

Had Mayfield stifled the impulse to candor, and ruled out the use of telephones or the mails, his problem would have been defined within limits that would have permitted him to venture a sale without committing a punishable offense against Federal law. His own knowledge of the circumstances would have had to dictate his best approach —whether to apply for a job, or whether he knew someone who might arrange an introduction with the right person at Colgate under some pretext. With his weakness for theatrics, perhaps he might have arranged to occupy a restaurant booth near the man he wanted to reach, and talked very loudly about his discontent with P & G, especially the marketing plans for Crest.

Mayfield seems also to have neglected the most important consideration of all, the form of payment. How much easier might it have been, rather than to have struck for cash, to have asked for a two-year contract to consult on marketing matters. Colgate could have studied the budget at the same time and table at which Mayfield read over the consulting contract. Only two or three persons in the company need have known what the contract was for. Mayfield would have gotten his money in an aboveboard way and then have been able to leave for Chicago and his home. If he had asked for one million bars of Palmolive soap he would have stood a better chance than to ask for cash in an airport men's room. Mayfield left Colgate no opportunity to actively consider his offer.

We may assume that nearly every executive who earns upwards of $15,000 annually knows something, or can render some service, that for the divulgence or performing of which someone is willing to pay. The agency in perhaps the best position of all to negotiate for such information or services is the executive recruitment firm, the "head hunters" hired to search out executive talent. A former official of the American Management Association has said that early in the 1960's, for some reason, the number of incidents in which valuable information was lost through recruitment efforts proliferated alarmingly, causing even some of the most reputable agencies to lose business they might otherwise have gotten.

All the same, bribery seems to hover in executive consciousness in much the same way as automobile fatality figures—an ever-present fact, but still something that happens to the other fellow. Each incident that is publicized, whether in the newspapers or around the lunch table, contributes none the less to the generalized anxiety of the security-conscious executive. This is particularly true because there is nothing equivalent to the National Safety Council to make the risk clearly visible and calculable, such as "in the three-day convention weekend just ended, a record 314 corporation executives accepted bribes totaling. . . ."

When it does happen, the effect can be unsettling. *Fortune* tells of the time that a vice president of a $300-million company found himself for the first time face to face with a real, live eavesdropper who had been hired to bug a Washington hotel room where he expected to hold a meeting. "A request for advice addressed to a friend, an investigator in a federal agency, brought an admonition to notify the FBI rather than the Washington police, against the possibility that the latter might be in on the deal themselves, as they had been in previous cases."

Chapter Thirty-Three

BOBBLES

Without wanting to discourage readers from holding seances with potential co- or sub-contractors, it must be said that today's team approach to technology has cost more firms more money through compromises than all of the broads, bugs and bribery put together.

—ANTHONY G. BAKER
Managing Editor, *Industrial Research*

1.

THE LOSS of a trade secret through inadvertence does not always, and perhaps not even usually, mean that the loss was accidental. It may mean only that the victim wasn't paying close attention to the motives of someone who interviewed him about a job or negotiated with him as if to buy his business. Records of the U.S. Court of Appeals, Fifth Circuit, in New Orleans contain an account of how much inadvertence once nearly cost a young Virginia electronics engineer, Charles Hastings. With the enthusiasm of the discoverer in search of capital, Hastings told an official of Phillips Petroleum that he had contrived a way to get a precise fix on the offshore position of seismographic mapping ships, the importance of which lay in its contribution to greater precision of geological data used in the search for offshore oil. Phillips, though, bought seismographic services from Seismograph Service Corp., and was its principal customer.

Seismograph, as it happened, had itself been looking, but with indifferent results, for a positioning system. After hearing a Phillips man's description of Hastings' Raydist system, Seismograph decided on a plan that was greatly to exercise Federal Judge J. Skelly Wright. As he saw it:

> Instead of going to Hastings as upright businessmen, Seismograph determined to steal his work. [Dr. James E.] Hawkins, an officer and director of Seismograph . . . immediately applied for patents on the system and variations thereof in the hope that the inexperienced and impecunious Hastings had not already done so. But Seismograph did not stop there. It sent its executive vice president to Virginia to learn more of Hastings' secrets and to offer him a brave plan by which they would form a joint venture to exploit the system. The brave plan was even reduced to writing and presented to Hastings for his consideration. Seismograph invited Hastings to its home office, the further to pick his brains and milk him of the information on Raydist he had been so long acquiring. During the time Seismograph was deluding Hastings with the offer of a joint venture, its own technicians, led by Hawkins, were perfecting their own version of the Raydist system based on the information Hastings had given them. By August 1, 1947, Seismograph felt it had no longer any use for Hastings, having obtained all the information it needed. Still it held the lure of joint venture before his eyes, so that he would not give his information to Seismograph's competitor, Offshore Navigation, and so that it, Seismograph, would have time to perfect its patent position. . . . Seismograph's president, Westby, even conjured up a fake demonstration, and had Hastings prepare equipment for the demonstration for Phillips representatives who were never even advised that a demonstration was to take place. Indeed, Seismograph even stooped to espionage on Hastings' patent counsel. Thus it was that Seismograph was able to perfect its Raydist system, which it called Lorac.

What gave Judge Wright the opportunity to compose this opinion was that having patented Lorac, Seismograph sued Hastings for infringing its patent with his Raydist. As may be imagined, Judge Wright dismissed the suit, with the admonition that a patent "obtained through fraud and dishonest dealings is unenforceable in a court of equity."

2.

In the judgment of the aforecited Anthony G. Baker,

> The best cover possible for a man with designs on a specific blackbox is that of being liaison engineer. It is he who can set up exploratory "systems integration" studies with another company that knows the secret of the third firm. The third organization may compete 100 per cent with the first, or only five per cent. But somewhere along the line, Co. 3 has had its own systems integration study, or perhaps was a co-contractor with Co. 2 during an earlier endeavor. At any rate, the mere existence of Co. 3's proprietary material in somebody else's shop often is but a step away from selling it on the newsstand.

Then, too, as pointed out by a research report published by the National Industrial Conference Board:

> Engineers and scientists who work in company laboratories usually belong to professional societies in which they are expected to read or publish papers dealing with their fields of specialization. Many researchers, too, in pursuing graduate degrees at universities publish theses that are built around knowledge they learn on the job. Such activities can serve useful purposes and are often encouraged by management. But there is a danger in discussing matters related to their work in such publications, they may unwittingly leak out trade secrets and other information they are required to keep confidential.

Security worthiness is a matter of temperament. There are men who drink to moderation, don't chase women, treat the telephone as if it were a public address system, never get drawn into divulgences by phony job offers, study carefully every statement they make for public consumption, and yet who in informal debate, a lively discussion over a lunch or dinner table, shrug off their closed habits and use willy-nilly whatever examples come to mind, secret or not, to make a point. I have heard securities analysts (stock and bonds) for institutional investors reply huffily to direct questions concerning their portfolios: "We at the Rock of Gibraltar Fund," they usually will say, "do not disclose . . ." followed by a long list of things the Fund does not disclose. Twenty minutes later, though, upon hearing their judgment challenged, if only by implication, they will describe at least one-half the decisions represented in the Fund's portfolio in order to make a case for their own investment philosophies.

Philosophers in general, and those devoted to the natural sciences no less than others, appear as if by nature to want to talk and to compare notes with anyone who can exhibit an intelligent interest, but particularly persons who indicate that they are occupied with similar problems. They are, in fact, members of a community that puts a high premium on this sort of sharing and exchange of knowledge. Baker remarks that the Pentagon gets upset because "many technical publications have better information on the status and course of complex developments than do most of the people who work on them. And nearly all the information is collected without particular privileges being accorded the reporter."

Another worrisome soft spot in a corporation's armor is the salesman. Anyone who spends a good deal of time outside the office inevitably arouses nervousness in executives with a strong sheep-herding instinct. Most salesmen have to spend their time beating the bushes. The entrepreneurial streak is strong in salesmen; when they say "we" to a customer, they often mean no more than "me." Many move restlessly from job to job and entertain constantly the dream of taking their accounts and going into business for themselves. Also, they like to talk a lot. The boss never knows how seriously they will take his injunctions to regard certain matters as confidential. Anxiety from this source has grown more acute in recent years because in hiring salesmen, industries with complicated things to sell emphasize knowledge of subject matter more than they do personality.

3.

Sales and trade shows put the performance-oriented company in a box. Trade exhibitions are showcases; a company that signs up to show its stuff should put out the best it has. This is why at the 1966 annual Music Show of the National Association of Music Merchants in Chicago there could be found two dozen or so Japanese from the home office in Tokyo of Sony Corporation. They came prepared with cameras and sketch pads. A *Wall Street Journal* account would suggest that they might have had trouble, though, getting a clear shot of the displays.

"RCA had some 25 industrial designers, engineers, sales planning and product planning people combing the exhibits in teams. Most had note pads and measuring tapes. . . ." Also, Zenith conceded to having a "dozen or more" sleuths at the show, and "two Magnavox designers confessed they were part of a 10-man inspection team. Motorola had a crew of agents headed by its general production manager, and Westinghouse had patrols in the aisles."

And guess what? Peter Munk, president of Clairtone Sound Corporation, put his exhibit on an invitation-only basis. "He posted a Pinkerton guard at the entrance to keep out the bad guys."

Perhaps relief from these banes will come, like antibugging devices, only after a great many executives attend industrial espionage schools, such as those established in San Francisco and Tokyo. Presumably, when everyone knows the tricks of the trade, none of the tricks will work. In the meantime, corporations turn to specialists in security systems, like Norman Jaspan.

The hardware of security systems is advancing almost as rapidly as the penetration technology. The ultimate device will be a thing about the size and shape of an old Electro-Lux vacuum cleaner that jams all taps, detects all transmitters, gives an indication as to who within its range is telling a lie, and sounds an alarm when anyone uninvited comes within its outstretched wavelengths. Until it is invented, security systems installers make do with separate contraptions for each of these various functions. Probably the simplest security system to buy and install for business conferences is a steam bath; not a dry air sauna, but a good wet steamy sweat room. The hissing noises and humidity combine to make bugs either ineffective because of background noise, or inoperative because the vital miniature parts become soaked with moisture.

Since 1960, Pinkerton's has run a research and development department directed to studies of the numerous mechanical, electrical and electronic anti-intrusion and protective devices coming into use. One of the department's earliest triumphs was Pinkerton's purchase in 1962 of an electronics manufacturing concern in Webster, Massachusetts. The Pinkerton Electro-Security Company, a division of Pinkerton's, Inc., now manufactures under exclusive patents a space alarm operated on radar principles and using the registered name "Radar-Eye." The alarm quickly opened a market in business and industry, and subsequently a more compact and perhaps better known model, The Minuteman, became popular for small stores and household use.

It would appear to be only a matter of time when these gadgets will reach a standoff, the bug followed by the anti-bug, followed by the anti-anti-bug followed by . . . until once again corporations will be safe from the spies of competitors and the temptation to spy on their competitors. The equipment will very likely be expensive, befitting the special market it will be meant to serve. Then, a corporation may stash away its customers lists, credit ratings, personnel inventories, dossiers, contracts requiring disclosure of all inventions made by employees, and the like, without having to fear that they will be stolen. That won't leave security agents much to do except to create what business they can out of making sure that the rest of us aren't thieves and liars. I haven't any doubt that private enterprise will someday also put on the market a moderately priced electronic security device, something Sears Roebuck can offer, that we can use to protect our own trade secrets, check our phones, see that we aren't being bugged, and the like. The period of time that worries me, because it is the period of time I occupy, is the time between now and the day that the Everyman's Minuteman is put on the market.

Chapter Thirty-Four

PRIVACY RECONSIDERED

The catchword "preparedness," which originally meant a state of readiness for a problematical war, has of late come to be applied to an ideal state of national efficiency, not in reference to any particular future event but to the whole future history of our country. The expression was obviously used in this broader sense by the National Academy of Sciences when last April it voted unanimously to offer its services to the President "in the interest of national preparedness." The offer met with a hearty response in official quarters and set on foot a train of events that are pregnant with possibilities. . . .

—*Scientific American*, 1916

Things have come to a pretty pass when religion is allowed to invade the sphere of private life.

—WILLIAM LAMB, Viscount Melbourne

1.

THERE IS ONE EASY TEST the Congress might make to see how seriously Americans feel about their privacy. It is suggested by the testimony taken in the Gallagher Committee hearings from Abraham Carp, director of selection for the Peace Corps. The test would be for the Congress to propose and take up as if seriously a law to require every citizen who drives a car across a state line, or who makes use of any highway constructed substantially with Federal funds, to submit to psychological tests, including the Minnesota Multiphasic Personality Inventory used in screening Peace Corps applicants.

The proposal is unalloyed by a distinction between rights and privileges, since a driver's license is as much a privilege as employment in the Peace Corps. The argument for the law may be made by changing a few words in Dr. Carp's deposition:

"We can help to identify people through the use of these tests whom everybody would agree it is wrong to put behind the wheel of an automobile. And there is some likelihood that if we did not use the test, we might in fact have issued them driver's licenses, to their own harm as well as to that of pedestrians walking city sidewalks, some with babies in strollers, and to other motorists on the road."

In getting up a lively debate, we could certainly rely on the public-spirited help and great skill and experience in these matters of the automobile manufacturers and auto clubs, the Iron and Steel Institute, the American Association of Advertising and the proprietors of the engines of communications, to mention but a few. The contest might have the collateral benefit of enriching the always-depleted coffers of the American Civil Liberties Union, which has been a partisan in many legal contests involving claims of injury to privacy.

That the proposal will not be taken up is due not to any lack of intrinsic merit, but to absence of a Senator with the right qualifications. He would first have to possess a pixyish streak. When Robert Novak asks him on *Meet the Press* how he makes his proposal jibe with his previous statements on privacy, he ought to be able to quote with a straight face Proverbs XXVII, 15: "Iron sharpeneth iron; so a man sharpeneth the countenance of his friends." What's more, in order to get the proposal taken seriously enough to cause a few campus uprisings, he should have a large personal following together with substantial power in the Congress. And, finally, he should be planning to retire from office, but without having made his intention known, and have no further ambitions to political office.

The opportunity seems entirely too remote to offer promise for a remedy soon of the defects in the feedback system we have come to occupy. Corporations will continue to look upon the information which comes to them by request, or that is manageable, as stock for their inventory, but upon much other information as if it were a security threat. They continue, that is, to exhibit the tendency known to anyone who stays off a bathroom scale when he sees that he has to let his trouser belt out another notch.

Witness as a particularly telling example the operational problem that has been called to their attention by the Civil Rights efforts of recent years. The problem, properly stated, is "Here is a tremendous reserve of unused energy. How do we avail ourselves of it?" Instead, as a rule, corporations, including labor unions, have tightened up into preoccupations with how "to deal with the problem." The Federal Government has effectively compelled some three dozen contractors to comply with Federal fair employment regulations, which means there are that number of companies wearing expressions as if they had been made to swallow castor oil. To know something of the size and shape of the bugs and banes that disturb the night thoughts of these creatures is not to know how much weight they ought to be given. A spook, too, is real if its consequences are real. As is also true of living, breathing organisms seized by fear or suspicion, the goblins cherished by corporations weigh whatever the person afflicted by them says they weigh.

Some banes, to be sure, enjoy an existence independent of the mind of those persons afflicted by them. Under the terms of the security doctrine, however, the distinction is not productive in a discussion of the right to privacy. Again like a nation-state at war, the corporation merely need show that a danger is plausible in order to make it seem imminent, and therefore "real." The way this process works was demonstrated during the 1950's when what remained of the Yankee doctrine crumbled under the weight of the security doctrine. Or, perhaps more accurately, when the security doctrine became a thumb on the scale of justice Mr. Justice Holmes had in mind.

Beginning in 1949, we may recall, the community formed by the largest advertisers and the managers of broadcast communication effectively hampered, and in some cases prevented, the employment of numerous actors, writers, directors and others connected with the performing arts patronized by corporations. This practice, which in many instances constituted a blacklist, arose because a coterie of cheapjack gossipmongers called into question the loyalty and patriotism of these employees, based on previous political activities of the accused.

Thus over the back fences of the community in which corporations live the security conscious passed newsletters, lists or whatnot containing the names of "controversial" persons. No arguments, even in support of fear, can get along without some sort of sustenance from a *sequitur* or two. In the case, say, of a performer who made his living as a tap-dancer, it might be hard to make a tenable case that the performer was an espionage agent tapping out code messages, so it was argued that part of the money he earned would go to help the Communist conspiracy.

Advertisers and networks had a more difficult time giving flesh and blood to the spook. The explicit threats of American Legion posts to boycott their products and programs gave some body to their contention that the security of their investment in good will was jeopardized, but breathed no life into the threats themselves. Therefore, they elevated to national prominence a Syracuse grocer with three stores who really did stop buying goods from advertisers who employed the lepers of controversy. More than that, he put up signs around the store telling his customers why he stopped offering their products.

Eventually a balance was worked out. The Anti-Defamation League of B'nai B'rith instituted clearance procedures, a sort of jerry-built due process. The ADL would satisfy itself that the unemployed performer was not a Communist, and then persuade others on an informal "board of directors" which included a Hearst columnist or two, the security agent for Batten, Barton, Durstine and Osborne, and a scattering of freelance protectors of the nation's security. This process only helped to harden the practice into respectability. Thus, the feedback system fell back into a new equilibrium; the "community's interests" were defined.

The first victim of blacklisting was Jean Muir. She has since been exonerated, notably in magazine stories hailed as courageous, but which appeared so long after the fact that they were courageous in the sense that it is courageous to suggest that Thomas More was wrong in his accusation concerning the slayer of the two princes in the Tower of London. One of the articles, however, mentioned the sponsor, General Foods Corporation, who complied in having her discharged from the cast of the Henry Aldrich show. In 1965, in fact, when she was interviewed on an American Broadcasting Company show about her harrowing experiences, all mention of the sponsor was blipped out of the tape.

This may be viewed as a warming instance of mutual redemption, of forgive and forget, save for the fact that the corporation, like the Crown, has the power of self-redemption, at least here on earth, and Miss Muir does not. The incident cost her a considerable part of her real-time life program. So far as one can perceive in the sales figures, it cost General Foods scarcely a night's sleep. For as Adolph Berle remarked long ago, what the medieval corporation had that the giant corporation, public or private, does not enjoy today is, as he puts it, "the conscience of the King."

Joseph C. Harsch, writing in *The Christian Science Monitor,* points out that,

> The motorcar masters of Detroit are correct when they say that today theirs is "the most important industry in the economic picture of the United States." And one may hope that they will police and regulate themselves without Government coercion, for self-discipline is always preferable, at least in theory, to outside discipline.
>
> It will, however, be a new departure if they do. To date, no industry in its moment of being the biggest and most important, has yet managed to teach itself humility. The grace has had to come either from disciplines imposed by an outraged public, or from successful competition.

2.

Those who are perhaps most devoted to maintaining the guarantees of the right to privacy are reluctant to adopt the only term which gives the right its specific gravity. For the critical issue is, privacy of what? Its defenders take as the critical term in the discussion of privacy the rights of the *individual* rather than the term which comprehends, but is more than, individuality, the *person.* This represents a form of the literalism which caused William Howard Taft to reach the decision he did in *Olmstead.* It has more recently led a majority of the Supreme Court to hold that forcing a motorist to yield a sample of his blood to determine if it contains some specified amount of alcohol is not the same as making the motorist incriminate himself with a spoken confession.

Thus by some curious standard the placement of a wiretap device more than halfway through an apartment wall is breaking and entering; the injection of a needle attached to a syringe to extract the occupant's blood is not. This is presumably because due process clauses in the Constitution make mention of property, but make no mention of the live epidermis. The effort to treat privacy as being privacy literally of the biological individual leads to an endless, fruitless attempt to legislate out of existence technology that will no more be legislated out than will alcohol, mood-changing drugs or the automobile.

I suspect that the reason many of those occupied with restoration of personal rights are reluctant to accept the concept of person as defining those rights is an association suggested by Walter Lippmann in *The*

Good Society. There, Lippmann argues that the person is the conviction toward which "men have fought their way in the long ascent out of the morass of barbarism. Upon this rock they have built the rude foundations of the good society." The person he conceives as an "inviolable essence" in the recognition of which religious experience is somehow entailed; this fact, he says, is what moves collectivist regimes to be "profoundly irreligious."

Deliberation over the question of privacy suffers, in short, from the great fear among civil libertarians of terms which smack of origins in a time in which theology was taken seriously. Thus, rather than recognize the corporation for what it says it is, essentially a new and workable model of its medieval ancestors, the utilitarians enlisted in the cause of individual rights will insist that corporations are no more than fictions in the eyes of the law, as if by their insistence they will make the consequences of corporate behavior equally fictional.

That this is the case is further indicated by remarks Professor Beaney, of Princeton University, made to the Gallagher Committee. Privacy, he said, almost apologetically, "is important to many people, not just to artists or creative people. It is important to all of us who have serious work to do, who regard the human being as something more than a number in the population total, and you don't have to bring in religious reasoning to justify this." Indeed not; all you have to show is that in the absence of respect for persons, the security of the great corporation is worthless.

A direct test of the health of an automatic feedback system is the capacity of the smallest component within the circuit to receive and send signals. John Platt, professor of physics at the University of Chicago, tells why this should be so in a discussion of "social chain reactions":

> Business and military organizations are already using methods such as "operations analysis" and "game theory" to multiply the effectiveness of intelligence in organizational situations and in conflict situations. . . . The key word in what I have to say is *amplification.* I believe that this concept has not been sufficiently emphasized in thinking about how intelligence can make itself effective. We see its importance as soon as we consider how, in the biological world, the brain directs the activities of an animal or a person. The brain is a rather small organ. Yet it receives information from the senses and makes

> decisions that are amplified and carried through the metabolizing pathways of the nerves until they are amplified again in the muscles and serve to trigger the full physical powers of the body into achieving what the brain decides is needed.

Professor Platt believes, for example, that by applying much the same principles as managements of corporations use to "amplify" their intelligence, small groups can set in motion counter-thrusts, or as he says, provide "a social chain-reaction with positive feedback." In this way,

> In a democracy, even outside official channels, there are opportunities for small groups to be surprisingly effective . . . thinking they see a better way of doing things, they are sometimes able to enlist and guide the additional forces of other men in a tremendous self-amplifying process until the result is achieved.

This would seem to require at minimum, though, the capacity among the citizens for carrying on the activity denoted to the Greeks by the word *sponde,* a drink offering. This word became *spondere,* to promise, and *respondere,* to undertake in return, as, for example, to make answer for himself, as well as for the law, or the language, or journalism, or teaching the young, healing the sick, or for honest weight at the meat counter. The capacity to undertake pledges and to respond, i.e., to answer for the pledges, is customarily denoted as responsibility, and its lack as unresponsiveness, or more accurately, despondency.

Without that wish, and without confidence in that capacity among its citizens, the "multiple interconnected chain reactions" break down. A vital constituent in that capacity and confidence is a lively feeling of solicitude for one's own reputation, which in turn is not possible without a confident sense of the truth of one of Westbrook Pegler's dicta, as cited by Murray Kempton, that every man's reputation is "his own rag doll to play with."

3.

Eyewitnesses at the U.S. Marine invasion of Guadalcanal in the last Great War relate that a number of men on the beaches dug in and froze, as if out of fear. Officer grades responded in the way they were trained to respond, by pointing a hand weapon at the immobilized man's temple, and ordering him to move. The personal courage exhibited in these incidents, by the man holding the gun and by the man who summoned himself to move, seem to me to exceed the grasp of any terms of common experience, and therefore of any nomenclature, commonsense or occult, by which we hope to account for why men do what they do.

I confess to wonder even more at yet another and in many ways more singular discovery. Since the war in which the Battle of Guadalcanal figured prominently, we have committed large numbers of troops to two other wars. To neither of them have we committed, though, the civilian dedication marked by Humphrey Bogart winning the North Atlantic for Warner Brothers, meatless days, new-fashionless seasons, debutantes at the USO, Rosie-the-Riveters and "Praise the Lord and Pass the Ammunition." From this experience we conclude that even without glamour, Ernie Pyle and Bill Mauldin, our young men will go forth to die in battle.

What's more, we have learned that even a man whose parents have never been permitted to vote in an election, who has been given no grounds for great expectations from the economic or political system, and who has not received nor seen many persons he knows receive substantial due process from constituted authority; even that man may be plucked from where he lives, tested, classified, labeled, reprogrammed by basic training, put aboard a conveyance, and taken to confront any enemy that authority appoints.

Short of having a pistol pointed at his head, which would be a personal matter between him and the man who would have to pull the trigger, he is impelled only by a series of binary, off-on, plus-minus choices. At any one of many steps he may choose either the organized disavowal of the community and jail or to go on through to where he may have the opportunity to combat a stranger for survival. Having done that, he is begrudged by many of his fellow citizens the protection of the Illinois National Guard if he chooses to march in Cicero. That he gets it is a tribute to the same process that sent him to fight for his country.

Encouraged by these examples, we seem to have been lulled into supposing that we can dispense also with the everyday courage of our citizens. I can think of no other reason to explain why the courts and legislatures permit the executive branch of the Federal Government, and our industrial giants, indiscriminately, yet systematically, to loot private citizens of the substance of and principal motivation for personal courage and capacity for mutual trust.

I am speaking not of the class of professionals who know the ins and outs of the corporate structure, and know how to make it work for them, or at least not against them; but of the run of citizens, the man who applies for loans and jobs, is "audited" all unawares while on the job or speaking over a telephone, who may be fingerprinted when he goes to buy a hunting rifle, who is forced to listen to the sweet "we've got you now, haven't we?" woman who wants to know why the telephone bill hasn't been paid in advance; the man who fills out his own tax form, serves on juries without much protest, submits to a polygraph test because he needs the work, and to a credit check because the man who sold him insurance wants to make sure he'll get his commission.

No man or woman of high school age or beyond, who by design or whim of circumstances—by winning a beauty contest, joining loudly in debate on issues of public policy or reporting on Unidentified Flying Objects—catches the attention of others, may ever be sure where the information is stored, when it may be retrieved out of a corporate memory and displayed again, or in what connection.

I should think it might prove instructive, operationally speaking, were a foundation to find some room among its concerns, provided that it could find someone competent who was also interested, to see if there is a relation between the rising incidence of homosexuality among males and the mounting voyeurism of the Government and subsidiary private corporations. Loss of control over his own reputation may easily create in heads of households the symptoms referred to as "loss of a sense of identity," said commonly to be at the paternal root of the homosexual's pattern of behavior.

Meanwhile, the organism to which they give substance develops a nervous system that delivers to the brain nothing more than it asks for; with no sign of pain or upset or danger. It may go on betraying itself as casually as a bulldozer uprooting trees for new billboards, never the wiser. Who is to gainsay it? A man strapped in a chair with electrodes checking his vitals to make sure he isn't lying?

Chapter Thirty-Five

SECURITY RECONSIDERED

Mr. Jansen believes that if a computer could be programmed for Violent and Non-Violent language, we would be able to determine precisely the amount of belligerency behind any diplomatic note. For example, in the course of his research he found that "Violent" words in international communiques rose sharply in 1914. Ah, if only we had known. . . .

—J. OSTROWSKA

. . . Messrs. Brown and Campbell are probably at least partly correct in their large claim that the modern development in automatic engineering is the consequence of a point of view which finds satisfaction in unified schemes for their own sake.

—ERNEST NAGEL, *Self Regulation*

1.

"THOUGH CURIOSITY is a constant element in social life," Professor Alan F. Westin writes in the *Columbia Law Review*, "many social scientists have observed a rise in recent decades of a particularly dangerous form of curiosity to which the term 'voyeurism' has been applied. . . . Many social commentators believe there has been a rise in general voyeuristic tendencies in American society, caused by lessening of direct experience with creative life and greater reliance on pseudo experience." Another possible explanation is contained in direct mail solicitation for subscribers made by *Consumer Reports*. "If ever you feel you're being 'had,'" says the message on the outside of the envelope, "welcome."

The invitation put me in mind of a large billboard once maintained high over Michigan Boulevard in Chicago by Dad's Old Fashioned Root Beer, obviously as a taunt. The message consisted of a single question in large, black letters against a yellow background: "Have you had it lately?" I think Hugh Hefner missed a bet by not leasing the space after Dad's relinquished it to ask, with the appropriate bunny symbol: "Are you getting yours?" And in smaller type:". . . Who is stopping you?"

Paranoia appears to be a condition of survival against the competition of substantially unpredictable adversaries possessed of guile and energy. The arousal and maintenance of certain expectations concerning the extent to which the adversary will *not* go, or the means of which he will *not* avail himself, is requisite to a reduction of paranoia among competitors, and hence to the release of energies for constructive action. When a nation confronts an enemy whose actions offer no acknowledgment of the need for such expectations, it is itself given to a certain degree of disabling paranoia. The problem is to keep it within bounds. The problem is complicated, though, by another phenomenon.

If a competitor stands greatly in fear of his own tendencies to violate these expectations, whether in fact he yields to them or not, he is likely to fear that others, including those less in fear of their own inclinations, will, and at a cost to his own legitimate aspirations. Thus paranoia becomes self-serving.

To anyone who feels as if he is being had, two questions become matter for continuing concern. One is, Who is getting it, and how? And the other is, What are *they* up to? To anyone afflicted with these concerns, the likelihood of their making anything happen diminishes about in proportion to the intensity of the concern.

A divorce lawyer I know attributes the high divorce rate of recent years to the fact that a great many men and women grew up believing that everything was possible and that if they didn't make it happen, the fault was theirs. Since this is an intolerable premise to live with when not much is happening, they look to fault the closest thing at hand: the husband or wife.

There is yet another form of indiscriminate curiosity abroad that is more amorphous and less easily contained. It is this curiosity which inclines me to suspect that privacy, conceived of as a right, may end without so much as a whimper. It may be tsk-tsked to death in the course of some such investigation as indicated in this passage from the *Journal of Business* published by the Graduate School of Business of the University of Chicago:

> The general research procedure was this: Three hundred twenty-five Chicago area college students surreptitiously observed another member of their own families in their homes over the nine-day period from Saturday morning, May 16, 1944, through Sunday evening, May 24. Each selected one other member of the household (usually a parent or spouse) and was to make as many observations as possible within the nine-day period, though a twenty-five-observation-hour limit was imposed to keep some control on the quality.

A philosopher of social organization will be peering through a two-way mirror at a Puerto Rican who has applied for help from the Federal Government, and thus been asked to volunteer for research. It will occur to the researcher how awful that these devices intended for legitimate research have been put to use for "commercial" or "trivial" purposes. Richard Lukens, who administers lie detector tests under charter of industrial security, will understand. For he knows that as soon as the New York State legislature gets around to establishing licensing standards for polygraph operators, the public will be more content and comfortable with them.

These members of a new class of intellectual entrepreneurs have a claim that transcends the claims of either side in the contest of wills over the meaning of due process. It is a claim to the acquisition of information for its own sake, rooted, as all the rest, in the "community's interests." One of these entrepreneurs will be preening himself a bit over the fact that he has been given an XYZ clearance by no fewer than three separate Government agencies, thus enabling him to land a fat Government contract. It will occur to him that something ought to be done to stop the indiscriminate use of tape recorders, polygraphs and two-way mirrors in the hands of amateurs and journalists.

Information is extracted from our citizens as if to place them under an injunction of *caveat vendor*. The line at the bottom of the form says the applicant may go to jail, or not get the loan he is applying for, or be dismissed from the job he is in, or denied the one he wants, if he does not answer truthfully. If not that, the suggestion is made that non-truthful answers will defeat the beneficent purposes of the research to which he has been asked to contribute, sometimes by his boss.

Of course, if he needs the job or money so badly that he feels it necessary to take a chance on a small omission or exaggeration he is, as every loan and personnel officer knows, just playing the game. Whose game?

2.

"It's a computer world," says the headline. It sits at the top of four pages of advertising by National Cash Register Company in the September, 1966, *Scientific American.* Whose world is the computer world?

> It's what's happening all over. Computers are taking on the tough jobs—the time consuming jobs—to help managements worldwide solve their operating problems. Advanced management science applications are helping solve today's problems and anticipating those of tomorrow.
>
> Linear programming, for example, can consider all variables of all possible investments and determine how funds can best be allocated to provide the greatest return.
>
> Or Multiple Regression Analysis, to take another example, can predict a particular factor—such as the probable risk on a potential borrower in the credit field—on the basis of a measured set of variables—in this instance, sex, age, family background, income, etc. [There's that "etc." again.]
>
> PERT (Program Evaluation and Review Technique) is being used on every NCR computer from the largest RMC to the smallest 315. It can forecast potential time lags on such projects as building construction.

On another page, though, Systems Development Corporation reminds National Cash Register in a two-page spread: "systems are for people." Says SDC: "As people strive to shape their environment in today's complex society, they look to a computer resource: *information* [emphasis SDC's]." Just to be sure: What is information? The expert on that subject is A.T.&T. Its ad says that, "If someone tells you your own name, he . . . transmits no information: You already know it. He doesn't resolve any uncertainty for you."

> This idea—that whatever resolves uncertainty is information—was used by Dr. Claude E. Shannon during his years at Bell Telephone Laboratories to define and measure information for

> the first time in a way that was usable to scientists. Starting from such basic concepts, Shannon built a theory which has many applications to problems in communication and in other fields. In 1948 he published his classic paper, "A Mathematical Theory of Communication."

From SCM Corporation we get some idea of who will resolve uncertainty for businessmen. "To turn knowledge into useful business information, turn to SCM," says SCM over nearly a whole page; and, at the bottom of the page: "Information alone—even in the midst of an 'information explosion'—is of little use to the businessman until that information can be controlled and acted upon." Until, that is to say, it can be converted into intelligence.

Who will resolve the uncertainties the rest of us feel when we pick up the telephone? Will SDC ("systems are for people") do that for native organisms while SCM does what it can for corporations? It doesn't look promising:

> In addition to developing information systems, SDC's work also includes the design and conduct of training programs, and applications of such techniques as systems analysis, simulation, and computer programming. These are among the activities we undertake for the Air Force, Army, Navy, and NASA in such areas as space surveillance, command and control, anti-submarine warfare, and air defense system training and exercising.

There's one thing we have to say for SDC:

> You may be interested to know that SDC is an independent, nonprofit corporation chartered in the public interest. During the past five years, more than eight million dollars—two-thirds of the fees received by the corporation—have been used to support an extensive *independent* research and development program in the information sciences, a significant part of our total R & D effort. The program's results are freely and widely disseminated.

To whom? Has the Congress been holding out on us? Does it really know all about systems and the way the executive branch keeps its books, but is just playing dumb? Until I see more evidence, I shall have to conclude that the Congress is not much better off, member by member, than other native organisms. Like most of us, they are children of progress and are therefore also forced to the habit, especially annoying to them, of having to assume that the President knows something we don't. I must come back, therefore, to testimony given by Dr. Frank Stanton before the Senate subcommittee investigating juvenile delinquency.

3.

Childhood is an experience which, by itself, makes no one an expert on the subject except children, and they are too inexperienced to be much heeded. Thus it is "a sad fact," as Dr. Frank Stanton told the committee, that "we don't have adequate research" to measure the extent of television's influence on the young, and that there is "a whole host of forces at work." I give Dr. Stanton this. A child is perpetually submerged in an ambience of messages, a low hum punctuated by shrieks, made up of words, actions, songs, pictures, glances, moods, mutterings. They come, to mention only a few obvious sources, from parents, clergymen, teachers, Boy Scout leaders, ringleaders, playmates and *their* parents, social workers, shopkeepers, books, magazines, movies, radio, as well as from television.

They instruct, wheedle, cajole, exhort, threaten, promise, praise, blame, inspire, excite, titillate. The gun or stick toted by a policeman conveys meaning as much as does the opening shot from "Gunsmoke"; a shout from a parent, a wail of a siren in the middle of the night, a screechy teacher, the face of a clown, a pediatrician's hypodermic syringe, are as much messages as a rollicking episode from the *Man from UNCLE*. Dr. Stanton must know, however, that the most compelling of these, and the ones to which a child is most vulnerable, are the artfully prepackaged messages which give form and structure to the rest.

No child, in William Hazlitt's commendable formulation, "is truly himself but in the ideas which others entertain of him." While Dr. Stanton awaits the fruits of further research, a parent, to help his progeny obtain a sound idea of themselves, must monitor the racket of messages as best he knows how. Some he excludes or postpones (or tries to); some he uses; with some he must compete; some do not matter much one way or the other.

For the American parent this task has probably never been more exacting than it is today. This is not only because the noise has gone up in volume and intensity but also because the experience of one generation is so difficult to make relevant to the next. My children's growing pains may be at least as acute as mine were, but their hazards, and the sources of their woes and hopes, are contained in things and situations which for me did not exist.

I know even less, surely, than Dr. Stanton, who holds a Ph.D. in psychology, whether television has a greater influence over children than did the comic books, radio programs and movies which research suggests have been displaced in their attention. I venture that it has, because it is as accessible as all sin, more literal, more intrusive and done with such great technical skill that it is more likely to be accepted as a true depiction of what makes the world go 'round. To prevent it from becoming a twenty-one-inch mirror, by which a child takes to reckoning himself and his possibilities, is another tax on a parent's already heavily taxed energies—in days when parents have a tough time making something out of their own experience.

To whom may we look to do for us what SCM does for business? How about the executive branch? It is almost too easy at this point to examine utterances from that branch concerning Federal wiretap policy, or successions of statements about the progress of the war in Vietnam, or presidential speeches about the state of the economy and the real meaning of employment figures. Let's take instead a statement made by Orville Freeman, Secretary of Agriculture, to a group of congressional candidates in the summer of 1966. He was offering some advice on how to handle questions about consumer prices:

> Slip, slide and duck any question of higher consumer prices if you possibly can. Don't get caught in a debate over higher prices between housewives and farmers. If you do, and have to choose a side, take the farmer's side. It's the right side and, besides, housewives aren't nearly as well organized.

The citizen is left overwhelmed and underinformed. He hasn't any choice but to place his confidence in his chosen authorities. Trial lawyers claim that juries heed too closely these days the charges given by judges, as if for some clue to how the judge believes they should decide. One hears it said often these days that "the President must know what he is doing; he has the information" or "J. Edgar Hoover knows what he is talking about" or "there is scientific evidence to show that. . . ." (As an instance of scientific authority, I am assured by the firm of Moore & Schley, Inc., that "Food technology is the final major phase of IMC's current work. The company has achieved major progress in a substantially improved food sweetener. Derived from natural products, the agent is claimed to be 1,000–3,000 times sweeter than sugar. Development work is continuing in an effort to reduce a slight after-taste.")

This is no less true of the run of journalists. I have heard clutches of them berating the best men engaged in their calling as being senile or "leftish" or "off their feed" for questioning the utterances of cherished authorities. There are, it must be said, numerous exceptions. Even so, newspapers alone are not geared to the job of doing for us what SCM does for corporations, except slowly. This is particularly true when the question is whether birth control pills are safe, or when the National Aeronautical and Space Administration assures us that although things seemed to go wrong in a space mission, a "real-time interface" or some such, view of things actually establishes that the whole shoot was an enormous success.

At the same time, not the citizen nor the Congress nor newspapers can jar loose in time information which corporations use to manage their own affairs, but which are considered too dangerous for the rest of us to know. A man may buy a car which, as the manufacturer's operating experience comes to indicate, may for engineering reasons suddenly spin out of control. The buyer of the car goes confidently about taking his family for Sunday drives, blissfully ignorant of the defect until informed by mishap or by the chance that his dealer gets time to call the car in for remedial work.

He may never learn why General Motors Acceptance Corporation turned down his application for a loan, or why he was denied a job in Government, or a chance with the Peace Corps. Nor is he made privy to information entering into decisions which, by means of the "amplification of intelligence" of which Professor Platt wrote, affect him vitally.

Chapter Thirty-Six

A PROPOSAL

But Thou wouldst not deprive man of freedom and didst reject the offer, thinking, what is that freedom worth, if obedience is bought with bread? Thou didst reply that man lives not by bread alone. But dost Thou know that for the sake of that earthly bread the spirit of the earth will rise up against Thee and will strive with Thee and overcome Thee, and all will follow him, crying, "Who can compare with this beast? He has given us fire from heaven!"

—FYODOR DOSTOYEVSKY,
The Grand Inquisitor

. . . legislatures are ultimate guardians of the liberties and welfare of the people in quite as great a degree as the courts.

—OLIVER WENDELL HOLMES

Courage is the thing. All goes if courage goes.

—SIR JAMES MATTHEW BARRIE

IT IS HARD to stir out of the coals of recent Congressional hearings concerning invasions of privacy an argument that will avail against the security doctrine. A case in point was the effort by the Gallagher Committee in July, 1966, to defeat the proposal for setting up a National Data Center to contain all of the information in the Federal Government's files concerning every citizen. It might include schooling, grades, military service, personality traits, credit rating, income, employment and other impedimenta. The purpose for which this machine was proposed, by the Bureau of the Budget, is of course to provide data for operations research and planning in management of Government. Against the spectre of a national data center, the committee mobilized Vance Packard, the author; a professor of constitutional law at Yale, Charles A. Reich, and a number of scare phrases. The thought of all these dossiers "neatly bundled together into one compact package is appalling. We cannot be certain that such dossiers would always be used by benevolent people for benevolent purposes." Packard added the thought that "The Christian notion of the possibility of redemption is incomprehensible to the computer." And Professor Reich: "We are establishing a doctrine of no second chance, no forgiveness, one life, one chance only." To which one might add that when a person dies, the only "authoritative" account, the only fingerprint he may leave behind for generations and generations to know about, is a dossier in the National Data Bank he has never seen.

It was a good try. It may even compel the Bureau of the Budget to a compromise, a pilot plant perhaps to demonstrate how well the machine will protect the privacy of citizens. Once that is done, it will grow, and grow and grow. . . . And the reason it will grow is that it is an engine of the time, as much as Watt's steam engine was to his, and no more to be denied. To try to deny it is a misdirected use of political capital and energy.

Any advance in the cause of privacy it seems to me has to be measured by the extent to which it relieves paranoia and dissociation in the body politic. I don't mean to suggest that anyone we know is paranoid. *They* are paranoid; we are not. Should you doubt this, listen to them, any of them, debate the desirability of a police review board, the poverty program, Federal Aid to Education (particularly those discussions which touch on school busses for parochial school children), whether LSD should be added to the list of drugs outlawed from the pharmacopoeia, whether it was right or even "tactically wise" for Martin Luther King to march in Chicago, or whether there is any merit to any book which refers to scientists as "the new priesthood."

However, since we are involved in their problem, we should help them with it, particularly since they are ganging up to deprive us of our privacy. To that end, and seriously now, it appears to me vital that the Congress stake out a larger claim to the "lifeblood of a feedback system," which is to say, information. The institution through which to advance this claim exists, although feebly undernourished to the point of being faintly ludicrous, in the Library of Congress.

I confess I haven't an inkling of what it might cost to convert the Library of Congress into a genuinely effective information storage and retrieval system appropriately staffed; perhaps as much as the cost of a month of warfare in Vietnam. It would, however, do wonders for the confidence of the Congress. I should think the Congress might, having voted that money, also vote itself some money for spending on work by think companies to help them in keeping track of what goes on at the administration, and aid them in their own initiatives. This might have the further benefit of inducing some schizophrenia in the leading think companies, and cause them to meditate from time to time on the utility of the separation of powers in Government.

Once that is done, it would be a simple matter to place the National Data Center where it belongs, in the Library of Congress. Once it is installed there, steps may be taken to relieve the Government of the demeaning and demoralizing practice of talking behind the backs of its citizens. The first step would be to make the Center contain every single scrap of information concerning any citizen, by name, now resting scattered around the nation's capital in agency and departmental files.

I mean by this that when the Internal Revenue Service is through with a tax return, it must be turned over to the Center. Similarly all of the information contained in the FBI files; all census information; everything. Nothing traceable to an individual citizen ought to be retained by the several departments and agencies. We must assume that none of the various persons working in these agencies squirrels away in his desk drawer a personal storehouse of information; that would be something of a scandal with or without the Data Center.

The Center, once placed under the jurisdiction of the Library of Congress, should be given adequate appropriations and staff to run it, including persons needed to examine applications for information from the center. Information and statistics of a general nature, or of a kind that would give the recipient no opportunity to learn who contributed it, ought to be available freely and expeditiously to anyone who wishes it. Operations research would thus not be hampered in any way, and the cost of keeping duplicate information strewn here and there throughout the Government would be substantially reduced.

Anyone wishing to see a dossier on a particular individual should be required to obtain a court order. I take it from testimony given by proponents of a new wiretap policy based on court approval that this requirement will not significantly hinder law enforcement practices. There is one exception I would make to the general rule. The machine, I should hope, will incorporate the latest technology, which means that it ought to be able to print out a dossier on request in a matter of moments. Therefore, *any* citizen upon showing proper identification and paying the copying cost should receive on request a copy of his dossier.

If he sees anything in the dossier which he believes is untrue or which in its context reflects unfairly upon him, he ought to be able to file information to that effect in the dossier, pending a hearing. A commission selected by the President should be constituted in each of the Federal Court districts to hear appeals and view evidence, and to make a determination as to whether the dossier ought officially be changed. This, I believe, will discourage inclusion of loose talk in the files. It will also help to assure the reliability of the information used for operational planning.

Moreover, except on petition from the subject of the dossier, all information in the Data Center concerning a citizen ought to be destroyed within three years following his death.

I believe that the solicitude that these measures would instill among Federal agencies for the information they handle would help to imbue private citizens with a greater solicitude for their own names and reputations. Which brings me to my second proposal. That is, that American Telephone and Telegraph Company be held to account for the integrity of its circuits and instruments against any intrusion by anyone for any reason.

The company ought to be made liable for civil damages when wires are tapped without its knowledge, and to criminal prosecution for a tap installed with the company's permission. The FCC's most recent order against eavesdropping ought to be left to stand, if only to drive up the price of eavesdropping so as to limit its practice to persons who are serious about it. I see no hope for accomplishing anything except further disrespect for the law in trying to legislate against eavesdropping by law enforcement agents. They will do it, and there is not much to be gained by making them lie about it.

A precedent for the third proposal I want to make was set by three automobile insurance firms in June, 1966. The firms, Nationwide, All-State and State Farm, told the Insurance Commissioner of Maryland that they would from that time on inform applicants and policyholders of the reasons for denying them insurance, or refusing to renew policies. This form of accountability ought to be made general. If a credit bureau sells information that a citizen has created, the citizen ought to be able to obtain, free of charge, the same information that is sent to clients of the credit bureau.

I would propose that this be made a matter of law as a part of general Federal Protection of Privacy legislation. Beyond that, I believe the Congress ought to examine whether mailing lists should be bought and sold quite as freely as they are; it may be desirable to permit a person who subscribes to a magazine, for example, to ask that his name not be included in any lists for sale. This would at least introduce a negotiable value into information that is now freely circulated for profit.

Operations methods, as we have seen, are powerful because they embolden the user to ask questions that would otherwise be impractical. It is useless, however, if the questions aren't asked. Once the Congress makes it known that it considers the right to privacy "the most comprehensive of all rights," it will receive numerous suggestions more fertile than these few very modest urgings. Once these measures are instituted, they ought to have a salutary effect by example and public pressure on the conduct of private corporations.

"Men born to freedom," Mr. Justice Brandeis said, "are naturally alert to repel invasion of their liberty by evil minded rulers. The greatest dangers to liberty lurk in insidious encroachments by men of zeal, well-meaning but without understanding."